Rurally
Screwed

5/31/12

Enjoy!!

Rurally Screwed

My Life Off the Grid

with the Cowboy I Love

JESSIE KNADLER

B

BERKLEY BOOKS, NEW YORK

THE BERKLEY PUBLISHING GROUP
Published by the Penguin Group
Penguin Group (USA) Inc.
375 Hudson Street, New York, New York 10014, USA

Penguin Group (Canada), 90 Eglinton Avenue East, Suite 700, Toronto, Ontario M4P 2Y3, Canada
(a division of Pearson Penguin Canada Inc.) • Penguin Books Ltd., 80 Strand, London WC2R 0RL,
England • Penguin Group Ireland, 25 St. Stephen's Green, Dublin 2, Ireland (a division of Penguin
Books Ltd.) • Penguin Group (Australia), 250 Camberwell Road, Camberwell, Victoria 3124, Australia
(a division of Pearson Australia Group Pty. Ltd.) • Penguin Books India Pvt. Ltd., 11 Community
Centre, Panchsheel Park, New Delhi—110 017, India • Penguin Group (NZ), 67 Apollo Drive,
Rosedale, Auckland 0632, New Zealand (a division of Pearson New Zealand Ltd.) • Penguin Books
(South Africa) (Pty.) Ltd., 24 Sturdee Avenue, Rosebank, Johannesburg 2196, South Africa

Penguin Books Ltd., Registered Offices: 80 Strand, London WC2R 0RL, England

This book is an original publication of The Berkley Publishing Group.

The publisher does not have any control over and does not assume any responsibility for author
or third-party websites or their content.

FIRST EDITION: April 2012

Library of Congress Cataloging-in-Publication Data

Knadler, Jessie.
Rurally screwed : my life off the grid with the cowboy I love / Jessie Knadler. — 1st ed.
p.   cm.
ISBN 978-0-425-24568-2
1. Knadler, Jessie.   2. Country life—Virginia—Rockbridge County.   3. Farm life—
Virginia—Rockbridge County.   4. Rockbridge County (Va.)—Social life and customs.
5. Rockbridge County (Va.)—Biography.   6. Knadler, Jessie—Marriage.   7. Married
people—Virginia—Rockbridge County—Biography.   8. Cowboys—Montana—Biography.
9. Women professional employees—New York (State)—New York—Biography.
10. Career changes—Case studies. I. Title.
F232.R68K59   2012   2011047721
975.5'852—dc23

PRINTED IN THE UNITED STATES OF AMERICA

10 9 8 7 6 5 4 3 2 1

Penguin is committed to publishing works of quality and integrity.
In that spirit, we are proud to offer this book to our readers;
however, the story, the experiences, and the words are the author's alone.

To Jake

CONTENTS

Part Three

Part Four

AUTHOR'S NOTE

"Off the grid? You don't live off the grid." That's what my mom said the first time I told her the subtitle of this book. "'Off the grid' means no electricity," she pointed out. "It means relying on a generator, living nowhere near a paved road." She's right. I'm not exactly a mountain survivalist. I enjoy electricity. I live on a paved rural highway. I've never worn a deer pelt. I drive a Volkswagen Passat. By "off the grid" I meant simply in relation to the life I lived in New York, a life where I never dreamed I would end up eating squirrel one day.

While we're on the subject of semantics . . . This is a true story, but it is not entirely nonfiction. I have taken liberties for the purpose of driving the story forward. In most cases, names have been changed. Some places have been altered, conversations and experiences condensed and combined, and some events changed or taken out of sequence. A few characters are composites. In Chapter 2, I have taken experiences and impressions from four different magazines and rolled them into one fictitious publication staffed by fictitious people.

Thanks, Mom, for keeping me straight.

Was I climbing upward toward some sort
of well-balanced maturity or sliding downhill
into a slothful indifference?

—BETTY MacDONALD, *The Egg & I*

Part One

One

The Allure of
Manly Men

In the mid aughts, I thought I knew who I was. I was a thirty-year-old fashion magazine editor. I went to clubs (those that were left, anyway). I drank frequently and smoked socially. I still tried to rave. I was a woman bordering on irrelevancy—which is to say, I possessed the self-awareness to not question why acid wash was ironically desirable among hipsters but I looked kind of desperate whenever I tried to ape the trend. I kept a journal about my drinking, smoking, dancing and acid-washing, and if you were to open up that journal to a page marked March 23 of that year, you would find the beginning of a story, an adventure that would change the course of my life forever. Or bring me right back to square one, I'm not sure which.

That story began one Saturday morning at the unholy hour

where darkness meets dawn, outside a dilapidated warehouse in Bed Stuy. Its squeaking metal door crashed open and I, laughing so hard I could barely see, stumbled from the darkness of an unlit stairwell onto the sidewalk, causing my two friends Hush and Maria to laugh not with me, but at me. It was a social dynamic I was probably a little too comfortable with. We were cackling at something that seemed extremely funny two seconds prior but had already been forgotten in the haze of booze we'd been consuming since eleven o'clock the night before.

The night had started out so innocently. The three of us had met for dinner on the Lower East Side where Hush struck up a conversation with a group of disheveled music industry types who shared our long, appropriately rustic communal table. They said they were headed to a warehouse party in Brooklyn where one of their friends, a DJ from Mexico City I had actually heard of, was spinning, and would we care to join? I looked at Hush and Maria but their expressions said bedtime was imminent. I made a sad face. There was no need to articulate my consternation. This was becoming an all-too-familiar scenario: They wanted to go home, I wanted to hang in there until there was no more glow in my glow stick. Good dance music in New York was more likely to be heard at a health club than a club-club, and that was a big reason I now spent so much time reaching for the stars to electronic music at the cardio dance fitness class at Chelsea Piers.

Maria looked at me, exasperated. Even though she was a few years younger, she had recently dimmed the lights on her get-drunk years and tucked herself under a cozy afghan of yoga and sound nutrition and early nights so she could endure the long hours required for her job as an editor at *Finance Daily*. Maria was a hypercompetitive perfectionist, an overachiever whose biting, dry humor sometimes made it hard to tell whether she loved me or felt sorry for me. I think she loved me because we hung out often. We took a lot of yoga classes together and traveled quite a bit, though I wouldn't say our relationship was built on warm, fuzzy feelings or some notion of quirky girl power. It was built more on the fact that we made each other laugh, usually at each other's expense (but mostly mine). She said she was known as "the edgy one" among the starched shirts in her office. Which was true, if you considered books like *Take a Hike! With Poles!* and *50 Strokes for Superior Swimming* cutting-edge reading material. Maria was on a quest for physical and professional perfection, and damn if she wasn't perfect in nearly everything she attempted, even if she'd sometimes say all she *really* wanted out of life was to own a shack on the beach where she could sell Mexican meats. Why she picked that dream goal eluded me, but I got the feeling she wanted the shack mostly because she didn't own one already. If she did, it would probably be in an off-site owner capacity, and she'd staff it with a bunch of Mexican workers whose activities she'd carefully scrutinize via a bank of closed-circuit monitors linked to her New York office. All this is to say, Maria was more likely to find her spiritual, cathartic release not on some grubby, creaky dance floor in Bed Stuy but at a Bikram yoga class in Park Slope where she lived.

Hush, who was my age, was a little more like me in that she couldn't quite dispense with the partying yet, though we both felt increasingly inept trying. Hush had been raised in a strict Mormon family of wildly high achievers and was regarded as the black sheep of her family because she wasn't into finance or high tech (her masters in philosophy from Columbia was considered as frivolous as bathroom reading). Because of, or in spite of, the family label, she had assumed the role of restless reactionary by wandering outside the confines of her upbringing to smoke pot, have sex, and date men who were no good for her—rebellious expressions that belied a deep conservatism that would emerge in later years. Hush was all heart, generous and kind to a fault, and sharp as they come. She was also so concerned about clothes that she never wore the same outfit twice; she considered it bad luck. Her signature look veered toward caps, scarves, vests, leather pants with grommets and sneakers, but never in the same permutation. She had more clothes than H&M—most of her finds came from there—and she rarely paid more than twenty-five dollars for any of it. Hush wasn't even her real name. It was Julie. Julie had decided a year ago that she was too artistic and tough for a normal name, so she changed it to something that better complemented her Patti Smith meets Punky Brewster vibe. And I happily obliged her request. One day I called her Julie, the next day I called her Hush. I saw the name change as her boldly asserting her own true identity, which I considered the rightful act of claiming the American Dream.

It reminded me to a lesser degree of my own identity conversion from Patagonia-wearing teen transplant from Missoula, Montana, to New York City magazine editor. Even as a fresh-faced Montanan new to the city, gallivanting through the slushy streets of downtown Manhattan in January 1992 in a hideously practical ski parka and a neon fleece headband equipped with handy ear flaps, I was determined to join the ranks of round-the-clock hipsters around me. I spent more than a decade shedding the ski parka for a well-tailored trench. I wanted to live the life I felt certain I was meant to live, that I was *destined* to live. And as every New Yorker knows, Manhattan is nothing if not the city of self-invention. And self-delusion, as Maria liked to point out, which was why she refused to call Julie Hush, which really pissed Hush off.

Hush also had a thing about leaving the island of Manhattan; it was like asking her to board a Peter Pan bus for Kansas City. Why would she leave? She lived in a rent-controlled one-bedroom on the corner of Fifth Avenue and Twelfth Street—pretty much the center of the universe—so there was no way she was going to Bed Stuy. There was no reason for her to go to Bed Stuy.

Or maybe she would. At least that's what her face registered when the guys next to us teased us for being a bunch of old ladies. And next thing I knew, we were all piled into cabs on our way to Atlantic Avenue, with Maria insisting the whole time she'd stay for an hour, tops. But as we were led up the steps to the top floor of the run-down warehouse, the bass from behind the double doors becoming louder and heavier and more tremulous with each step, I had a feeling the night might—please, please, dear sweet Jesus!—get out of control. And when the doors burst open to reveal a rainbow of pulsing lights, sweating bodies and music so clear and loud it made me shiver, I knew we wouldn't make it out of there until morning.

And now, as we stumbled up the dreary industrial street toward the skyscrapers of Manhattan, we resembled three wastrels—dehydrated, blinded by the early morning sun, pasty, jittery from the night's debauch. Hush was inexplicably holding a cheerleader's baton. My ears rang and I could still feel the bass reverberating up and down my spine.

"God, I hate Brooklyn," said Hush. In the throes of a blooming hangover she was alternately giddy and irate. She appeared even thinner and paler than she her normal sylphlike self. Her long brown hair jutted out in spirals underneath a denim cloche hat.

"I can't feel my feet," said Maria.

"I know," I said. "I haven't danced like that in a long time."

"No, I really can't feel my feet," she said, her pitch set to shrill. "There's no circulation in my feet."

Maria sat down on a stoop and kicked off her shoes, nerdy-chic pumps that looked like what a cobbler in a fairy tale might wear, only with a slightly higher heel, and roughly massaged her feet. Hush and I stood over her, casting shadows.

"*And* I missed my Saturday morning yoga class," Maria said. "I'm too old for this. I can't believe it's morning. I need a cab."

"Yet you hung in there!" I said, not wanting her to leave. "When was the last time you stayed out all night?"

"When I studied for the SAT." She looked up at me, pained. "Can you try hailing me a cab?"

Atlantic Avenue looked vaguely apocalyptic this early in the morning. There were no cabs. We kept walking, which I told them suited me fine because I was in no hurry to get home—Jeff might be there.

"Jeff—the great cyborg masturbator," cracked Hush, using one of my more colorful nicknames for the man I had been dating for the past ten months. "Jessie, now *why* haven't you dumped him?"

I winced because there was no simple answer to that question. Or maybe there was a really simple answer, but one I was too incapacitated to give. From all outward appearances, Jeff satisfied the checklist of what constituted a winning "significant other" for a thirty-year-old woman in New York City. He was an architect, the boyfriend profession of choice for every status-conscious woman in New York. What woman doesn't want to date an architect? Which is precisely why I think Jeff became one—it sounded cool. Although he worked long hours, I never got the sense Jeff was particularly passionate about his craft, other than the look of awe he'd get on his face whenever we'd pass one of the warped, sparkling monoliths that rose along the West Side Highway. I eventually caught on that his admiration was more about the moneyed lifestyles those buildings contained than respect for the buildings' modernist construction. He was tall and slender and handsome in a Club Monaco model sort of way, and he was scrupulous about his appearance. He wore his wispy jet-black hair in a carefully crafted vertical tousle. He grew up in the suburbs of Des Moines, yet his tastes were unquestionably urbane—Helmut Lang jeans, state-of-the-art Japanese stereo equipment and sculptural bedside tables from Moss. Even the candle on the mantel in his bedroom had to be rotated just so. He attended art openings, bought slick photography books, dined weekly at trendy restaurants like wd-50 and drank sidecars. Hush thought he was gay the first time she met him.

But I thought he was cultured. I was intrigued by his fastidiousness. He demanded "the very best," which I assumed summed up his attraction to me. But over the last few months I'd come to suspect that Jeff's obsession with visuals, with the way things looked, masked a bleak, cold emptiness inside. Hence my nickname for him, "the cyborg." He had no real friends, except for me. He lived in a distressed Victorian home on the outskirts of Astoria—a strange domicile for an architect—with three weird older guys. At first I thought his choice of housing was because he spent all his money on expensive trinkets and dinners out, but the longer we were together I realized it was more than that.

When he wasn't working, Jeff spent most of his time alone in his bedroom looking at online porn. (The giant desktop computer on his bedside table was one tip-off.) When I mentioned this, Hush and Maria both looked at me blankly like, "Yeah, and . . . ? Welcome to earth." All men, they reminded me, were addicted to porn to some degree or another, at least according to all the women's magazine stories devoted to the topic. But Jeff's habit went beyond *Butt Pirates of the Caribbean* type of ick. Jeff's preference was for Lolitas, nymphets. Not Miley Cyrus, but Noah Cyrus. I first became suspicious when he bought me a pair of little girl underpants printed with unicorns and rainbows a few months ago. At first I thought it was just kinky. But the idea of my Club Monaco boyfriend sauntering into the Big K on Astor

Place and rifling through the little girls underwear looking for the perfect package of "big girl panties" with his long slender fingers disturbed me, to put it mildly. He'd say things to me like, "You're so small, like a little girl, so petite." I got the sense he wanted me to act young, to be young, which made me feel edgy and paranoid. It was around then that I became aware of a cloudiness behind his eyes, a perpetual mist of post-orgasmic pleasure and shame. He plodded when he walked, his brow was knitted, and his shoulders were hunched around his ears, like he was carrying a dark secret, one he kept locked on a separate hard drive in his bedroom in that creepy *Grey Gardens* house in Astoria.

My suspicions were confirmed the day he left the house briefly to run an errand and I sat down on his bed to check my email. I jiggled the mouse to bring the monitor to life and was met with a department store webpage of young girls modeling in their underwear. It was all perfectly innocent—if you were a mom of tweenage daughters, not a twenty-nine-year old childless male with a creepy aura. I hesitated, debating whether to check his recent history, but I was too afraid of what I might find. So I left the house before he came back, too disturbed to confront him. The sick part? As much as Jeff repulsed me, I actually felt sorry for him. There was something about him that seemed like a little boy lost, so he groped himself for reassurance. I knew I'd have to confront him one of these days, but for now I was incapable of doing anything. So when he'd called me the previous day to ask if he could come over after work to talk, I choked. Out of equal measures pity and dread, I said okay, telling myself this was the night I would break up with him. This was the night I would drop the hammer. But even as the thoughts formed in my head, I knew I wouldn't go home at all. He'd let himself in with the keys I had lent him, wait up for me all night, and leave in a huff once he realized I wasn't coming home. I could blame it all on losing track of time, having too many cocktails, and *then* dump him by text. It was an outrageously deceitful, cowardly move, but justified, I thought, when weighed against his larger moral offense.

"I don't know why I haven't dumped him," I answered Hush. "I really don't know.

"Atta girl," said Maria. "Taking the world by storm."

"How about let's stop talking?" I asked.

We finally found the C train to ride back into Manhattan. Maria got off at Hoyt to make her way to the F train for Park Slope. Hush and I got out at Fourteenth Street to grab a goji berry juice before going our separate ways. On our way in to the shop, a woman in her early twenties emerged from the store. She had long dark hair and wore a tight, cleavage-baring lululemon yoga top. Maybe it was because she was talking loudly on her cell phone about some girl she knew who'd slept with Kanye West, but there was something performative about her demeanor. I half expected a camera crew from Bravo or VH1 to come trailing behind her. She was blithe and indifferent, a calm produced by the gratification of her every whim. Our soiled appearance came into sharp relief by comparison: Hush and I looked like a pair of crack whores in her presence. We parted to make way as she jostled past, trailed by the scent of Chanel and self-entitlement. We watched her stride down the sidewalk and hail a cab.

"Wow," said Hush.

I often professed not to understand this shellacked and pampered breed—what it would look like if Wall Street and reality TV had a baby. But the truth was, an anthropologist studying young people living in the city's gilded age just before a major economic collapse would classify me as a member of this very tribe. I lived in West Chelsea. I didn't have a boob job, but my teeth were laminated a brilliant shade of Benjamin Moore white. I lived for my next tawny spray tan. I was an editor at one of the top-selling women's fashion magazines in the world and had made a successful, well-paid career out of editing and writing stories about "Why Men Can't Keep It in Their Pants." I was deeply competitive at Kundalini yoga yet considered myself more ethereal, more spiritually *at one* than the average person. I asked waiters questions like, "Is this beef grass-fed?" and "The pear galette—is it really organic?" And now I was spending $13.75 on something called goji berry juice.

I winced when I realized the only real, substantive difference between me and that girl was the size of our breasts.

Hush and I walked outside with our jumbo juices, sucking without restraint. As we said our good-byes on the street corner, I became wistful.

"Geez, I wonder if we'll ever have another night like that again in our lives," I said, showing my laminated teeth in a semblance of a sad smile.

"You say that like it's a bad thing," said Hush.

"I'm just saying . . ."

Hush came in for a hug and handed me the baton. "Seriously, this thing with Jeff? Please end it. Soon."

My parched lips stuck momentarily to my teeth. I grasped the baton.

I took my time walking over to my building on the corner of Twentieth Street and Tenth Avenue. It was a bright and sunny morning. Flowers and trees were just starting to bud. A sudden blast of cold wind from the Hudson swept through the streets, causing bundled up West Villagers out walking their hypoallergenic dogs to clutch their weekend *Times* more tightly. I stopped at a quaint coffee shop on the corner of Jane and Hudson and took my time sipping a cappuccino. Surely Jeff wouldn't be so undignified as to wait around for me into the breakfast hour. He'd *have* to be gone by now. Only someone with no self-respect would tolerate such abuse.

A guy in his early thirties with curly, strawberry blond hair and alpha nerd sunglasses stood on the curb outside the coffee shop impatiently smoking a cigarette and drinking a latte. He looked like an anguished writer—pissed off and broody. My type. I thought if I smiled he might like me. Just as quickly, I wondered if he too had a thing for Lolita porn. I finished my cappuccino and shoved off for home.

As I lumbered up the stairs to my fourth-floor apartment, I could already hear my next door neighbor Steve belting out a musical theater rendition of "Cat's in the Cradle."

I put the key in the lock and opened the door to my darkened studio apartment. The blinds were drawn. There was an animalistic odor—confirmation the apartment wasn't empty. The room was illuminated by the acidic glow of an open laptop. Jeff's form lay bunched in the sheets. The laptop clicked shut before I had time to shut the front door.

"Oh, hey," I said. I felt awkward, like an interloper in my own home. "I wasn't sure if you'd still be here."

"Yeah," Jeff yawned with exaggerated effort. A long, lanky arm stretched for the ceiling.

I stiffly walked into the room.

"Where were you?" he asked, still pretending to have been awakened. The room was dark but I sensed his distorted expression—contrite, angry.

"I waited up for you all night," he said. "I wouldn't have come over if you weren't even going to be here. Why are you holding a baton?"

I looked down at the cheer stick in my hand. "Oh, it's something I got from Hush." I lamely rotated it in my fingers. "Look, it twirls."

There was a painful silence. Jeff looked at me furtively as he rolled out of bed in his boxers. He reached for the pair of jeans folded neatly across a nearby chair. I watched him dress slowly and deliberately in the half darkness and wondered if this was the part where I was supposed to say something. Maybe he wants to be caught. Maybe he wants to be reprimanded like a naughty schoolboy. Maybe my role in this sordid relationship was to fulfill some weird childhood psychosexual drama of his. I twirled the baton a bit more forcefully and walked over to the window, opened the drapes and raised the sill.

"What do you have going on today?" I asked, plopping on the

couch and turning on the TV as if there wasn't the slightest bit of tension in the room. Spencer Pratt and Heidi Montag preened and posed for the cameras during an *Access Hollywood* rerun.

He stood before me like a six-year-old sent to the principal's office. His shoulders were in their usual hunched position. "I was hoping we could spend a little time together," he said. "I haven't seen you in a week. Jessie, where were you last night?"

"I was out with Hush and Maria," I said. "I told you I wouldn't be here."

"You told me you were going out to dinner with your friends. You didn't tell me you were going to be gone until"—he glanced at his cell phone—"nine o'clock the next morning."

"I lost track of time."

"'Lost track of time,'" he repeated derisively. "You know, you treat me like such shit sometimes."

"That's because the theme song to *The Little Mermaid* plays in my head whenever I look at you."

"What the hell is that supposed to mean?"

"Nothing."

We glared at each other, caught in an unintentional stare war. He finally blinked, losing another of our silent battles, yet as impaired and passive-aggressive as me. I turned back to the TV.

After what seemed like forever, he finally picked up his computer bag and said, "I don't know how much longer I can keep doing this."

I rolled my eyes, incapable of engaging him further. He walked toward the front door and, with one hand on the door-knob, paused. "I'll try giving you a call later."

"Okeydoke," I said, not taking my eyes off the screen.

As soon as he shut the door, I waited a moment before walking over to the door and double-locking it. As I looked in the peephole to make sure he wasn't loitering in the hallway, my next-door neighbor began singing Joni Mitchell's lyrics, "They paved paradise, and put up a parking lot."

I slumped into the closest chair and wondered if the reason I couldn't confront Jeff was not so much fear but curiosity; if perhaps his self-loathing and creepy behavior intrigued me more than it disturbed me. It was almost as if Jeff had become a puzzle I felt compelled to solve precisely because his perversion was so shocking and incomprehensible to my relatively straitlaced world order (save for the occasional crazy night out). Maybe *I* was the one with the problem? After all, Jeff and I were guilty of the same crime: Pretending the elephant in the living room—or rather, the one-eyed monster that had probably besmirched my sheets— didn't exist. I considered that I should probably explore this issue in my next session with Dr. Neimi. But I knew Dr. Neimi would just look at me placidly while daintily picking lint off his double-twill trousers. Sitting before Dr. Neimi was like facing off with a garden gnome.

I pulled myself up and stripped the bed, being careful not to touch anything but the corners, and threw the sheets in the laundry basket. As I remade the bed, I heard the ping of my Black-Berry. I opened the email and saw it was from a photographer friend of mine, a fellow Montanan who frequently shot for top publications in New York. We had kept in touch over the years because there weren't many native Montanans working in big media. Laurie said she had a story idea she thought I might be interested in, about a rodeo called the Bucking Horse Sale. It took place every May in Miles City, Montana, and amateur rodeo stars competed on never-before-ridden horses and bulls. "It's dangerous, exciting, there will be lots of broken bones and cute cowboys," she wrote. "What do you think? Would *Glitter* be interested? Maybe something like 'City Girls and Cowboys— Can it Work?' or 'The Allure of Manly Men?'"

I sighed. I already knew such a story wouldn't fly at the editorial idea meeting on Monday. I could already hear the raspy voice of *Glitter*'s editor-in-chief asking, "But where's the celeb angle? Is Jake Gyllenhaal going to be there? Not even Carrie Underwood? Why can't we find a similar rodeo in Santa Monica that has celebs?"

I hit the reply button and typed back:

Hey Laurie:

Great to hear from you! The rodeo sounds awesome! As much as I'd personally love to write a story like this, it's probably not a right fit for *Glitter*. The editorial focus here is more about honoring one's quirky individuality while hewing closely to our prescribed fashion dos and don'ts than exploring the untamed American West.

I deleted that last sentence and rewrote:

Unless of course there's a strong celeb angle (Jake Gyllenhaal, Carrie Underwood, Jewel), or the Bucking Horse Sale relocates to Santa Monica. Is there a chance the rodeo may relocate to Santa Monica? Otherwise, thanks for thinking of me! Feel free to pitch me anytime . . . and happy trails?

Best,
Jessie

I hit send. I probably could have finessed the response a bit more, but I figured it was better to be brutally honest with Laurie than give her the usual "We just did a similar story a month ago so it will be awhile before we can revisit this topic."

Sleep was finally coming on fast. I opened the medicine cabinet in my bathroom and popped half an Ambien. I took a long hard look at my reflection. It wasn't so long ago that my looks were compared to a young Meryl Streep, a compliment that flattered me greatly. But after having been awake for more than twenty-four hours, the only thing I saw in the mirror was my future and the future said, "Hi, I'm Lady Elaine from *Mr. Roger's Neighborhood*. Won't you be my neighbor?" My eyes looked sunken and beady, and my cheeks looked hollow, which made my ordinarily patrician nose—at least that's what I called it—seem massive. I couldn't look anymore. I walked out of the bathroom and collapsed in a heap on my partially made bed.

Two

Orgasm Face

On my way to the editorial staff meeting the following Monday, I swung by the snack room for a packet of fruit chews but the candy got stuck halfway out of the vending machine. I pounded my palm against the glass a few times, then dug around in my pocket for change for a hot chocolate. As I sipped, I reread the slip of paper scrawled with the story idea I'd concocted moments prior.

I sat heavily in one of the few remaining chairs around the conference table and slurped my drink. Sitting through editorial meetings made me feel like I was two hundred years old and choking on yogurt—the weight of feigning enthusiasm over earnest story ideas like "10 Reasons Why Funny Women ARE Sexy" and "The Good Girl's Guide to Sex!" being bandied about the table. Something had happened to my brain during my long tenure at women's magazines. I wasn't sure if it was because my mind moved a million clicks faster than my mouth could keep up, or if I had edited one listicle, charticle, gridicle and relationship quiz too many. But I had developed a bizarre inability to speak before higher-ups without stuttering, which the creative director eulogized in a drawing of me with a stream of "Er, ah, duh, durs" coming out of my mouth. I ignored what the characterization might portend and hung the picture up in my cubicle anyway because it looked exactly like me.

Danica sat to my right. Danica and I shared the same title but she was well on her way to world domination, which instinctively made me dislike her. A zebra-print bound notebook, newspaper clippings, a folder of papers and three different colored pens were neatly arranged on the table in front of her.

"Geez, Danica, are you pitching ideas or planning a blitzkrieg?"

She looked at me with a raised chin and blinked.

"Should I dim the lights for your PowerPoint presentation? Perhaps you require the use of a laser pointer?"

"I wouldn't want to be in your shoes," she said cryptically.

I crushed my empty paper cup in response and scanned the rest of the faces around the table, as well as those who pulled up chairs beside it. Most of the more seasoned editors, the ones who had been on the masthead for an astonishing five years (which was like fifteen years in this industry), wore blasé, bored expressions. Younger staffers looked like they might crack from a lethal mixture of fear, enthusiasm and Red Bull. I found it ironic that despite the magazine's unrelenting edict to dress to the nines for every occasion, the women who put it together month after month were, with the exception of the fashion department, a decidedly no-frills bunch. Practically everyone, myself included, wore a variation of the same utilitarian uniform: jeans, T-shirts, boots, minimal jewelry, scant makeup, and with hair that lacked bounce and sheen.

"Is the editor in chief coming?" someone asked.

"No, she had to run up to nine," said the editor in chief's second-in-command, a gruff, boxy redhead in her mid forties who embodied the librarian aesthetic of the editorial side. My feelings for this woman were summed up in my nickname for her—Number Two. Today Number Two wore a snap-front shirt, a brown prairie skirt and chunky motorcycle boots—an uncharacteristic display of style meant to approximate the current boho trend, except on her it looked like clothes she'd pulled from a box marked "The 80s" in the back of her closet.

"Yeah, maybe their snack machine is working. Stupid thing took my fruit chews," I whispered to the lifeless creature next to me. Her name was Liz. Liz was a reporter who transcribed hour-long interviews with skin-care experts word for word.

"No, that looks like throw-up," Number Two casually informed the harried assistant art director as he presented another page layout for her inspection. She impatiently sipped from a bottle of Italian spring water as the meeting got underway.

"Okay, so we're assigning the big porn package for the September issue," Number Two declared. "Why men look at it, how often and what does it say about you, et cetera, et cetera. Kaitlin, you're writing. Danica, you're editing."

I made a face like a toddler presented with a plate of boiled brussels sprouts. "Porn! Porn! I'm sick of porn!" I groaned. When I reopened my eyes, I noticed everyone around the table looking at me.

"Is there a problem, Jessie?" Number Two asked.

"Uh, no, no problem," I said. No problem except every "porn package" I'd ever read—and I'd been reading a lot of them lately—followed the same pitiful arc: Don't worry if your guy wacks off relentlessly to women other than you; he still loves you *and* your quirky personality *and* your cellulite! But I wasn't bitter at all.

"Oh my God, Audrey, this is hilarious!" Number Two laughed wickedly. She was responding to the story idea, "What Does He Think of Your Orgasm Face?" pitched by the new junior editor and current office "It" girl, a polished but salty blond who looked like she'd grown up riding expensive ponies in some upper-income enclave in New Jersey.

A murmur of laughter rippled around the table. Danica crinkled her nose disdainfully.

"Ha! Love it! Love it!" Number Two cried as she scribbled notes. "We need more ideas like this! Unexpected! Funny. Outside the box. Editor in Chief is going to love that! Let's assign it for the August issue." Number Two turned to me, all trace of humor drained from her face. "Jessie, what have you got?"

Emboldened by her request for outside the box ideas, I

fumbled with the slip of paper in my hand. "It's an idea I've, ah, been developing for a while now: 'Discover His New Moan Zones With a Scarf.'"

Number Two shook her head and commenced The Number Two Eye Roll—pupils penetrating the ceiling while her lower lip opened and closed like a ventriloquist's dummy. "Oh, you mean like 'Discover His New Man Map With a Feather' that ran two years ago? Does anyone else have ideas that *aren't* blatant rip-offs of old stories?"

My ears felt hot as I sunk deeper into the bowels of my chair. Danica sat up taller, more regal.

Number Two's verbal beating caught me off guard because I assumed my pitch was more or less on par with what other editors on staff were coming up with. That is, it veered toward the crazy because the entire magazine went that way. So I could not understand why "The Great Porn Package" and "What Does He Think of Your Orgasm Face?" were lauded while my Moan Zone story was publicly stomped. And it's true, I stole the Moan Zone idea from an older issue I found wedged between two bookcases near the freight elevator, but it was my understanding that recycling stories in magazine-dom was par for the course. It was like how every fashion story about skirts and cargo pants were called "Skirting the Issue" and "Precious Cargo," respectively, and how "The New Military Look" or "Untamed Safari Trend" were both dusted off and updated every few years. What was the big deal? But I got the feeling Number Two's public teardown underscored a larger point: That is, the higher up the masthead I rose, the worse my lady magazine skills became. My flailing performance was laid bare in all its magnificent glory when another senior editor—Number Two's personal mercenary—pulled me into her office right after the meeting and informed me my work seemed "glib."

"Uh, not sure what you're talking about," I said.

The Mercenary's chin rested in one hand, her caramel-lacquered nails were perfectly manicured. Her mouth was a slit and her carefully sculpted brows grazed her hairline. She was obviously going out tonight, as her usual brown mock turtleneck and tan slacks had been swapped for an outfit that might actually be featured in the pages of the magazine. She wore her curly brown hair in a chic but tousled updo. Her form-fitting brown sheath, with slick chocolate platforms, reaffirmed my conviction the only color this woman ever wore was brown.

"Call me crazy, but I get the feeling you're not serious about what we do here," she said, pausing for effect. "Or maybe you really don't get it. And your copy—your copy is . . ."

She shook her head and picked up one of my recently edited articles, titled, "Bedroom Games Guys Love."

"'During foreplay, playfully throw your panties in his face,'" she read, then enunciated the next sentence slowly. "'But give a quick check to make sure they're clean first.'"

She dropped the manuscript on her desk and squinted her eyes. "'*Give a quick check to make sure they're clean first*'? Um, ew?"

"Oh, well, the throw-the-panties-in-his-face thing was one of Editor in Chief's pre-approved ideas," I explained. "She wanted that one in."

"She wants throwing-panties-in-his-face," the Mercenary

leveled. "She'd freak if she read anything about checking for cleanliness."

"But . . . isn't that something the reader might want to do?" I asked, somewhat confused. "I mean, that's what *I* would do if I threw underwear in some guy's face."

I chuckled nervously like we were in on the joke together; that, of course, tossing a pair of used undergarments at someone might come across as a tad impudent. I had actually pondered the issue for some time during the edit and concluded that if a man threw his stained, holey skivvies that had been hugging his testicles all day into my face, I would not like that. Ergo, if we must advise something this wacky, let us provide a helpful caveat.

"Oh God, stop, just stop." She held up her palm and tried to crinkle her eyes but her forehead was Botoxed so tight it would have taken a chisel and a space heater to melt. "It just points to a level of taste that seemingly isn't there."

I hated when people used the word "seemingly" in conversation; it's a word only ever used in print by writers and editors who want to sound smart.

"Yet . . . we're advising the reader to throw dirty—" I stopped, realizing this was not a debate for polite company, particularly with a woman four lines above me on the masthead. "But no big deal!" I shrugged and smiled brightly. "I'll just take it out!"

"Jessie, I'm sorry, but your work just isn't at the level it should be," she resumed.

"Are you firing me?"

"No, we're not firing you," she said sadly. "We're reassigning your stories to another editor for the time being."

A few weeks later, all but two of my stories had been reassigned to other editors and I found myself writing the table of contents—an assignment usually reserved for editorial assistants. Clearly the wheels had been set in motion to make me quit, but I couldn't quit until I found a new job. In the meantime, Danica was promoted to features czar, which meant she was effectively my superior and it was only a matter of time before I'd be reheating her cappuccinos. And "It" Girl Orgasm Face increasingly spoke to me with the clipped authority of one who now edited most of my former stories.

My professional death spiral came to a head the following Sunday when one of my superiors called me that evening as I watched a *Law & Order* marathon, nursing a bottle of Côtes du Rhône.

"Listen, we have a major emergency on our hands," the editor said.

Did the offices burn down, perchance?

"We just found out that Britney Spears got married in Las Vegas," she said. "This is a huge story. We're supposed to finish shipping tomorrow"—magazine speak for sending the final edit of the issue to the printer—"and we want to crash in a story about the news."

I didn't like where the conversation was headed, but I was flattered that of all the editors on staff, she chose me to crash in the story. Maybe there was hope for me in women's magazines after all.

"I need you to do the sidebar," she said, referring to the lowliest, most junior-level writing assignment in all of magazine-dom (other than the table of contents). "I need you to go to Penn Station tomorrow—early, six a.m.—and ask commuters if they think Britney has lost her mind or not. We want a poll. With numbers and statistics and quotes. Talk to about a hundred people. Have it to me by nine." Click.

I guzzled the remainder of the wine.

Filled with rage and self-loathing, I arrived at Penn Station at nine the next morning. Blocks of sullen commuters swarmed around me as I stood stupidly off to one side with a pen and a notebook in my hand. Everyone looked pissed off, harried and insufficiently caffeinated as they blew by me to their big important jobs uptown and downtown. Even the secretary contingent, dressed in their scuffed pumps and cheap navy London Fog knockoffs, looked like they had more purpose, more reason for belonging in New York City than me. I tugged at the underwear being siphoned up my hindquarters. The few people I approached looked at me with such utter contempt that I slunk into a seat at the nearest Au Bon Pain. I ordered a giant latte and proceeded to make up the results of the poll—89 percent for insanity, 11 percent against, which sounded about right—and a bunch of quotes. Then I called Hush.

"Hush, I'm touching the delta of my despair," I said as she picked up the phone.

"What?" I could hear her clicking on her keyboard, deep in an instant message.

I explained where I was and what I was doing. "I can't take it anymore. And, uh, I meant to tell you . . . but I think I found the cyborg doing that thing he does after I left you guys that morning a few weeks ago."

I had managed to keep this nugget of information to myself because I knew it would have invited questions about a break-up that hadn't, for reasons I couldn't quite articulate, occurred. But now, in my despair, I revealed the full depth of my misery.

"Oh, no!" She laughed. "But you dumped him, right?"

I couldn't think of anything clever to say so I remained stoically quiet on the line, mouth ajar. I heard her stop typing.

"Don't tell me," she groaned. "Jessie, come on! You didn't break up with him?"

"God, I can't even dump a pervert," I moaned. And then it hit me: I can't even dump a pervert! Shit! I dropped my head onto the table and inhaled slowly, intoxicated by the scent of old coffee and chemicals. I had reached the nadir of my existence: I am a pervert-loving, Britney Spears beat reporter. Twelve years in New York had amounted to this.

"I have to quit," I hissed. "I have to go freelance."

"'Freelance,'" she scoffed. "And then you can move into a cardboard box. Why not just wait to be fired or laid off so you can collect unemployment?"

"Because I don't want to wait to be demoted to the office janitor in the meantime." I said. "I have pride . . . though . . . I suppose dating a perv might suggest otherwise." I explained that I had to leave the magazine not so much because I sucked at my job, but because I was too deep, too thoughtful to be part of a culture that pushed such regressive stories as "What Does He Think of Your Orgasm Face?"

"Well, maybe you *should* leave," she said. "You've been really unhappy for a long time now."

I winced. Hush's habit of not sugarcoating the truth was one of the reasons I loved her but was occasionally rankled by her. She had this way of confidently highlighting some less-than-flattering part of myself I'd rather not be reminded of. I wouldn't have described myself as "really unhappy," which sounded so depressing. More like, "caustically content," a designation that connoted a wry and jaded outlook on an otherwise glamorous life. But there it was: "Really unhappy." And now I really had to leave.

"Why don't you write for us?" Hush said. "The editor in chief is desperate for ideas."

Hush was the photo editor at a men's magazine called *Outdoor Adventure*. Nobody had ever heard of *Outdoor Adventure*. It wasn't sold on newsstands. It was owned by a giant tobacco conglomerate and mailed for free to smokers or anyone who'd ever filled out a coupon or entered a cigarette sweepstakes. In other words, it wasn't a real magazine, but a place where dilettantes, deadbeats and an oddly high proportion of hysterically funny theater performers went to earn a paycheck until they landed their big break.

The irony was that this "fake" magazine published real stories. Writers on sizeable budgets were flown around the country to report on under-the-radar subcultures and demanding physical activities romanticized by manly smokers (that their readers could never perform such activities without the aid of an inhaler was another of the magazine's many absurdities). For someone like me, who'd all but forgotten how to write after spending my career editing departments with names like "Couples Corner!" and "You! You! You!," Hush's suggestion was appealing. She had ended up there herself as a refugee of *Vogue*, and loved it. It only published four times a year, which meant she could roll into the office at ten thirty, leave at four and take off every obscure holiday on the calendar.

"But don't call him unless you have ideas," she said.

I wasn't sure what a "Couples Corner!" editor could offer, but then I remembered Laurie the photographer's pitch for the Bucking Horse Sale—an under-the-radar event featuring amateur rodeo riders in an "exotic" location—my home state—with probably lots of hardened smokers present. It was perfect. I spent the next two days hunched over my computer at home crafting the perfect proposal. I pitched it as an exposé of an event not hampered by typical rodeo governing bodies' rules and regulations. The Bucking Horse Sale was truly a grassroots event where anyone—young, old, feeble, fat—who was ballsy enough to get on an unbroken bull or horse was welcome to compete. No professionals allowed. There was no other rodeo like it. I wrangled a meeting with the editor in chief so we could go over my story proposal face-to-face. The desperation in my voice must have gotten to him because after he mulled it over for what seemed an eternity, he finally sighed, "Alright, but don't screw it up." Two days after that, I gave my notice at the women's magazine. I was officially a freelance writer.

And from there the story became a lot more interesting.

Three

Under the Big Sky

A few days before leaving for Montana I was invited by the publicist for a fancy Upper East Side stylist to get my hair cut for free—the unspoken trade-off being that I use him as a source in my next riveting hair-care exposé (I didn't bother to tell him I'd just quit my cushy magazine job). I went to the salon requesting a disheveled rocker 'do but came out with Park Avenue matron hair—an outlandishly curled bowl cut. It looked horrible.

All the barrettes and bobby pins I had to wear to keep my hair under control kept rubbing against the oversized DJ-style headphones I wore during my flight to Montana. I was listening to a Madonna CD that featured a lot of songs about the "hard issues"—war, consumerism, religion, addiction (not her issues, of course, but other people's)—sung to hyper-produced, bubble-gum beats.

She was singing a song about not wasting time, about being a strong and powerful lady, when the plane broke through the clouds and I looked out the window to see the sparse, unforgiving landscape of Eastern Montana thousands of feet below.

As her lyrics pulsated into my head, a mist of a thought presented itself: I probably couldn't afford to waste any more time either. I was thirty years old, and my existence amounted to a series of conventional, almost formulaic milestones that seemed to define what it meant to be a thirty-year-old single woman in New York City at the dawn of the twenty-first century. In therapy—check. On antidepressants—check. Popping Ambien—check. Smoking too much weed and drinking too much—check and check. A history of professional unfulfillment—check. Dating a porn addict—check. Dating a Lolita porn addict—astonishingly, check. That I still hadn't ended it with Jeff was testament to how emotionally paralyzed I'd become.

One of these days I will dump him by text.

One of these days. One of these days had become my mantra. *One of these days* I'll dump Jeff. *One of these days* I'll figure out what I'm doing with my life. *One of these days* I'll quit therapy. I couldn't quite connect the dots as to how I'd ended up in therapy in the first place when I actually loathed talking about myself and my problems to strangers. I wasn't even capable of coughing up the angst and anxiety required for a full-blown panic attack, a condition that seemed to afflict a lot of my more psychologically delicate—and come to think of it, successful—friends. And murkier still, what real problems did I have to discuss? After a year's worth of sessions with Dr. Neimi, the only psychological breakthrough, the only cognitive revelation I'd come to was that a) I required two glasses of wine before going to sessions and b) I was suffering from ennui. That's it. I was depressed because my life was shallow and retarded. I had agreed to go on medication not to work through my malaise but because I got off on the act of popping pills. Putting a tab of Wellbutrin on my tongue and swallowing it, chasing it with a glass of wine and an Ambien digestif—I delighted in the ritual of it, the routine. One pill in the morning, a few cocktails after work, a puff of weed in the evening, another pill before bedtime. Everything would be fine as long as I had my chemical salves. This sounds like I had the makings of a very fine drug addict, except that I was obsessed with exercise and the pursuit of firm buttocks. Sinewy, sculpted muscles aren't, it turns out, compatible with hangovers.

I peered out the window and saw a bunch of tiny, dark brown dots scattered across a terrain of beige when it hit me. I was living the life of a cow, just like one of those brown dots mindlessly munching scrub grass down there. I was merely following a well-trod chute, led by millions of dissatisfied, chemically dependent Manhattan women before me. I didn't consciously make my own path; I went wherever I was poked and prodded. And to where was I being prodded? Where did this chute end? Marriage (maybe . . . eventually), more meds, a house upstate, couple's counseling, two-point-five kids with behavioral problems and wheat allergies, different meds, a Volvo, divorce, another Volvo, death.

"Care for a drink?" the stewardess said to my stricken pallor.

"Uh, Coke, please—make it diet."

As I guzzled the Coke, I convinced myself that being on this flight to Billings, Montana, was testament that I was now taking control of my life. Madonna's words, however tone-deaf and incongruous they were to the scrappy, masculine landscape below—were an apt soundtrack to my state of mind. I deserved a life of purpose. A life of adventure. I felt certain there was no one who could write a better story about a rodeo—a subject I knew precisely zero about, but whatever—than me.

I cranked up the volume as the plane hit the tarmac. Billings' airport occupies the rimrocks overlooking the city. When I looked out the window, Montana's biggest city spread out before me like a faded, dusty quilt, punctuated by a handful of tall buildings and a few cell-phone towers.

I grabbed my bags and exited the plane. Anticipating a line, I made a beeline for the car rental counter, though there wasn't a wait. The older woman behind the counter offered me a Mazda MPV. The thought of pulling up to a raucous Montana rodeo in a suburban mom car didn't quite gel with the powerful aura I was trying to fashion. Almost as a joke, I asked if she had any four-wheel-drive vehicles for the same price.

"Let's take a look," she smiled. "Well, whaddya know—we got a new Jeep Cherokee I can let you have for the same price." She gave me a wink. "Don't tell anyone."

I didn't want to jinx myself by asking questions. I just thanked her, took the keys and told her it felt good to be back in my home state as I headed out to the parking lot.

After plugging in my iPod jack and re-queuing Madonna, I drove through downtown Billings, past frontier buildings, diners, offices and a gas station called The Town Pump. The clustered buildings of downtown gave way to Billings' yawning industrial side, where most of the city's real economic hustle and bustle took place. Every building I passed seemed to specialize in dirt or rocks, sod or silage, trucks or trailers, all manned by cowboys, truckers, good ol' boys or a hybrid of the three. It was mid May, which I'd forgotten in Montana could still feel like the tail end of winter, and I realized I had seriously under-packed. I turned on the heat. The light from the late morning sun gave the earth a flat, gray cast.

As I got on the ramp for I-94 heading east for the three and a half hour drive to Miles City, a familiar wave of melancholy washed over me.

I'd always had a love-hate relationship with my home state. I loved it because it was beautiful and my family still lived there, but I disliked it because I'd never felt like I belonged. I guess this is how every small-town kid feels before jettisoning for the city, but growing up, I always felt gypped of excitement and drama, like I was constantly waiting to be invited to a cocktail party that would never be thrown (for starters, Montanans back then didn't drink cocktails, they drank beer.) Both my parents were raised on cattle ranches, which meant I spent a lot of time as a child standing around vast, empty fields at various family functions asking,

"Now what?" That question—"Now what?"—that feeling that there must be something more important going on elsewhere, anywhere but here in this field, in these sticks, next to someone's broken down pickup truck, defined my youth. And here it was again, already coating my consciousness in its familiar film forty-five minutes after landing in the state's capital cow town.

As industrial businesses became fewer and farther between, replaced by sprawling alfalfa and wheat farms dotted with tiny tractors, I considered that my western upbringing could probably be envied by some, at least among those who like books like *A River Runs Through It*. My grandfather was the last living cowboy. He rode a horse every day of his life and smoked hand-rolled Prince Albert cigarettes (he could roll with one hand while the other grasped the reins). My grandma Rose was still spry enough to leap across a creek at the age of seventy-seven. My mom, Barb, was a barrel racer, a feisty, red-haired whippet who used to challenge boys to arm-wrestling contests—and win—back in high school. My dad's arms as a teenager were so muscular from bucking hay bales all summer he was incapable of scratching his own head. I have a cousin who walked down the aisle at his own wedding wearing Wranglers tucked inside his cowboy boots.

And who was I? I hated horses and was obsessed with *Vogue*. I got a paper route at age twelve so I could afford Esprit mini-skirts and Guess jeans at the mall. In my family, I was known as "the materialistic one" because I craved money, lots of money, to buy *things*, wasteful things—perfume, jewelry, shoes, matching bras and underwear, Archie comic books and, when I was a little older, liter-size bottles of Bartles & Jaymes wine coolers. My older brother's friends all thought I was pretentious and a bit mean—characteristics I patterned after my secret hero, Veronica Lodge. I almost preferred *not* to be liked because it was further evidence I wasn't meant for small-town life. I was edgy and sophisticated. Complex. Avant-garde, maybe. I purposely wore mismatched clothing, my feeble way of signaling to the world that I was meant for bigger things, important things. My desire for outsider status was made clear to me the day my jazz dance teacher, who'd lived in New York before coming home with a cocaine addiction, offhandedly told the class that the number of nightclubs in New York rivaled the number of muggings and drug dealers, and I yearned to be there. In diary entries from that time, it was clear I thought New York City was supremely glamorous and bohemian and dangerous while Montana was a plate of meat and potatoes—gristly, dull and constipating. It was a place where cable access shows like *Bass Fishing in the Northwest* were too strong a lure to compel Montana men away from the TV when company came over.

The Montana man. Also known as "the cowboy."

As I sailed past acres and acres of calves trailing their mothers, I thought about the type of men I grew up with. Montana men were strong but mostly silent types who seemed more enamored of their trucks and horses and—in the granola crunchy town of Missoula where I grew up—carabiners and mountain bikes than they were of, well, me. In this world, the idea of sweeping a woman off her feet was an anomaly. It was a man's world, an unvarnished cowboy mentality shaped by the ruggedness of the terrain and the harshness of the winters. It was a place where size—Big Sky, Big Fork, Big Mountain, Big Timber—was the only thing that mattered. Overt displays of femininity, on the other hand—manicures and pedicures, enjoying having a door opened for you, preferring *not* to lift things that exceeded your body weight—were seen as some sort of character flaw. I always had the sense that the women in my family were either expected to behave more like men, like cowboys—tough and stoic, know how to swing a hammer, open your own damn door—or morph into Mary Kay–wearing martyrs who sat around eating cheese dip and complaining about the emotionally unavailable men in their lives. It's why my mom now drove a massive Ford truck with vanity license plates that read "UNCLBARB" to subconsciously signal which side of the Montana lady divide she was on.

Neither role ever appealed to me, so I moved east a month after my seventeenth birthday and didn't look back, except for the occasional letter home that usually began with endearing salutations along the lines of "Dear Hayseeds!!!" and went down the toilet from there.

I had left Montana because I didn't like my options . . . yet here I was again, back in my home state, looking for new ones. I seemed to have a hard time finding an identity that fit.

As I saw it, there was only one solution to my current existential crisis: make out with a cowboy. A touch glib, yes, but I honestly felt a run-in with an all-American he-man, the archetype of my home state—a guy who probably had a better chance of opening a beer bottle with his teeth than sweeping me off my feet—was just the thing I needed. Making out with a rowdy cow puncher in some backroom bar in Miles City would help purge me of Jeff, help rid me of the listlessness and complacency that had come to smother me like a body bag. I didn't care if the cowboy was a monosyllabic redneck, I didn't care if he had a gun rack, I barely cared if he had a missing tooth. I didn't care one bit because I was flying back to New York—to a new outlook, a new beginning—on Monday.

I pulled into the town of Forsyth, about forty-five minutes west of Miles City and the only place I could find a vacant room within a fifty-mile radius of the rodeo. Forsyth had the bones of a 1910 frontier town—it boasted about eleven enterprises—bars, a grocery store, a café—running parallel to a railroad. The hotel room itself smelled dusty and stale. When I opened the drapes to allow in some light, the neon Kum & Go sign at the convenience store across the street beckoned me, like an invitation. (Kum & Go, The Town Pump—what would come next? The Tug 'N' Squirt?) From out of the Kum & Go's doors stepped two teenage boys, each holding enormous plastic Mountain Dew cups. One of the boys reached into his back pocket for a can of chewing tobacco. He snapped the can twice in his hand and shoved a wad in his lower lip, followed by a long draw of Dew. I was definitely back in my home state, a place where for some, a pinch of Kodiak passed for a serving of vegetables.

My BlackBerry chirped. It was Jane, the photographer who would shoot the story. Laurie, who had originally pitched the idea, ended up not being able to do it after being hired to shoot the Bucking Horse Sale for another publication. Jane and her assistant, Cody, had driven nearly seven hours from Missoula that morning. We agreed to meet at the Eagles Club for a drink before heading over to the rodeo, which had started that morning. While we talked, I caught my reflection in the mirror and almost didn't recognize the Upper East Side matron staring sourly back at me. I hurriedly changed out of my New York uniform—skinny jeans and boots—to something that would counterbalance the hair: cargo pants, iridescent sneakers and a T-shirt depicting a guy wearing a mullet and aviator shades next to the words "You party?"

The Eagles Club was located just off Main Street. It was approaching three o'clock by the time I got there, but happy hour was already in full swing for the handful of laughing, co-ed bikers who plunked coins into one of the many Keno machines lining the wall. At the bar, a couple of old timers slumped over their beers while a Rubenesque bartender munched a bag of Cheetos, carefully selecting one cheese curl at a time with her French-manicured fingertips. At the far end of the bar sat a woman who had to be Jane—she was the only one who looked like she could be from hippie town Missoula—and Cody. I pulled up a stool between them and ordered a vodka on the rocks.

The bartender scrunched up her eyebrows. "You want a glass of *just* vodka with *just* ice in it?"

"Yes, Grey Goose, please."

I sensed a wisp of annoyance coming from my new colleagues as they sipped their Budweisers. Both were in their mid forties and presumably old friends. Cody was reed thin and tall and wore high school math teacher glasses. Jane had an earth-mom vibe and wore black Birkenstocks with red wool socks. She had short brown hair and glasses, and had on a southwestern wool coat.

"So, what's the game plan for the weekend?" asked Jane.

I watched the bartender fill a mug all the way to the top with vodka not labeled Grey Goose. She slapped the drink before me and explained she was out of "grey good, or whatever," and walked to the far end of the bar.

"The plan," I said, taking a small sip, "is to capture that hyper-kinetic masculine cowboy iconography. I want to provide a picture of the untamed American West so I envision full-saturated, full-bleed, really close-up, vivid color action shots. Think horses mid-buck with the bottom of their hooves coming straight for the camera, that sort of thing."

"I don't have health insurance," Cody said. I could tell he wasn't warming to my charms.

After we planned our strategy, I paid for the round and we walked outside. The temperature was surprisingly balmy. Streams of sunlight melted holes in the clouds. Main Street Miles City looked like a larger, more deluxe version of Forsyth—a collection of Old West–style buildings featuring old cafes, supply stores, Western-wear boutiques and a high percentage of bars. We heard that for the next two nights, the entire street would close to traffic for a giant street festival with live country bands, dancing, barbecuing and barhopping.

We drove separate vehicles to the Eastern Montana Fairgrounds about a mile west of town. The parking lot was packed.

From inside the arena could be heard the muffled calls of the announcer. Vendors selling T-shirts and bumper stickers saying things like "I go nuts for Wrangler butts" and "Save a horse, ride a cowboy" were lined up out front. I called Bob Dixon, the sale's organizer, who met us outside the front gate on his ATV four-wheeler.

Bob was dark-haired, bearded and portly with a permanently placid expression. He gave us a little backstory on what he kept referring to as "BHS." Since the 1950s, he explained, every third weekend in May, horse buyers and rodeo-stock contractors from all over the country descended on this cattle town of 8,500 to bid on unbroken horses and bulls.

"We get horses here that have just come off the prairie and their owner can't even get a saddle on 'em," he explained as he handed us our press passes—laminated cards with the word "PRESS" typed on the front. "There's a lot of broken arms, broken legs—it's not a whole lot of fun for some cowboys. But some stock, you just can't break. Just like some men don't want to get married." He winked as Jane snapped his picture. "They're rogue personalities, wild. So they end up here."

What separated the BHS from other rodeos, he said—and why it attracted 4,000 spectators every year—is that professional rodeo riders won't risk their necks on untried stock (a broken arm tends to end a cowboy's season pretty quickly), so the cowboys who competed tended to be fringe amateurs—ranch hands, urban tourists on a dare, cowboys chasing a dream—anyone ballsy enough to get on an untamed bronc or bull. It sounded like a recipe for litigation but Bob said in the sale's five-plus de-cades, there had never been a single lawsuit. "Suing just ain't the Montana way," he said.

Bob led us into the rodeo. The stands were filled to capacity. Beer-drinking spectators milled about the paved promenade be-tween the bleachers and the ring. The crowd looked to be an even mix of tourists dressed in exaggerated western finery—leather jackets with fringe, ostrich boots, giant silver belt buck-les, turquoise pinkie rings—and low-key locals. Bob pointed to the main chute on the opposite side of the arena. It sprang open and a horse and rider exploded into the ring, ricocheting like a 1,200-pound bouncing ball. Within seconds, the animal cata-pulted the cowboy off its back—but the cowboy's foot got tan-gled in the stirrups. Helpless, the rider was dragged facedown in the dirt like a child's rag doll until the horse was eventually sub-dued by three men on horseback.

"That horse all but pulled a knife on our cowboy!" called the announcer as the cowboy was carried from the arena. "That's what we call gettin' wild and woolly Miles City–style."

A sign advertising the services of a local chiropractor hung over the chute.

Bob rode off as Jane, Cody and I entered the gate demarcat-ing "backstage," the area behind the ring where the competitors hung out. The gate was guarded by a grinning deputy. He checked the cards around our necks, which seemed like a mere formality since the entire fairgrounds, behind and in front, was crawling with slap-happy good ol' boys who looked like they'd been double-fisting cans of Coors Light since that morning. As we got closer to the chutes, cowboys preparing to ride unspooled large swaths of surgical tape, which they wrapped around their chests, arms, legs and hands. A lot of them wore Kevlar vests, some wore face masks, a few lay in the dirt with their eyes closed and heads resting on their saddles, as if in meditation. Perched on a nearby fence were groups of cowgirls—or what Cody described as "buckle bunnies," groupies wearing white cowboy hats and pink lip gloss and sipping Coors Light, their Wrangler-clad bottoms hanging like ripe fruit over the fence rail. I never understood why women wore Wranglers. They made their hindquarters look three times bigger than they actually were. My outfit, by comparison, made me look like the hip girl in a Volkswagen Beetle commercial. I glanced at the ground and noticed I was the only one wearing sneakers. The sun was blazing so I took off my jacket and hung it on a fencepost. A cowboy strode by with both thumbs extended. "Hell, yeah!" he said. I blushed and realized he was commenting on my T-shirt.

The testosterone in the air right around the chutes caught me off guard. I had become so inured to the neutered sexual relations that existed between men and women in Manhattan's media world that I almost forgot how unabashedly tough, virile and dirty cowboys were by comparison. I felt foreign and exotic.

Five feet away, a cowboy with chiseled cheekbones lowered himself onto the back of a shaking bull in preparation to be detonated into the ring. He was surrounded by a group of guys, all wearing equally tense expressions. The chute rattled and shook as the bull—somebody identified him as Kojak—struggled to free himself. The cowboy closed his eyes and mouthed a few words in prayer as he wound his hand around the rope. It was a poetic, almost tender moment and it was the first time I grasped the severity—the lunacy—of the event: *This dude thinks he's going to ride a bull.* The gate went up, and the bull blasted into the ring. It kicked its hind legs to the sky and swiveled its massive head around in an attempt to horn the cowboy. In an instant, the rider was airborne and then crashed into the dust, landing on his tailbone. The bull turned and charged as the cowboy scrambled to his feet and launched himself over the fence. My heart pounded, and I found myself cheering wildly with the rest of the crowd. The cowboy smiled big and waved his cowboy hat toward the stands while rubbing his tailbone with his free hand.

Invigorated, I looked around for someone to interview. I noticed the cowboy who'd been dragged facedown in the dirt by the bronc. He was sitting off to the side by himself staring into space. I strode over, Jane in tow, and asked his name.

"Zip. Zip Henderson," he said. He had jet-black hair and an intriguing gap between his two front teeth. He was from Dickinson, North Dakota—or "NoDak," as he called it. I told him who I was and asked him to relay what had happened.

"Don't want to talk about it," he said.

"Why?"

"'Cause if I talk about it, then it becomes real and fear takes over."

"That's pretty deep for a cowboy," I said. He glanced in my direction, as if just noticing me. "Seriously. What happened?"

"I said I don't want to talk about it." He got up and walked off.

"Alright, Zit," I called after him. "Nice talking to you."

"Where you from?" a husky male voice asked from behind me.

I turned to face three young cowboys lying laconically in the dirt, almost like they were sunbathing with their clothes on.

"New York."

"New York?" one bellowed while his friend whistled conspiratorially.

"Get a rope!" a passing cowboy chimed in, citing a line from an old salsa commercial. I think I was the only one who picked up on the dated pop-culture reference, which made me feel considerably older than the post-pubescent cowboys lying at my feet.

"What's a New York girl doing in Miles City?" one of them asked. All three looked at me skeptically, or maybe it was the sun in their eyes.

"I'm a reporter," I said. "I'm writing a story about the Bucking Horse Sale for a magazine called *Outdoor Adventure*."

"Never heard of it," said the cowboy in Bollé shades.

"Yeah, well, it's pretty elite."

I took down their names and phone numbers, had them sign model releases and motioned Jane over to take their pictures. As she photographed, I noticed a pair of golden chaps to my right. The wearer had his back toward me as he stretched out his legs. Upon closer inspection, and without making it too obvious that I was looking at his butt, I noticed the chaps were made of light brown leather and accentuated with shiny gold fringe and gold overlays. They had an old-world flair about them—like the kind I imagined rodeo cowboys from the '20s and '30s might have worn. He had one of those T-shape bodies—narrow in the hips and broad in the shoulders, the kind of physique male models and gay guys pay to have personally sculpted at the gym. This guy probably got his by punching cattle. Under his chaps he wore Wranglers and had on a big silver belt buckle and a blue plaid shirt. He turned and caught me scoping him out. It was the cowboy with the chiseled cheekbones who'd been ejected from Kojak moments prior. He nodded his chin and lightly touched the brim of his hat, a gesture that reminded me of something Robert Redford might have done in *The Horse Whisperer*. I took it as an invitation to walk over and verify it was he who'd been dumped by the bull.

He rubbed his tailbone and grinned. "Yeah, that was me." He took off his hat. His sandy blond hair was cut high and tight, military style. When he smiled, the corners of his mouth pulled up high, exposing a row of super-straight pearly whites, an indication of superior orthodontic work. It was a clue he wasn't from around here.

"Did it hurt?" Without a doubt, the dumbest question a reporter could ask a bull rider. "Or is it the kind of thing you can't think about or else the fear takes over?"

"Uh, no."

"How long have you been riding bulls?" I asked. His eyes were deep and kind and chocolate brown.

"Two years," he said.

"Is this your first time at 'BHS'?" For some reason, I put the "BHS" in air quotes, thinking he'd get I was trying to be "ironical."

"Yeah, first time at 'BHS,'" he said, matching my air quotes and raising me one. "How come you ask so many 'questions'?"

"I'm a reporter," I said. "From New York."

He gave my shimmering trainers a once over. "Yeah, I'd say that's about right. You're the only one here with twinkle toes." He looked at me suspiciously. "I hear New York women are nothing but trouble."

I couldn't tell if he meant to put that last sentence in air quotes too. "Funny, I've heard the same about Montana men."

His long, skinny legs, long arms, big hands and close-cropped hair reminded me of Woody from *Toy Story*—in a good way.

"What about you?" I asked. "You're not from around here either."

"How do you know?" He looked skeptical, almost like I'd insulted him.

"Well, for one thing, there's no chew stuck in your teeth."

"What can I say, I aim to impress."

"I'm impressed."

He said his name was Jake, he was twenty-five years old and from Virginia. He'd been living on a ranch for the past year and a half, pursuing his dream of cowboying on a real life cattle ranch in Eastern Montana. From this bit of information I deduced a) he was too young; b) he was probably a poser; c) but cowboy posers generally don't have the guts to ride bulls so maybe he's not a poser; and d) what did I care how old he was?

"How come you ride bulls?" I asked. "And not broncs?"

He pondered the question. "Bulls are more of a challenge. Broncs just want you off. But bulls—bulls want you off *and* they want to kill you with their horns. So it's more of an adrenaline rush."

I scribbled notes, aware that if I was going to make out with a cowboy this weekend, it should be with him. I asked for his contact information under the pretense of needing it for follow-up questions. He said he didn't know it—he'd been on horseback on the ranch for so long he never bothered to learn it. I followed him over to a white flatbed Ford truck parked in the grass behind the ring. I was admiring the way he walked—casually but with authority, arms imperceptibly floating a few inches from either side, like a college jock. He dug around the cab before handing me a slip of paper scrawled with the number. I took it and coyly asked him if I'd see him later that night at the street dance.

"Maybe," he said.

It wasn't really the response I was looking for, but it did seem like the cowboy thing to say.

Four

The Aircraft Carrier
and the Party Boat

That night, Jane, Cody and I made our way to the Bison Bar, which we'd been informed was the unofficial post-rodeo party headquarters, the place to experience BHS bacchanalia. It was only eight o'clock but most of the bar's patrons—spillovers from the rodeo—had been drinking since noon, so there was much stumbling and slurring on display. A heated arm-wrestling match was underway at a nearby table. That the two strong arms locked together belonged to women didn't faze anyone. Everyone was guzzling light beer. Live music drifted in from the street to compete with the Brooks & Dunn wailing on the jukebox.

My entire body was wrinkled, from my face to my socks. I had interviewed what felt like one hundred cowboys that afternoon and as I looked into the giant mirror hanging behind the bar, I wished I'd driven back to Forsyth for a quick shower, or at least to run a brush through my hair. My nose was sunburnt. I looked tired from the flight. I wondered if I'd run into Jake, but I looked so worn out it was just as well that I didn't. Besides, the bar was so packed with skinny cowboys in snap-front shirts that it would be impossible to pick him out of the crowd.

Just then I felt a tap on my shoulder. I turned around and there he was—Jake the skinny cowboy in a snap-front shirt, holding a can of light beer.

"Wanna beer?" He smiled.

"Hey, I didn't expect to see you," I said, taking the can. "How did you find me?"

"I kept my eyes on the floor, on the lookout for twinkle toes. And a girl as pretty as you stands out."

He was courting me. I blushed. Cody rolled his eyes and he and Jane disappeared into the crowd.

"Well, did you get all your interviews done?" he asked. He was all cleaned up and showered. He had a nice complexion, smooth and sun-kissed.

"Yeah." I had to shout to be heard. "I feel like I'm ready to ride a bull myself."

"Good," he said, grabbing my hand. "Let's dance."

He pulled me through the crowd toward the front door and onto Main Street. My hand all but disappeared in his scratchy, oversized palm. My heart pounded a bit as he led me to the middle of a roped-off dance floor facing the band and wrapped his free hand around my lower back. Everyone around us was touch-dancing and two-stepping. Laughter and music tossed all about us. Eyes sparkled from the reflection of street lamps.

"Uh, I don't know how to two-step," I stammered as he cupped my fingertips in his. I felt stiff and awkward. My rhythmic sensibilities were, for better or worse, deeply rooted in the bleeps and bloops of robot music. I had no clue how to partner dance and could envision myself stomping on Jake's toes.

"That's okay, pretty girl!" he shouted above the music. "Neither do I!"

He pulled me close and deftly moved across the floor, with a confidence that belied the absence of knowing any set foot pattern. I willed my nervousness to wear off and moved forward, responding with a slight smile. As the country song increased in tempo, dancers' feet stamped the floor, bodies spun and brushed together, hands joined and separated. Jake's eyes lowered one moment and looked intently into mine the next. He clutched me even closer as he twirled us around with the centrifugal force of an amusement park ride, and I couldn't help but laugh. The song ended with Jake dipping me backward before pulling me up so my face was mere inches from his. "Wanna keep dancing?" His eyes were ablaze and he grinned like a kid.

We danced for another hour before the band announced a beer break. Jake scooped my hand in his and we strolled to a bar at the far end of Main Street, where we found a seat at a quiet table in the corner. He helped me out of my jacket and pulled out my chair.

"You'll be alright by yourself for a minute?" he asked, presumably in the event some drunken cowpuncher would try to grab me while he was gone. I couldn't tell if Jake was serious or if he was appropriating the manners of a sixty-four-year-old Southern gentleman in an attempt to score. I was totally out of my element.

"I'll be fine."

He returned with two Budweisers and sat down heavily in his chair. "Yessiree, Jessie, you're a sight for sore eyes." He slid me a beer. "It's been a long time since I've seen a girl as pretty as you."

"Thanks. It's been a long time since I've seen a guy with such fucking awesome manners."

He made a face.

"Your manners," I repeated. "They're, like, really fucking good."

"Jessie, that's some potty mouth you got there."

I wasn't sure what he was referring to until I became aware of a subtle aftertaste of the F-bomb in my mouth. "Sorry. How is it that a cowboy doesn't have a 'potty mouth'?"

"I don't know—my mama? Sunday school? And I went to the Virginia Military Institute in Lexington, Virginia. They go heavy on the manners there. We had to take a class on how to treat ladies."

"Did you like college?"

He grimaced. "Let's put it this way—VMI is a great school to be from; it's a terrible place to go to."

I'd heard of this school. It was one of those ultra-conservative, predominantly male bastions of order and discipline not unlike

West Point or the Citadel, where they "tear you down to build you back up." A place where misogyny, I assumed, was a prerequisite for getting in, and classes in "how to treat ladies" more than likely reinforced antiquated gender stereotypes. But Jake didn't strike me as a military hard-ass with homoerotic leanings. He seemed more happy-go-lucky than masochistic.

"Let me guess, you got an A."

"If you say so," he said.

"A guy like you? All the cowgirls around here must chase after you."

"They try, but most of them aren't that good-looking. Besides, I don't get hung up on girls. I don't even like girls."

"How can you not like girls?"

"'Cause I like women."

Maybe it was because I was coming off a relationship with a man who shopped for little girls' underwear at The Big K, but a giant crescent moon shape took hold of my mouth. Here was a twenty-five-year old male who was actually a grown man. A grown man who actually had a preference for grown women. How novel. There would be no rainbow and unicorn underpants with Jake.

We talked until last call, paid our bill and walked outside. The streets were nowhere near empty. Cowboys and cowgirls stumbled out of bars in varying degrees of inebriation, their mates for the evening locked in step. Whoops and hollers punctuated the brisk night air. A cowboy was passed out on the sidewalk and girls laughed as they stepped over his prostrate body. Seeing all the wastrels around us, I realized Jake and I looked the same as everybody else attempting to walk a straight line up Main Street, though I was more or less sober. I felt like just another lonely heart in need of a hookup; like a Boomer Gone Wild trying to lure her young buck for the evening back to her Winnebago— pathetic. I'd been thinking about getting Jake alone all evening and suddenly when it was time to make my move, I choked. I didn't want to ask him back to my room. The man didn't even swear; he'd probably think I was "unladylike." The truth was, I'd never even had a one-night stand. They always seemed sad to me. At the same time, I couldn't get back on the plane to New York without some kind of symbolic purging of the last few years— Jake was my talismanic shortcut to renewal.

We stood under a streetlamp that cast a yellow glow all around us, like we were in the floodlights of an alien space ship. Moths danced and darted overhead. "What would you say if I invited you back to my hotel?" I asked. "I mean, it's really more like a *motel* and it kinda smells like urine, but—"

He put his hands on my upper arms and sighed, like he had something important or depressing to say.

"I'd say I don't normally do that kind of thing."

My heart dropped. The one time I work up the gumption to ask for a one-night stand—*from a hot, twenty-five-year-old bull rider!*—I get rejected on the basis of moral grounds.

"But . . ." He smiled softly. "I don't know. Something about you, about tonight feels right." He wrapped his long arms around me, pulled me close and kissed me. His lips felt hard and a little uncertain as his palms encased my back.

"Are you . . . religious, by any chance?" I asked.

"I'm a Christian, yeah."

"Ah."

That explained the hesitation. Sex should be saved for when the promise ring has been removed or better yet, one is married. I'd never made out with a Christian before. I mean, maybe I had, but never anyone whose religious affiliation was strong enough to bring up at a time like this. Still, what did it matter? Jake could have been a Christian, a Hindu, a conch-carrying pagan— what difference did it make? We were the proverbial two ships passing in the night—an aircraft carrier passing a party boat. I could already see the encounter becoming fodder for the next cocktail party I went to, which suddenly made me depressed. I kissed him harder.

He followed me in his white truck back to the hotel in Forsyth, where we collapsed on the bed and began fervently peeling clothes off each other. *So he's moral,* I thought as we fumbled for zippers and buttons, *but he's not a monk.* Yet he remained a gentleman throughout. His touch was gentle and sweet, loving and tender. I placed my palm on his chest for a pause, and asked if he minded if I had a quick toke of weed, a crumb of which I'd packed in my shoe.

I felt the tautness of his chest relax. "I guess not," he said unconvincingly as he rolled off. "You do what you need to do." I quickly loaded my miniature pipe disguised like a tube of Lancôme lipstick and took a long inhale of smoke while Jake studied my feigned insouciance. Through the smoke, I could see from his unperturbed expression that despite his good character, Jake understood the language of one-night stands as well as I did;

I knew he didn't like what I was doing, but he knew there was no point passing judgment on a party boat merely passing by.

Any reservations he had about my smoke break were quickly subsumed by the weight of our bodies refolding and tightening into each other. During the night, he placed his hands on my shoulders and gently pushed my torso away from his until his elbows were straight, as if to get a better look at me through the darkness. "Where did you come from?" he murmured. "Jessie K, are you an angel?" He slowly swayed my chest back to his, like I really was an angel fluttering to earth. All I could do was breathe him in, absorb the smell of sweetgrass and fresh rain that emanated from his bare skin.

When I opened my eyes early that morning, Jake was already out of bed getting dressed. I looked at the bedside clock: four-thirty a.m. His body was illuminated by a shaft of soft gray light coming from a slit in the curtains. I watched him pull on his Wranglers and snap the buttons of his shirt. No doubt about it, the man was smoldering.

"Leaving already?" I murmured.

"Yeah, I gotta be to work at five-thirty and the ranch is an hour and a half drive from here." He sat down on the bed beside me and ran a hand through my hair. "I'm already late."

I sat up, acutely aware this was how all one-night stands had to end: one person leaves, the other gets left.

"I'm glad I met you, Jessie." He leaned over and kissed my cheek.

"Maybe I'll see you today at the rodeo?" I asked.

"Can't. I have to work all day."

I couldn't tell if he was trying to get away from me—though of course he was; he was late for work. But I still felt rejected. Dejected. I'd known Jake for less than twenty-four hours and already felt like one of those needy, codependent women who call their boyfriends fifty times a day to find out what they ate for lunch.

"Maybe I'll see you at the street dance?" I asked, trying to sound casual.

"We'll see," he said.

As soon as the door closed behind him, I jumped out of bed and darted to the window to watch him go. He bounded down the steps two, three at a time. When he got into the truck, I saw a dog's head peek up from the passenger side—he'd had a dog in the truck all night. Jake warmly patted its head as the dog leaned closer to nuzzle his master's face. As the diesel engine roared from its night's respite, both Jake and the dog looked up to see my face peering from the second-floor window. He gave a little wave, put the truck in reverse and drove off in the direction of Miles City. I followed the white truck as far as I could before my eyes came back to the enormous Kum & Go sign across the street.

Five

Cowboy Up

That afternoon at the rodeo I suspended my usual organic piety by ordering a corn dog from a concession stand and devouring it in a way that elicited leers from a group of teenage boys nearby. No matter, I thought, as I tossed the polished skewer toward a trash can—and missed—and wiped a daub of mustard from my lip. I am not here to entice pimply-faced rednecks with the way I attack fair food, I am here to find Jake. Though I knew this was a conceit; I knew Jake wouldn't be here. He said he wouldn't be here. But I couldn't resist fantasizing that maybe, just maybe, he would have pleaded with his employer for the afternoon off to spend one final day with me, the mysterious woman with the strange haircut, before I flew back to New York on Monday. This shadow of possibility, this ray of hope, led me to look for his handsome face under every cowboy hat, on the back of every bull and behind the wheel of every pickup truck at the Bucking Horse Sale that afternoon.

By one o'clock I was ready for a nap.

Reporting from the front lines of an unfamiliar subculture was more challenging than I'd expected. By three o'clock, I had given up trying to understand the specifics of how the Bucking Horse Sale worked. Half of my interviewees were too drunk to provide coherent answers to my probing questions and the other half were too preoccupied to talk to me. I figured I'd call Bob Dixon once I got back to New York to fill in any remaining reporting holes. In the meantime, I told Cody and Jane to pack it in.

Cody looked at his watch. "Already?"

"Yeah, I have what I need," I said. Besides, leaving now would give me ample time to drive back to Forsyth, take a shower, expertly apply makeup and resume my hunt for the cowboy.

"Whatever you say, boss," he said as we nonchalantly watched another cowboy get launched from the back of a bucking bronc. Cody was dressed in a beat-up, faux-leather Members Only jacket from the early eighties. His thick auto-shading glasses, currently black as oil slicks, gave him a slightly menacing aura. "Gotta look your best for lover boy tonight."

Jane, who still wore her nubby wool socks and black Birkenstocks, just smirked. I had intimated that I'd hooked up with a cowboy the night before and they'd been teasing me about it all afternoon. The three of us had developed something of a rapport by now, boosted by my confession that I too was a Montana native. Cody's brusque attitude toward me had thawed somewhat. I was glad enough he liked me, but I found his provincialism annoying. He was the type of Montanan who considered himself a member of some elite tribe. To him, this great state was "the last best place," "God's country," and being a true Montanan—not some recent transplant from the coasts—was like being a descendent of Sitting Bull or Custer. To me, it was a mindset born of xenophobia, and it explained why so many vehicles with Montana plates bore the bumper sticker that read "NATIVE." Cody probably owned several. Even with my native credentials, I sensed that Cody had more or less decided I was a fast and loose New Yorker on the prowl for fresh cowboy meat.

We collected our belongings, said good-bye to Bob Dixon, who was still smiling beatifically astride his four-wheeler, and made our way to the jammed parking lot.

On the drive back to Forsyth, I couldn't help but congratulate myself on a job well done. I had come to Montana looking to hook up with a cowboy, and found a cowboy I actually liked. Not just liked, but *really* liked. It was almost a farce because Jake was 10,000 miles in the opposite direction from what I considered "my type." His profile would never have appeared on a list of potential love matches on an online dating site. Such a search would have yielded the expected collection of "creative" types—cinematographers, photographers, DJs, hipsters who said things like, "One of these days I'm going to finish that screenplay"—the tenuously employed, basically. I couldn't quite square where a Christian ranch hand fit into this pantheon of former flames. I chuckled when I thought that Jake probably listened to Toby

Keith. He probably voted Republican. He probably owned a gun and his dog was named something like Ratchet or Wrench or Skidder.

But I was getting way ahead of myself. It didn't matter where Jake fit. It didn't matter if he owned five machine guns. It didn't matter if he proudly displayed a pair of metal bull testicles from the rear hitch of his truck. Because I probably wouldn't see him tonight. I'd probably never see him again.

It was in this state of hopeful exuberance that I showed up to the Bison Bar that evening. I had managed to clean up. I wore shiny red lip gloss and smoky eye makeup. My skinny Joe's Jeans were tucked inside a pair of vaguely expensive looking (in the right light) Carlos Santana slouch boots. I wore a cap-sleeved stretchy black top that showed off my "cleavage" (a slight exaggeration) but the bar was so cold I was forced to keep my jacket on. Otherwise, I looked more or less middle-class Manhattan.

A small group of cowgirls whooped and hollered and ran to the dance floor as a song called "Redneck Woman" came on the jukebox. One of the girls assumed the rump shaker position—bent over, hands on thighs, buttocks wagging suggestively at a gathering of cowboys near the pool table, stringy hair covering her sozzled face. A cowboy jumped up and mock-humped her from behind, which he concluded by waving his cowboy hat in the air.

I turned to Jane. "You going to shoot that?"

Jane obliged by documenting this cross-cultural mating dance while Cody took in the spectacle, a look of bemused longing on his face. I surveyed the bar for Jake. He wasn't anywhere. I suggested we leave so we could document the scene at other saloons up the street.

"Sure, whatever," said Cody. He knew this was all a ruse for me to find the cowboy, but he kept his mouth shut; I think he enjoyed hitting the Miles City bar scene—he seemed like a bit of a loner who didn't get out much. But Jake wasn't at the second bar. Or the third. Or the fourth, fifth or sixth. It was nearing eleven o'clock, and Main Street was once again a carnival. I began to pick at the skin around my nails until they bled, a nervous habit I'd had since childhood. Last call was just around the corner. If I didn't run into Jake within the next hour, I wouldn't see him at all. It occurred to me I had his phone number so I could always try calling him tomorrow, but he said he worked in the fields—*worked in the fields*—and probably wouldn't get the message. Did cowboys return phone calls? Besides, I didn't want to call. I wanted another chance encounter. Phoning him seemed desperate for a woman just visiting for the weekend.

We ended up at the Olive Hotel, a fancy frontier-style inn at the far end of Main Street. It had a saloon that looked like something out of *Deadwood*, all distressed dark woods. It was less crowded than the other bars, with a clientele that skewed older—more boomers than young bucks.

It was now midnight and I knew I had to abandon my search or risk becoming depressed. I wasn't going to see Jake. I had had a one-night stand. That's all it was. I got what I wanted. But instead of feeling refreshed, I felt a funk coming on. So typical—

girl deludes herself into thinking there was genuine chemistry with one-night stand, when one-night stand was probably two-stepping with someone else right now.

"Wanna beer?" Jane asked.

"Yeah, sure," I said. "Gimme a bag of Funyuns while you're at it. And a jerky stick." I was starving. I hadn't eaten anything but the corn dog all day, and figured I might as well eat my weight in bar snacks now. I gravitated toward a table in the rear and sat with my back to the door so I wouldn't reflexively gape at every person who walked in. Cody took a seat next to me while Jane joined us with drinks and snacks.

"No cowboy tonight?" Cody asked.

"I don't know what you're talking about."

"Chin up," he said. "You New York women move too fast anyway."

I rolled my eyes and gnawed the head off my jerky stick. Without thinking, I turned around and glanced at the door. That's when Jake walked in. I nearly choked on the meat byproduct in my mouth. He spotted me immediately and smiled big. As he strode over to our table, my eyes fixated on the small patch of tanned flesh between his neck and the open top snap of his shirt, where a silver chain peeked out, which I knew held a small cross that hit at his sternum.

I willed Jane and Cody to disappear.

"How ya'll doing?" Jake asked as he took a seat next to me. His hand grasped mine underneath the table.

Cody and Jane inspected the bull rider, trying to ascertain what I saw in him besides his Chippendales physique. Jake referred to them as "Miss Jane" and "Mr. Cody," a folksy touch that sounded like an affectation to both me and Cody, judging by Cody's affable smirk. But it was charming.

After a round of chitchat, Cody and Jane finally took their cue to leave. As soon as they'd gone, Jake turned to me and took both my hands.

"You are absolutely beautiful," he said. "Even with that hunk of meat in your teeth."

"Oh!" I fumbled to extract the gristle. "I'm sorry."

"Don't apologize. I like a woman who eats jerky."

"I was about ready to go back to Forsyth," I said after he'd given my teeth the all clear. "I was beginning to think I'd never see you again."

"Not me," he said. "I knew I'd find you. I've been looking for you for three hours, walking up and down Main Street, going into every bar."

I laughed. I couldn't believe the man was actually willing to admit that he'd spent three hours stomping up and down Main Street looking for me. I remembered his unsolicited honesty at the Bison Bar the night before. Now he was coming through with several more ladlefuls of the stuff. What kind of strange disorder was this? I couldn't tell if Jake's lack of cynicism—a new and foreign lexicon—was for real or an act. He was like an artifact from a more wholesome era. And in the circles I ran in, wholesome was an insult. It was like calling someone "squeaky clean" or accusing them of harboring a secret collection of Disney figurines in a special hutch in their basement.

"How was work today?" I asked.

"Work was good," he said. "Though I couldn't stop thinking about you."

There it was again—the wholesome thing.

"You should come visit the ranch before you go. You'd love it there."

"I'd like that," I said, recalling images of myself as a sullen twelve-year-old, freezing my butt off in an empty field, softly crying.

The bartender announced last call. Jake got up to fetch two more beers while I tried to smooth my curled nest of hair.

"So—how does a Virginian end up in Miles City?" I asked after he'd sat back down.

"By driving." He took a swig of Budweiser. "I drove nonstop two winters ago. Just me, my dog and my horse."

"That sounds like a long drive for a horse."

"Yeah, but Socks could handle it," he said. "The only part where I got into trouble was driving through South Dakota. The temperature was twenty below and the diesel in my truck froze up. I broke down in the middle of nowhere. Eventually some guy drove by who gave me a ride to the mechanic. I had to wait two hours before my diesel thawed, then we pumped the diesel out of the tank because it was still so cold it would only freeze again, and refilled it with straight kerosene."

I reached for a response. "A truck can run on kerosene? Isn't that like lantern fuel?"

"Yeah, though kerosene doesn't have as much power as diesel," he explained. "You get less mileage per gallon on it. But you can blend kerosene with diesel. It's usually a four-to-one ratio—

four gallons of diesel to one gallon of kerosene will keep your fuel from gelling. That's what I did."

There was a long pause. I sipped my beer.

"Did you grow up in Virginia?" I asked.

"I'm not actually from-*from* Virginia." He winced. "I grew up in Baltimore. In the suburbs."

"Oh."

I wondered if Jake told people he was "from" Virginia as a way to gain traction with the farmers and ranchers of Miles City. Admitting his suburban roots probably wouldn't ingratiate him to the good ol' boys around here.

"I went to college in Virginia. Lexington, Virginia. It's a small town, about seven thousand people. Horse country. Very rural. I loved it there. I got very involved in the local community and ended up staying two years after graduation. I lived on a horse farm, where I worked as a farm boy for a competitive horse-woman."

"Is that where you learned to cowboy?"

"Yep. It's where I bought my first horse. It's where I had my first bull ride."

Aha. Jake the cowboy and Jessie the carefully crafted urban sophisticate were more alike than their opposing wardrobes suggested. Two individuals who brazenly claimed new identities, each traveling cross-country in opposite directions to find them. The East Coast suburban boy who dreamt of life on horseback moved west to compete at rodeos; the Rocky Mountain girl who longed to work in fashion magazines ditched her Western upbringing with the subtle finesse of a battle axe.

Upon further ten-second psychoanalysis, Jake's transformation meant he wasn't a cowboy by birth, but by choice—a cowboy in spirit. This was a crucial distinction because it meant he didn't have good-ol'-boy genes. His was not redneck DNA. (See: The outstanding orthodontic work.) It meant that no matter how many bulls he rode or diesel engines he stoked with kerosene, his suburban roots probably, surely, wouldn't allow him to toss empty beer bottles out the window of a speeding truck while yelling "Yeehaw!" or order personalized checks emblazoned with cock fights. This was a big relief since I'd been around enough cowboys to know that underneath the romantic, rugged exterior usually lurked someone more like Larry the Cable Guy.

"So you *became* a cowboy. What were you like before?"

He pondered the question like he couldn't remember such a time. "Mmm, don't know. A cadet? An Eagle Scout? I'm also a lieutenant in the Army Reserve. And I was always into construction. I like building things. I can fix just about anything too."

"What did your family think when you suddenly came home from college wearing a cowboy hat?"

"Don't know, never asked." He leaned back in his chair and cracked a smile. "But my mom laughed at me the first time she saw me in chaps."

Like Julie's name change to Hush, there was something refreshingly daring about such a blatant identity conversion, however disingenuous some of his family members probably thought it to be. But Jake's transformation didn't strike me as disingenuous. It seemed authentic, from his rough-hewn hands to the way he wound his hand with rope on the back of a bull. He moved like a cowboy. He spoke like a cowboy. He even drove across "SoDak" in a truck fueled with kerosene like a cowboy. He was a ranch hand in Montana! What other cowboy credentials were there? And in some ways, choosing to be a cowboy was more spirited than merely being born into it. The learning curve was a lot higher.

"I guess you can't call yourself a real cowboy unless you cowboy in the west. Is that why you moved to Montana?"

"That, and I had a—what do you call it? A stalker? This lady was after me. She wouldn't leave me alone. I had to get away from her."

I was intrigued but I resisted pressing for details as I didn't need the image of a knife-wielding ex-girlfriend interfering with my romantic moment.

"How about you?" he asked. "You like New York?"

I picked at the label of my empty beer bottle. "Mmm, it's okay. I've lived there for almost twelve years now. I'm getting really bored of it."

"What, did you move there when you were thirteen? How old are you? How the heck can a person be bored of New York City? Isn't it where everything happens?"

"Yeah, I guess so," I sighed, skipping his first question. "If you like going out and drinking and partying every night and blowing all of your money on rent and kombucha tea and having nothing to do on the weekends but go to yoga and shop at H&M—it's great."

He looked at me the way I'd looked at him during the diesel conversation.

"How old did you say you were again?" he asked.

"But I'm really from Montana—born and raised."

"No kidding," he said. "Jessie K from Montana. I knew there was a reason I liked you."

"Yep. I grew up in Missoula. One set of grandparents own a five-thousand-acre cattle ranch near Bozeman. My grandma Rose is like the original pioneer woman—tough as nails, very spirited . . ."

"So you ride?" His eyes lit up.

"Ride, like a horse? Oh yeah, sure. I grew up riding. Love horses. I had a horse named . . . Dokken." Actually, my younger sister, Cassie, the horsewoman of the family, rode a horse named Dog Kicker while I watched music videos by the likes of '80s hair band Dokken inside the house, so I was within the realm of truthfulness.

"Great! We can go for a ride while you're here."

"Though I haven't ridden in a really, really long time. . . ."

"Tomorrow, you come to the ranch, I'll show you around and we'll go for a ride. How's that sound?"

"Great!" I said.

There was no way I was getting on a horse.

Six

The Last Best Place

By the time I showed up the following day at Anderson's Ranch and Cattle in Kinsey, Montana, about twenty miles northeast of Miles City, it was already three o'clock—I was hours late.

Last night had been a repeat of the night before, with Jake following me back to the hotel before leaving in the wee hours of the morning so he could make it to work on time. Before he left, he drew me a crude map for how to get there. But once I got on the road after seeing Jane and Cody off around noon, I realized I could make no sense of his directions. They were incomprehensible. I had spent the last two hours driving up and down every gravel back road between the main highway and the Yellowstone River looking for the ranch. I knew I was lost after being hit in the face by the stench of the county dump, so I turned around and drove all the way back to Kinsey, and asked a diner waitress if she'd heard of the place. Two old ranchers sitting at the counter overheard our conversation and said they knew the place well, and pointed me in the right direction. By the time I pulled into Anderson's long gravel driveway, which led to a modest, single-level brick house surrounded by towering trees that served as ground zero for the family-owned three-thousand-acre cattle ranch, I was so rattled I was sweating.

I got out of the Cherokee and was immediately surrounded by three happy, dopey dogs, one of which planted its muddy paws on the front of my jeans. "Damn you, get off," I hissed as I jostled him down. I walked up the concrete front steps, opened the screen door emblazoned with a metal A, and knocked on the door. The door featured three small diagonally cascading windows, hallmarks of a home built in the late '70s or early '80s. The door was opened by a tall older woman with short gray hair and glasses, who wore a Montana State University sweatshirt over a turtleneck.

"Uh, yes, hello, I'm a friend of Jake's. My name is Jessie. Is he still here by any chance? I was supposed to meet him around noon, but I got lost."

"Oh, you got lost," she said. "I'm afraid he's out working in the fields. I'm not sure when he'll be back. Maybe we can try to find him?" She disappeared into the house and returned a moment later with her jacket on.

"I don't want to put you out," I protested out of polite convention. "He gave me his number. Maybe we can call him."

"No, I don't think Jake uses his phone much. I don't think he'll answer. I'll come with you. It can be tricky to drive out there."

I looked at the sky. The puffy, optimistic cumulus clouds that had greeted me that morning had flattened to a dreary, low-lying gray blanket that seemed to promise rain. The damp grass and muddy paw patch on my jeans indicated it had rained already. There was a chill in the air, like winter wanted to leave one more reminder of its presence before retreating for good. I tightened my jacket around me.

We loaded into a beat-up old truck that had the words "FARM USE" on the back plates, and slowly rumbled onto a dirt road that cut through a field that looked like it contained some kind of crop—sugar beets, according to my guide, who eventually told me her name was Beth. The terrain around Kinsey was as flat as Miles City only less brown, more lush. Trees bunched heavily around the perimeter of each farm. Beyond the sugar beets, said Beth, was pasture for their herd of Red Angus cattle. As we made our way to a group of outbuildings in the distance, Beth explained how she'd come to know Jake. They'd hired him on the recommendation of friends in Virginia, she said. Three months prior to his arrival, Beth's husband, the rancher, passed away suddenly of a heart attack.

"Oh, I'm so sorry!" I said.

"I don't know what I'd have done all these months without Jake," she said. "He's been an enormous help, both in keeping things running on the ranch and in keeping me company." She looked at me rather gravely. "Jake's a very special person."

I responded with a tight smile, unsure whether this was meant as a validation of his character or a warning to back off.

As we rolled past the outbuildings into a second fenced-off

pasture, I could make out the figure of a man standing next to a horse.

"There he is," said Beth.

Jake had the horse by a lead rope, which he kept slack, and was jogging the horse around a large circle while he stayed in the center. With no tugging or pulling on the rope, Jake switched directions and the horse followed, as though he was commanding the horse by body language alone. We stopped the truck about eighty feet away, and watched him repeat this quick, synchronized dance several more times, man and horse turning in polite unison. Jake finally looked up and waved. He stopped the trotting horse and patted its mane a few times before coming over to the driver's side window.

He leaned in and beamed when he saw me. "Hey, pretty girl," he said, as if Beth's profile wasn't mere inches from his face. "I thought you'd forgotten about me."

"I got lost," I said.

"What, New York girls don't know how to read maps?"

"I'm not convinced that was a map," I said. "Looked more like chicken scratch."

He laughed. "Well, I'm just glad you're here now. Thanks for bringing her out, Miss Beth."

Beth nodded, then turned to me. "Are you going to be warm enough?"

I looked down at my stretchy jeans and Carlos Santana boots.

"Don't worry," said Jake. "We'll get her suited up. Well, come on, Jessie K, let me show you around."

I tentatively scanned the surroundings. Fence, grass, sky,

horse, truck—we'd already covered the entire farm spectrum, as far as I could tell. What else was there? I forced myself out of the cab. Beth rumbled off as Jake walked over and put his arms around me.

"Cold?" he asked.

"Yeah, freezing." He grasped my fingertips. "What were you doing with that horse?"

"Teaching him some manners."

We walked back to the horse so Jake could unhook its bridle. The horse defiantly reared its head a few times. Jake responded by wrapping his arms around the horse's face and hugging it very close to his chest. He held it there until the horse stopped trying to jerk its head.

"If a horse lets you hold him around the nose like this it means he's submitting to you," he explained. He rubbed the top of its head between the ears and murmured, "You think you're the boss, don't you?" He turned back to me. "I'm trying to show him he's not the boss."

"What, are you like the horse whisperer?"

He laughed as he released the animal. "I don't know, maybe. Sometimes I think I understand animals more than I understand people." He scooped up the bridle as the horse resumed munching grass. A dog—the one I'd seen in Jake's truck—came bounding toward us. His coat was damp, like he'd been playing in a stream, and his tongue was lolling out of his mouth. It looked like he was smiling.

"There he is," said Jake, sounding like a proud parent. "There's Cowboy."

"Cowboy." Of course.

Cowboy was a male border collie whose eyes were rimmed in black with upturned tips at the sides, like how a '60s go-go dancer might apply eyeliner. The markings gave him a distinct though slightly feminine appearance.

Jake picked up a stick and threw it. Cowboy raced after it and brought it back, promptly dropping it at Jake's feet.

"He's showing off for you," he said, then turning to Cowboy: "Roll over, Cowboy."

Cowboy immediately dropped to his belly and rolled over in the damp grass before returning his gaze to his master. "Now roll the other way," said Jake. Cowboy swiftly rolled in the opposite direction, like a soldier performing army drills. "Well done," Jake said as he patted the dog's head.

The wet grass was soaking through my boots. I began to shiver. The three of us walked to one of the larger outbuildings. Inside were a couple of tractors in varying states of repair. Table-tops and counters were strewn with greasy tools, machines, coffee mugs, hardware and paper towels. Oil spills covered the floor. The place looked like a farmer's paradise, as if its doors had never been darkened by womenfolk. A woodstove, to my delight, burned welcomingly in the corner. Next to the stove were a pair of green and yellow bar stools fashioned out of old tractor parts. The seats were vintage metal tractor saddles shaped to fit the contours of the rear end.

"I just built those," Jake said. "Finished painting them yesterday."

Even to my untrained eye, the craftsmanship looked flawless.

The paint job was meticulous. I could easily see them displayed at any farm-to-table restaurant in New York.

"You could sell these in New York for a thousand bucks a pop," I said.

Jake made a face and handed me a large wad of clothes. "Here, put these on."

I shook out the wad, which turned out to be a pair of men's insulated overalls with the Carhartt brand stitched on the front and a matching Carhartt hooded coat. Jake pulled a black knit cap onto my head with the authority of a parent dressing a clumsy child, and gave me a pair of men's insulated muck boots that were at least four sizes too big. Once attired, I felt small and ridiculous—like the immobilized, snowsuit-wearing little brother in *A Christmas Story*.

"Help, I can't move my arms!" I wailed from beneath the mounds of insulated canvas.

"C'mon, I want to introduce you to my buddy Wade."

We walked outside and crossed a swath of pasture toward a large barn. A light rain began to fall. At a corral by one of the buildings, several fat pigs rolled in the mud. One of the larger pigs trundled over to the fence and tried to push its snout through the boards into the legs of my overalls. I backed away.

"Looks like you have a new friend," Jake said.

"Sorry, Mr. Prosciutto, I have nothing for you."

I couldn't remember the last time I'd seen a pig. I couldn't remember the last time a pig had pressed its snout into my crotch.

We walked around to the front of the barn. At another muddy corral, we encountered a heavyset man in a Hanes T-shirt and red suspenders. He appeared to have his entire arm shoved inside the ass of a cow. I screamed. The man turned around and managed a strained smile, like he was rooting around for a lost set of keys.

"What is he doing?" I cried.

"He's AI-ing," said Jake, tickled by my shocked reaction. "How's it going, Wade?"

"Oh, it's going," the man drawled.

The cow calmly munched hay, as if the appendage inside her was no more significant than a blade of grass stuck to her tail.

"What's AI-ing?" I asked. I fumbled for my BlackBerry, thinking AI-ing was something Hush and Maria would need to see as a "not safe for work" jpeg.

"Artificial insemination," Jake said. "Wade's planting semen."

"Isn't that a bull's job?" I asked. I zoomed in with the camera phone and clicked away.

"It is, but this way we get to pick exactly which bull impregnates which cow so we can breed for traits we want," said Jake. "We order semen samples out of a catalog, like ordering vegetable seeds for a garden."

I envisioned a large turkey baster loaded with semen arriving COD from the post office.

"So does Wade, like, do this for a living?" I whispered.

"I don't know," Jake said, raising his voice. "Knowing Wade, he probably does it for fun. Wade, do you do this for a living?"

"Nah, I do a lot of other stuff," Wade said. "I work for MSU's ag research facility. I'm stationed in Miles City."

"Wade drops by whenever cows are in heat, which is synchronized to happen at least once, twice a week."

"Your arm must stay plenty warm."

"Yeah, something like that." Wade intoned, like someone who'd been fielding such comments his entire career.

We left Wade to continue the tour of the farm. As we walked, Jake held my hand, a gesture that caught me off guard. As we passed more tractors, old trucks, fences and gates, Jake made a point of meticulously explaining each part or machine to me—why these latches on that gate are used, how an old truck with manual transmission is able to shift gears without pushing in on the clutch, and a lot of other subjects for which I had zero comprehension. On some level he must have known a women's magazine editor wouldn't—couldn't—be interested. But I didn't particularly mind. I got the sense he just liked explaining things and it was ever-so-slightly refreshing to be around someone so mesmerized by gates.

The rain began to pour. "Uh-oh, this doesn't look good," he said. He pulled his cowboy hat tighter against his head and squeezed my hand. "This might not be the best day for a ride."

I tried to frown.

"What do you say we go inside and warm up? Do you mind?"

"I guess not—but only if you want to."

By the time we got inside, the smell of frying ground beef wafted into the mud room as we removed our boots and coats. Beth greeted us in the doorway wearing an apron and asked what we'd like to drink for dinner. I craved wine, but I settled for a Crystal Light fruit punch.

"Smells delicious, Miss Beth," Jake said. He led me by the

hand through the galley-style kitchen into a living room that seemed to sag like the rancher whose picture was displayed on an end table. The couch was old and faded. Two worn La-Z-Boy recliners were situated right in front of the TV, which played *America's Funniest Home Videos*. The mantel above the fireplace was lined with more photos; family photos from the '80s and '90s—department-store studio portraits of smiling young people against backdrops of the autumn harvest. A large elk painting hung on the wall.

"You two make yourselves comfortable while I finish up these burgers," called Beth from the kitchen.

"Sure thing, Miss Beth," Jake called. He turned to me. "Wanna watch TV?"

"Not really, but okay," I said.

We sat on the floor in our socks, drank our Crystal Light and watched unsuspecting dads get smashed repeatedly in the groin by innocent offspring wielding bats and sticks.

When dinner was ready, the three of us sat down to a small circular table in an alcove of the kitchen and helped ourselves to hamburger patties, boiled potatoes and peas. I was about to put a forkful of peas in my mouth when Jake stopped me.

"Let's say grace."

"Oh, right." I bowed my head and folded my hands.

"Dear Heavenly Father," Jake said. "Thank you, God, for allowing us to live another day and for blessing us so abundantly with good food, friends and family. Please offer guidance to Miss Beth as she moves on from the ranching lifestyle. Thank you also, Lord, for giving Miss Jessie safe travels out to the farm. May we live each day to honor you, God. Please bless us in your service. In the Lord's name we pray. Amen."

We raised our heads and briefly scanned each other's faces. Beth smiled. "Amen. Thank you, Jake."

"Amen," I added. I felt the urge to cross myself in solidarity, but instead asked, "Is this meat local?"

"It all comes from here," Beth said. "And the potatoes."

After dinner, Jake and I did the dishes before replanting ourselves in the living room, pretending to watch *60 Minutes* with Miss Beth. The intensity with which he played with my fingers and tickled my hands suggested he wanted to sneak off to a back bedroom as much as I did, but the need for propriety, it seemed, took precedence. After what seemed like an eternity, he finally announced, "Well, why don't I show you some pictures? Do you mind if we leave you for a minute, Miss Beth, so I can show Jessie some photos?"

"Sure, go right ahead."

We went into a bathroom just off the living room, which led to a second door that connected to spacious guest quarters on the other side, or Jake's room. This room featured another door to the outside. I noticed Jake made a point of keeping both the bathroom door and the door to his bedroom ajar so Miss Beth wouldn't get the wrong idea. Partially blocked by the door, I wrapped my arms around his waist and whispered, "You're too good."

"It's her house," he said quietly. "I don't want to be disrespectful."

The bedroom's feminine décor—floral bedspread, a wall

plaque that read, "Life is not measured by the number of breaths we take but by the number of moments that take our breath away"—was offset by its current inhabitant's uber-masculine sensibilities. Lots of Western art hung on the walls, the kind familiar to anyone who shops for art in mall parking lots, in homemade frames wound with barbed wire. Three extra-large hazard cones were stacked in the corner. A bookcase fashioned of driftwood was filled with photo albums and religious books like *Chicken Soup for the Christian Soul* and *The Purpose-Driven Life*. A RadioShack boom box sat on a dresser next to a bunch of leather CD books. As Jake rifled through his CD collection for music, I looked at a framed photo collage on the wall, which depicted a younger Jake at various stages of his life, a montage no doubt assembled by a proud and caring mama: A teenage Jake wearing a Boy Scout uniform earning his Eagle stripes; Jake holding a Christian Young Life banner; Jake wearing a wrestling singlet, crouched and ready to tear the arm off an opponent; Jake up to bat in a baseball uniform . . .

"Geez, you're like Mr. All-American," I said as I plopped on the bed. "I didn't know they made people like you."

"Like what?"

Electro-elevator music from a '90s-era Moby CD came on, a selection Jake erroneously assumed an ambassador from New York City might enjoy.

"I don't know," I said. "You're not like other guys I've met. You seem so . . . good? Like you've eaten a lot of Wheaties."

Jake looked skeptical and joined me on the bed. "Is that a bad thing?"

"No, it's not a *bad* thing."

It was a *new* thing. A new way of looking at the world and relationships. Without a fashionable grudge or layers of ironic cynicism to parse through, how would I communicate with this person? "I've just never met anyone like you, that's all. Question: Do you listen to Toby Keith?"

"'American Soldier' is one of my favorite songs."

"What's your favorite movie?"

"Of all time?"

"All time."

"Mmm, *Top Gun*."

"I see. Do you own a gun?"

"Yeah, I own a gun," he said. "I own six guns." He went to the closet and pulled out multiple gun cases of varying sizes and laid them on the bed. He opened the first case, which revealed a Glock. Four subsequent cases held a .357 magnum revolver, a 30-30 lever action, a 7mm magnum bolt-action rifle and a shotgun. He picked each firearm from its case and thoroughly talked me through the parts and features—how each one loaded, how to use the sight. He made me stand and hold each weapon as he explained the proper handling technique. The guns felt like alien metal in my hands. I felt awkward and foolish as he tried to correct my grip and stance.

Jake opened the sixth case, and picked up a weapon that looked like the kind used by the Taliban.

"Is that a machine gun?"

"Yeah." He worked the bolt to make sure there wasn't a round in the chamber. "It's an AR-15. It's modeled after the guns used by the army special forces."

"Jake! Why do you have a machine gun?"

"I'm a soldier. Soldiers have weapons." He looked through the sight and aimed it at a wall facing away from the center of the house. "Wanna hold it?"

"No, I do not want to hold it! Aren't those things illegal?"

"This is civilian-issue and perfectly legal," he said. "Don't worry. It's not loaded. They are pretty fun to shoot. Maybe one day I can take you out shooting."

I was pleased to know he wanted to hang out again, but less thrilled at the prospect of rendezvousing at a shooting range to fire machine guns, which sounded so redneck. He must have sensed my unease; eventually he put the guns away. He gently kicked the bedroom door closed another foot before pulling me onto the bed next to him.

"Next you're going to tell me you have a pair of metal bull testicles swinging from the rear of your truck," I said as he buried his face in my hair.

"You mean 'truck nuts'?" His breath tickled my neck. "Heck no. Those things are tacky as all get-out."

I knew I should have left that night. We both knew I should have left that night. I kept saying "I gotta go" between kisses, but our bodies ended up sticking together like magnets, charged by the knowledge we more than likely would never see each other again.

Next thing I knew, I opened my eyes and it was morning. Jake's sinewy body was curled around mine. His eyes were already open and staring softly into mine. "Good morning, beautiful," he whispered. "You probably shouldn't be here when she gets up. It'll be awkward."

I looked at the alarm clock. It was five in the morning. I had to leave immediately. My plane was scheduled to leave Billings at noon, and I had at least four hours worth of driving ahead of me. Jake and I dressed quickly, swapped addresses and phone numbers, and crept out to where my vehicle was parked.

"Are you going to get in trouble for last night?" I asked.

"I hope not," he said. "But it was worth it—Jessie K, this was the best weekend of my life."

"Me too." The earnestness of my response almost surprised me. "Do you think we'll ever see each other again?"

"I have a feeling we will," he said as he pressed a scrap of paper into my hand then wrapped his long, muscular arms around my waist and picked me off the ground, squeezing me so hard we both heard my back crack. I couldn't breathe, but I had never felt more secure.

As I drove down the driveway, with the image of Jake and Cowboy receding in the rearview mirror, I opened the scrap of paper in my hand. It was a Lipton teabag. On the inside he'd scrawled, "I'm gonna miss ya!"

Part Two

seven

Long Horns
and Asphalt

Three weeks after returning to New York, I met Maria one Saturday morning at a Kundalini yoga center in Soho. It was taught by our favorite teacher, Kaur Maur Khalsa Amsala—née Denise Cronk from Coxsackie, New York. Petite and precious, she radiated health; her face actually shimmered from daily applications of sunflower oil, which she frequently reminded the class was available for purchase at the front desk for $29.95. She wore a flowing white robe and a white turban adorned with an exquisite jade amulet. Hearing her melodic voice ("Imagine you're on a ride at the carnival! Only the difference is—the ride is you!") was like being wrapped in the downy wing of a pegasus. For me, exercise had always been borderline religion, but a session with Kaur Maur Khalsa Amsala was as close to spiritual transcendence as I'd ever known. She was my personal guru. I wanted to *be* her. Except that as I now sat on my sheepskin rug, eyes closed and staring into my third-eye point, pulses of blue light receding from behind my closed lids like paintballs shot to the horizon while I frantically beat my arms up and down over my head for eleven hellbound minutes, I couldn't help but laugh. I was thinking of something Jake had said when I'd tried explaining Kundalini to him the other night on the phone.

"Let me get this straight," he'd said. "You pay twenty-five dollars to some lady wearing a turban to wave your arms around like a chicken?"

"Um. Yes."

"Uh. Sounds more like kundacrap to me."

I laughed.

"What are you doing?" Maria mouthed as she beat her arms next to me. Her '80s-style blue terrycloth headband was damp with sweat.

"Kundacrap," I whispered loudly. Yogis turned to look at me. Kaur Maur Khalsa Amsala scanned the room to detect the disturbance in the class's energy flow. I didn't care. I would have shouted "KUNDACRAP!" at the top of my lungs had it been more yogically acceptable. My arms ached and my shoulders felt like they might rip from their sockets, but my heart chakra was open. I felt light and giddy and free. Blissful Kundalini energy radiated from my skull. Jake's first letter had showed up a few days after I arrived back in New York. It was short and sweet—he wrote it on a Post-it note—and part of it read, "I'm alive and I'm free, and who wouldn't want to be me? Still smiling thinking about you, pretty girl!" In a later phone call, he'd said that Miss Beth was in the process of selling the ranch and the entire herd so she could relocate to Billings; Jake had volunteered to drive twelve of her cows to new owners in upstate New York. He'd be here in a few weeks.

Out on the sidewalk after class, Saturday morning Soho shoppers were out in force, faces encased in black sunglasses of varying geometric configurations. "That class was a trip," I said. "I . . . feel . . . delirious."

"That's cause your eyes were crossed the whole time," she said. "You're dizzy."

Maria was as devoted to fitness as I was, but she maintained a skeptic's eye when it came to the more tutti-frutti aspects of yoga—and of life, for that matter. Maria was the kind of person who demanded tangible proof of everything, from wanting to know whether a glass of wine at a restaurant was the official four-ounce pour—which sometimes necessitated calling over the waiter with a measuring device—to the existence of God. I, on the other hand, was willing to suspend disbelief when it came to taking a magic carpet ride of self-discovery with Kaur Maur Khalsa Amsala.

On our way to meet Hush for brunch, we passed the boutique Miu Miu. I stopped and stared into the window, entranced by a mannequin wearing one of the line's signature ladylike yet subversive dresses, the kind that look appropriate for the office or a space station. On the mannequin's feet, a pair of impossibly high wooden platform heels in a graphic print brazenly clashed with the dress.

"I was born to wear Miu Miu," I breathed, not realizing Maria had continued up the block without me.

I let out a melancholy sigh. I'd always felt that because I *wasn't* decked out in Miu Miu or Prada on a daily basis meant something had gone horribly amiss in my life. I was suddenly overcome by an overwhelming desire to go in and buy some ridiculously overpriced bit of clothing, not only to lay claim to a lifestyle I'd somehow been denied, but to have something to wear for Jake that would demonstrate I wasn't conventional. I wanted to convey I was complicated. Intellectual. Quirky. Fashion-forward. Maria noticed I'd fallen behind and rejoined me at the window. I made her come inside with me as I browsed the racks of sheer, floaty, five-hundred-dollar summer dresses and displays of fifteen-hundred-dollar ostrich handbags before settling on a pair of bunchy, slightly baggy cream-colored silk underpants that had delicate lace trim sewn around the top. They were ambiguously sexy, like something a 1930s substitute teacher might wear, and, at $195, the only thing I could afford.

"Like a cowboy will get these," Maria said as I handed the cashier my credit card. "They look like diapers. Are you sure you don't want to go to Victoria's Secret?"

"Don't be disgusting." I made a face and clutched the small, structured Miu Miu shopping bag tighter. "I didn't buy them for Jake. I bought them for myself."

"Uh-huh."

We walked over to Le Pain Quotidien on Grand. Hush was already at the head of the line and waved excitedly when she saw us, her little body clad in a shimmering black vest, tweed shorts over Capri leggings, a herringbone cap and high tops, which gave her the appearance of a Dickensian street urchin. She called us over to cut the line, which prompted a chorus of agitated sighs among the upwardly mobile behind us.

"So . . . are you excited?" She asked as soon as we were seated and had ordered a round of eggs and bowls of café au laits.

"Yeah," I said. "Only thirteen days to go."

"A cowboy," she said. "That is so badass."

"A *Christian* cowboy," Maria interjected. "A Christian cowboy who prays and reads the Bible and listens to Toby Keith and owns six guns, including a machine gun. Did you see the necklace?"

"He's not some Bible beater," I reminded Maria. "He's a man of faith—very spiritual." I fished the necklace out of my shirt.

Hush grabbed the small, silver circle with a hole in it on its chain and pulled my neck to the middle of the table. "Yeah, I saw it—I love it."

Maria's silence conveyed something different.

I gave her a look. "Not all jewelry has to cost money, you know."

"Really?" Maria asked. "Cause I'm pretty sure this one cost ten cents."

"He shot a hole through a dime at eighty yards," Hush said. "You gotta admit . . . that is awesome. Did he use the machine gun to do it?"

"Jesus." Maria rolled her eyes.

"You shouldn't take the Lord's name in vain," I said.

"Look at you." Hush chided Maria. "You're jealous."

"No, I'm not jealous," Maria said. She turned to me. "I just don't want you to get your hopes up, that's all."

"What do you mean?" I asked.

"You've been talking about this guy nonstop for three weeks." She weighed her words. "And I'd like to remind you that what looks good in the sticks doesn't always translate to real life. I can't help but wonder if you're attracted to a Christian ranch hand because . . ."

"Because . . . ?"

"Because your last relationship was with a pervert," she said.

I lowered my face and slurped from the bowl of café au lait before me.

"I'm just trying to honor the pact, that's all," she added.

The pact. Maria and I had made a pact several years ago that gave us the right, when asked, to freely admit whether we genuinely disliked the other's boyfriend, and the other person wasn't allowed to get upset by the information. The agreement was born out of our mutual dread of being *that girl* who dated the guy everyone hated, but pretended to like. Apparently, the pact had evolved to sharing reservations about the other's love life even before there was a legit love life to speak of, and the asking part was a forgotten formality. But Maria had learned over the years to speak freely with me because I had a tendency to fly off like a spinning top—therapy, meds, the cyborg, two-hundred-dollar schoolmarm underpants. We both knew I had a tendency to go whichever way the wind blew. I had even voluntarily moved to Jersey City with an old coworker at one point, even though I knew she decorated her office with kitten posters and stuffed animals. I was also vaguely aware that she had sex with a rotating cast of mailroom guys in our office stairwell and liked to attend Harley-Davidson rallies to wrestle other women in coleslaw. I chose to ignore these code-red warning signs and moved in with her, not simply because I needed a place to live, but because I deluded myself into thinking it didn't matter where I called home since I was always working and going out anyway. Except that just as Maria had predicted, it turned out to be a colossally stupid decision that culminated in me walking in on my roommate having sex on the couch with one of the mailroom guys—right before he shielded his soiled member with my favorite silk throw pillow.

"No, no, that has nothing to do with it," I said. "I like Jake because he's different. He's unique. I've never met anyone like him."

"That's what I'm saying," she said. "Name one thing you two have in common."

"Well, we . . . there's . . . we both love to dance." I didn't mention he leaned toward Tim McGraw while I gyrated to Brazilian dance music. "We both like beef jerky. We both have a connection to Montana. And our carved cheekbones and prominent noses make us look like Aryan siblings."

The waitress set down three plates of eggs in various interpretations.

"Look, I don't want to undermine your budding romance," Maria said while cracking her soft-boiled egg. "All I'm saying is, when he starts skinning gophers for you, don't be shocked, okay?"

"Good grief, let me have my five-minute infatuation, will

you?" I said. "I'm sure I'll be back to dating emotionally unavailable man-tards on the F train soon enough. And I already told you—he's not a hick. He's from Baltimore."

After brunch, Maria caught the train back to Park Slope while Hush and I strolled over to the promenade on the West Side Highway. Ever since I'd returned from Montana, I'd stopped riding the subway. Not because of its overbearing smell, but because I couldn't handle the teeming masses anymore. I couldn't tolerate someone's thigh spilling over onto my seat, or having my face pressed into the back of somebody's musky coat during rush hour, or catching a whiff of some random stranger's deodorant. But it was the faces of riders that irritated me the most—we all moved like zombies, lifeless and inscrutable, shuffling from one train to the next, lost in our digital lives. I craved light and air. I had to walk. I could barely take a cab. I walked everywhere I went now. I walked to yoga, I walked to go out at night. I walked the thirty blocks each way to *Outdoor Adventure*'s editorial offices in Midtown, where I had accepted a "permalance" (temporarily permanent) assignment after the editor in chief had been impressed enough by my Bucking Horse Sale story. This was supplemented by other assignments from women's magazines—including the one I'd just left. So far, I was loving the freelance life.

It was a gorgeous June day. The promenade was full of joggers, walkers, chic downtown moms pushing Bugaboo strollers and pumped up men on Rollerblades.

"Don't listen to Maria," said Hush. "I think Jake sounds cool . . . a lot better than some of the guys around here."

Hush was coming off of a relationship with an actuary named Dennis, who came from a similar background but made a show of flaunting his "heretical" behavior. Hush was initially attracted to Dennis because he, like her, had wandered outside his religious community: He dabbled in drugs and had casual sex. But, unlike her, Dennis wasn't cool—Dennis was a tool. Dennis was the kind of guy who was genetically programmed to live in a high-rise apartment with a doorman on the Upper West Side: he wore rumpled khakis and sensible loafers and slurped six-dollar coffee beverages from domed plastic cups with straws. Dennis had decided some years ago that the Upper West Side was too conventional for such a deep and metaphysical stoner as himself, so he moved to the Meatpacking District in an attempt to be "edgy"—though Manhattan, and the Meatpacking District in particular, was about as edgy as a Hammacher Schlemmer catalog at that point. He ended up glomming on to Hush, who rode around town on a boy's BMX dirt bike, doodled on her walls, habitually went against the grain and revered clothing and the Church of Latter Day Saints in equal measures. That is, she was an individual in every sense of the word.

Dennis was a blank slate with entitlement issues. At first, his interest in Hush seemed like a sincere infatuation—he was always complimenting the way she dressed and giving her these avuncular little smiles—but it later revealed itself as a calculating attempt to appropriate her style. He even went so far as to invest in his own BMX dirt bike and rode it around Union Square while wearing a coonskin cap. Hush, Maria and I all laughed as we watched him pedal off, the actuary's chino-clad knees practically banging the underside of his chin as a long foxtail flapped from his fur-covered crown. Then a few months later, Dennis was done with Hush. One of the last things he had said to her was, "Thanks, Hush, for making me cool. And now I'm ready to go out and conquer the world."

Hush was a little sore about men these days. But she was tough and resilient and usually did an impressive job venting her frustrations at H&M anyway, which was where she was headed after dropping me off at my apartment.

The mailman hadn't come yet so there was no letter from Jake. I stumbled upstairs and opened the door to my apartment to hear my landline ringing. I rushed over to answer it.

"Hi, Jessie, it's me." The voice on the other end oozed a shaky confidence. "It's Jeff."

"Oh . . . hey . . . what's up?" I hadn't given Jeff a second thought since meeting Jake, who in one weekend had managed to restore my faith in men. Jeff already seemed like a bad memory.

"I'm just calling to say hi," he said. "I haven't spoken to you for a while. How are you?"

"I'm fine," I said. "Look, Jeff . . ."

"How's work?"

"Work is fine."

"I've missed you."

I turned on the TV.

"Hey, I was wondering if you want to go to wd-50 with me this weekend," he finally said.

"Look, Jeff . . ."

"I really need to see you. We . . . need to talk."

His tone suggested he knew I knew about his little problem and wanted to discuss it. Maybe it was a cry for help, an opportunity to finally confront his demons. Or maybe it was just part of the perversion. Whatever the motive, I wanted nothing more to do with this walking porn package.

"Look, Jeff, I don't want to see you anymore."

Silence.

"I met somebody," I said.

"Oh."

"Yeah."

"Who?"

"A cowboy."

"A cowboy?"

"Yeah, a cowboy. He owns a bunch of machine guns. We're probably going to get married."

A tad dramatic, perhaps, but it conveyed my point. The other end of the phone became a quiet hiss—the sound of a guillotine in free fall came to mind. I smiled serenely and delicately hung up the phone.

Jake rolled into downtown Manhattan two weeks later driving his F-350 flatbed truck and pulling a twenty-five-foot livestock trailer loaded with six calf-cow pairs. I had no clue how he managed to navigate the unwieldy farm barge through the cramped streets of Manhattan—or whether hauling livestock into New York City was even legal—but when I looked out my window down to West

Twentieth Street, there it was, his brawny diesel engine rumbling as cars lined up behind it all the way down the block, horns blaring. Jake jumped out of the cab and I laughed when I saw he was dressed in full cowboy regalia—tight Wranglers, a cowboy hat, big silver belt buckle. In West Chelsea, it made him look like a man on his way to the gay bar, Rawhide. He looked up to see me waving from my fourth-floor window.

"Come on, Jessie K! Let's go!" he called.

I grabbed my bag, scrambled downstairs and jumped into his waiting arms. We kissed as an idling driver growled from an open window, "C'mon, assholes!"

"Hang on a sec, bubba!" Jake called back as we both climbed into the truck. Cowboy, who rode between us, leaned forward to lick my face. The truck lurched toward the stoplight.

I could tell Jake was exhausted—his eyes were glassy and red. The cab was strewn with takeout bags and cups from Bojangles' and McDonald's. He'd been up for thirty-six hours straight. "Can't stop when you're pulling cattle!" he yelled over the diesel engine.

We made our way out of Manhattan through the Holland Tunnel and into New Jersey. Once we got onto the Jersey Turnpike, he pulled over at a truck stop and asked me to drive while he slept. I'd never driven a vehicle loaded with animals. But the truck had an automatic transmission and we were on a relatively straight highway so . . . how hard could it be? I managed to keep the vehicle between the white and yellow lines all the way to a dairy farm near the Canadian border, where we dropped off the cows. The next morning, we made our way back to Manhattan. We parked the trailer in the sprawling parking lot of a New Jersey shopping mall before driving the truck back into the city (which Jake discovered turned out to be illegal when he went to pick it up a few days later, though he managed to talk his way out of paying a heavy fine).

I was excited to show Jake the city. I was excited to introduce him to Hush and Maria. But I was also a little nervous. The closer we got to the Holland Tunnel, the more concerned I was that once Jake stepped inside my admittedly bougie little world, once he saw the way I lived—the drinking, the Kundalini obsession and the organic food fanaticism, plus the realization my teeth weren't really this white—he wouldn't like me anymore. He'd find my interests trivial and silly. He'd already inferred as much when he called it "kundacrap." And he'd probably shut the door forever once he found out I didn't walk hand-in-hand with Jesus.

Or maybe it was Jake who was silly. His penchant for saying things like, "I'm alive and I'm free and who wouldn't want to be me!" *did* sound alarmingly cartoonish the closer we got to the city. I glanced at him as he drove. He had his head thrown back and was singing along to a country song that ginned up nostalgia for some mythical America where people caught tadpoles in secret swimming holes. Maybe Maria was right. Maybe Jake was just a character of his own creation that might come across more like a caricature—*Crocodile Dundee* came to mind—against the hard, fast backdrop of New York. Maybe there was just too much space and light and air in Montana for me to have discerned it. The sheer size of his belt buckle, embossed with a pair of long-horns, meant introductions to my friends might feel more like show-and-tell than a normal social interaction.

"Are . . . you really going to wear that belt?" I asked him that night. We were dressing in my apartment, on our way to meet Hush and Maria for dinner at Sushi Samba on Seventh Avenue, and I didn't want to confirm Maria's every assumption about him the second we walked in the door.

Jake looked down at his waist and rocked on the heels of his boots. "What's wrong with my belt?"

"Nothing. It's just . . . so big. Like a dinner plate at Sizzler."

"How am I going to keep my pants up?" he asked. I looked at his Wranglers, which were so tight they looked like they'd been applied with spray paint. "But I won't wear it if it embarrasses you." He grabbed me by the waist and dug his long, calloused fingers into my sides, which made me laugh until I forgot about the belt.

Sushi Samba was packed with spray-tanned women in plunging necklines and well-fed men in untucked tailored blue shirts. I felt the entire room gawk at us as we made our way across the restaurant toward Hush and Maria in a far booth. Maria's expression was impassive. Hush, meanwhile, was laughing—laughing at Jake's Wyatt Earp getup, I knew, but she played it off like she was giggling over some innocuous thing Maria had said.

"Howdy, ladies," Jake said as he removed his hat and pulled out my seat.

I sat down and gave the girls an anxious smile. I was suddenly overcome with embarrassment over Jake's courtly display of manners and by his use of the word "howdy." I wasn't sure how to finesse these two worlds colliding—though I reminded myself we were all technically of one world, one Eastern seaboard world. Jake was a Baltimorean playing a cowboy . . . which suddenly seemed quaint and preening against the techno samba playing in the background. I ordered a Mojito Supremo.

"So, Jake, we've heard so much about you," said Hush, who was so gregarious she could chat up a serial killer. "I feel like I know you already."

Within minutes, the two were engrossed in a conversation about horseback riding and how New Jersey was one of the main equestrian states in the country, topping a chain of horse country that extended all the way to North Carolina. Hush peppered him with farming-type questions, which evolved into a fascinating Q&A about horseshoeing.

Maria didn't so much listen to their conversation as sub-contract to a dark recess of her brain the task of discerning whether there was anything worth listening to while she fiddled with her phone. I was almost flattered when she did eventually zero in on Jake, no doubt looking for signs of cowboy B.S. I studied her while she studied him, seeking confirmation I wasn't crazy for falling for a ranch hand. (I didn't study Hush—she genuinely liked everybody.) As expected, Jake was interesting and interested, and didn't feel the need, like a lot of men in a group of women, to dominate the conversation. Most of all, he was charming.

When Jake and I walked back to my apartment that night,

through the raucous throng of Manhattanites out on a warm Friday night, we passed a group of tipsy Wall Streeters, ties loosened, gaping at Jake's outfit from their seats around a cluster of outdoor tables. Jake squeezed my hand as we strode by.

"I know what they're thinking," he said.

"What?"

"They're looking at you, they're looking at me and they're thinking, 'I gotta get me one of those cowboy hats.'"

Jake wasn't the least self-conscious about being gawked at. On the contrary—he reveled in it. He delighted in standing apart. When we passed a group of girls in the Meatpacking District and one of them cooed, "Hey, *Brokeback Mountain*!" he shot back, "Hey, I'm a cowboy! Everybody knows those guys were sheepherders!"

My phone vibrated in my pocket. It was a text from Maria.

I like. Maybe skinned gophers not so bad?

I leaned in closer and put my arm around Jake's waist. He squeezed me tight and we kissed clumsily as we walked. A passerby noted, "Ride 'em, cowboy." I felt validated—drunk, but validated. I also felt ashamed for judging Jake, for assuming he'd disappoint me or embarrass me in front of my friends. I suddenly realized that unlike me, Jake didn't peer into the future and automatically assume the worst. His sensibilities were rooted in the present, a perspective that gave him a confidence I lacked. He didn't particularly care what people thought of him. It was not in the usual self-defensive way in which people say they "don't give a shit," which is usually the tip-off they're as fragile as egg-shells. He genuinely seemed at ease with himself and the world around him. I wondered if his lightness of being was the result of religion—if praying gave him the compass to remain rooted in the here and now, and not five, fifty, one hundred murky lengths ahead. I wondered if a similar state was possible for me.

Back at my apartment, with the sound of samba music in the background, Jake and I lounged on my bed, too giddy to sleep. On my bedside table was a copy of a health magazine with my latest article in it, "Learn to Love Your Imperfect Self." Jake picked it up and started reading, then stopped.

"What?" I asked.

"I mean"—he winced—"I think what you do is really cool and all, but some of this stuff is kinda cheesy."

His words stung. Not so much that I agreed with him, but because it really wasn't a nice thing to say—to my face, at least. I turned away.

"Well, we can't all live as authentically as you," I sighed. "You know, with the wind at our backs and cow shit under our feet."

"Hey, I didn't mean it like that." He tapped a finger on my back. "That story is just a little funny, that's all. I'm sorry if I offended you."

I turned to him. He made a goofy face in an attempt to ease the tension. "And you shouldn't swear," he added.

So Jake was more judgmental than I thought. But it wasn't a judgment born from superiority. It was a by-product of living purely, having surrounded himself with dogs and horses and hay bales and old tractors. He wasn't under the yoke of money or status and he didn't feel pressure to "succeed" in the typical bourgeois sense. He hadn't sold out, and was quite blissfully broke. I had sold out, and was paid well for it. He was a straight talker, which is what I loved about him, but it cut both ways because it also made him too honest.

✻

Eight

Burn the Ships

Terry, Montana, is a speck of a town. It is laid out like a tic-tac-toe board and about as interesting, located a stone's throw from the NoDak border. Jake had moved to Terry for another job on another parched cattle ranch. It is so flat and dusty in Terry the whole town should have dried up and blown away in the prairie wind years ago. Attractions included a public swimming pool, three bars, a prairie museum and a gift shop called Prairie Unique that lived up to its name, insofar as it was the only store within a fifty-mile radius that sold jigsaw puzzles and beer bread.

It was well over 100 degrees the entire two weeks I was there. While Jake worked at the ranch during the day, I stayed behind at his little yellow house on Washington Street and pretended to work on magazine assignments—"pretended," because he had no Internet connection or TV or air-conditioning or magazines or books other than his collection of Bibles and inspirational tomes for Christian men. In the afternoons, when we weren't rolling around in bed adding to the already stifling heat index, we wandered over to the pool to cool off. But the pool was so old and decrepit, the walls covered in a thick, green algae, I couldn't see my hand in front of my face underwater. The good citizens of Terry didn't seem to notice. They bathed in the pool's murky waters like vacationers to Club Med.

After a dip, we would amble over to the Roy Rogers Saloon, where we clinked beer cans with Terry's drinking elite—stout ranchers, gristly cowboys and wild women. On the weekend, we canoed a stretch of the Yellowstone River, but the river was so slow and torpid and infested with snakes and mosquitoes that we ended up paddling like Lewis and Clark to avoid frying to a crisp in the sun. One day, Jake took me to a shooting range near the Badlands where I surprised myself by hitting the bull's-eye nine times out of twelve with the Glock. Impressed by my marksmanship, he made me shoot the AR-15, the kick from which was like a punch to the shoulder—my arm ached the rest of the time I was there. There came a morning when I was finally persuaded to go horseback riding. We arose before sunrise, hauled two horses toward the Badlands, rode up to the highest peak and watched the sun peek over the eastern horizon. It was probably the most romantic date I ever had, but I was so frightened of my horse I practically blubbered the entire way—sliding sideways off my saddle like a helpless city slicker while Jake and Cowboy eyed me with great concern.

My two weeks in Terry were a retreat from the modern world and I loved it. Even though the town epitomized the very word "boring," I had the time of my life. I loved barreling toward the setting sun along backcountry roads, listening to country music while dangling my bare toes out the truck's passenger window, talking about our friends and families, our pasts and futures and where we saw the other in it.

On Sundays, we went to church, housed in a nondescript building on the side of a highway. The only tip-off it was a place of worship was the large "Cowboy Chapel" sign out front.

The large room was suffused with harsh fluorescent light that reminded me of the inside of a department store. The pastor wore Wranglers and short sleeves and the parishioners all looked unmistakably Montanan—tanned, creased faces and firm, weathered bodies that looked ready to wrestle a calf or eat more gravy. Everyone looked like they were on their way to a livestock auction.

I felt puny and inconsequential in the pews as the congregation stood to sing a series of lilting, unsteady hymns. I mouthed the words, eyeing Jake as he stood tall by my side, cupping the songbook in both hands and confidently singing along. The hymns concluded and we resumed our seats. The pastor waved toward us with a friendly sweep of his hand and singled us out for introduction. Every parishioner turned and gave us an amiable nod or hello. I hadn't been to church for at least sixteen years and I felt a little uncomfortable. I had officially soured on religion after witnessing too many rural Montanans speaking in tongues during church services as a child. I was brought up Lutheran in an extended family comprised of Mormons and Pentecostalists. My grandma Kate, a spirited artist with an otherwise loving soul, turned Pentecostal after deciding her former Lutheran faith was too candy-assed for her hard-line Christian sensibilities. She meant well, but she deluged my family with so many prayers and predictions about the coming apocalypse that all of us reacted, to one degree or another, like a dog too tightly leashed—we pulled in the opposite direction.

As I looked around the congregation, I wondered if anyone there really, truly believed, or whether they were merely following a script passed down by their parents and their parents before them. I glanced at Jake and in him I saw, or possibly projected, everything that is good and right about Christianity; he was the embodiment of love thy brother, turn the other cheek, do unto others as you'd have them do unto you. Or maybe I was falling deeper in love. He wasn't rageful or conceited, covetous or insecure. He seemed armored in perfect tranquility and calm. He was the first serious Christian I'd ever met who wasn't fanatical about it. He never proselytized, which piqued my interest and made me feel safe to dip my toe into religious waters. That Sunday's sermon turned out to be pleasantly short and sweet, though there was a certain tautological reasoning behind the message, which boiled down to, "The Bible is true because the Bible says so." I concluded I'd have to put off more serious religious exploration for another day.

When my birthday came around mid-month, Jake baked me a cake with my name on it. We shared a giant slice in the living room while Cowboy sulked on the steps out front. Cowboy was extremely sensitive and intuitive; he was the smartest, most well-behaved dog I'd ever met. Once he figured out I wasn't going anywhere—this interloper in his home, in his master's bed—he had decided he wanted nothing more to do with me. Where he once greeted me with a friendly wag of the tail, he now eyed me resentfully before quickly vacating the premises.

Jake played me some of his favorite country songs on his RadioShack boom box—tracks by Chris LeDoux, Darryl Worley, Steve Earle and Pat Green. I was expecting a bunch of overproduced ballads but this music was less polished, more gritty with an overriding message of accepting life as it is, not as you want it to be. Still, I couldn't resist mentioning I thought country music was cheesy. He changed the CD and put on some older stuff by Waylon Jennings and Merle Haggard. Already buoyed by a week of passion and firearms, it was music I could relate to. It was authentic, anti-slick and rebellious, wound with raw pain, hardship and humor. I told Jake he embodied both sides of the country coin: a squeaky-clean super Christian on the one hand, a go-it-alone nonconformist on the other. He didn't say anything. I took his reticence as another example that he wasn't one to ruminate over the nuances of his own personality. He picked at the last few crumbs of cake on the plate. Waylon Jennings's

"Are You Sure Hank Done It This Way" played in the background.

"Happy birthday, Jessie K." He sighed as the song ended. "Are you ever going to tell me how old you are?"

I winced. I had dodged the question for the past four months and I knew it was absolutely pathetic to continue.

"Just turned thirty-one," I admitted.

"That's what I thought."

"What—are you saying I look old?"

"No." He grinned. "But I think you care way too much about what people think."

My cheeks burned. I moved outside to escape the stifling heat of the house and took a seat on the concrete steps that passed for a porch. Cowboy lumbered off the steps to be further away from me. Jake joined me a moment later with his guitar. Cowboy snoozed in the grass under a nearby tree. Washington Street was utterly quiet except for the sound of a dog barking and bugs fluttering around the porch light. The stars spread across the black sky. I pressed my chin into the back of Jake's shoulder as he strummed and spoke the words of what sounded like a made-up song.

> *I'm sittin' here*
> *With my army gear*
> *My books, my hat, and my rope*
> *Wearin' Old Spice,*
> *Now ain't that nice?*
> *Thinking to myself,*
> *How much wealth*

Does one man need?
There's just one thing
That could bring
More riches than I deserve,
And that one thing
Is her.

I pressed myself into him more tightly. I wondered if he was trying to signal the kind of life we might have together—a life short on riches, long on love.

The moon, swollen and satisfied, roosted high above the first craggy steps of the Badlands to the east. The still air remained unmoved by the beating of my own heart. Cowboy contentedly whined during a long yawn. I was at peace. I was home. Anywhere near this man was where I belonged. I looked up at the stars and imagined the three of us from far above—specks of matter inhabiting the upper right quadrant of Terry's tic-tac-toe board, which must have looked infinitely smaller than a pinprick from space.

Jake wasn't much for the phone—I frequently had to pry information from him—but he was quieter than usual during a phone call in late November. I'd made the mistake of telling him I'd met an old friend, a raging queen, at a notorious gay club on the Lower East Side, where Chelsea boys with bionic erections danced naked on the bar. The other end of the phone became silent; Jake brusquely ended the call. I didn't hear from him for two days.

When he finally rang, he admitted my anecdote about hanging around a bunch of naked men—whether gay or straight—deeply annoyed him. I was taken aback by such provincialism. I guess, living in west Chelsea for so long, I'd forgotten how much of the country still had issues over uninhibited homosexuality. In my neighborhood, it was more common to see two men kissing on the street than a man and a woman.

He sighed. "But there's another reason I'm upset."

"What?"

"I wanted to tell you the other night but the way you were talking—about the men and the dancing—I just wanted to get off the phone."

"What?"

"Jessie, I got deployed."

"What do you mean, 'got deployed'?"

"Jessie, I'm going to Iraq."

I held the phone away from my ear.

"Jessie?"

My mouth opened but I couldn't speak. I sat down on the edge of my bed and pinched the bridge of my nose with my thumb and index finger, trying to drain reality from my brain. I'd conveniently chosen to ignore that Jake was also a lieutenant in the Army Reserve. All this time, I'd been thinking of him as a soldier in the abstract sense; that is, I could easily picture him wearing a camouflage uniform and one of those jaunty berets, and holding a gun, and looking devastatingly handsome, but I never considered him being called upon to perform the duties of an actual soldier.

"Well, that just sucks," was all I could muster.

After we hung up, I stared at the ceiling for a long time. I'd never been a believer in love at first sight, thinking that sort of thing was a device used in fairy tales and Nicholas Sparks novels, but the more I got to know Jake, I knew he was the one for me. In a very matter-of-fact, biological though indefinable way, I had identified him as my soul's match even though we were opposite in nearly every way. But the rational part of me acknowledged we had spent a total of twenty-six days together, hardly enough time to determine if this was more than a heavy infatuation. And it would certainly be impossible to ascertain this with him out of the country for a year and a half. Who knows what ravages would be inflicted upon his body and soul in Iraq? It was too much for me, too real, too soon. My heart sank as I realized it was probably time to think about an ejection strategy, which I delicately broached during a phone call the following evening.

"You don't quit when something gets hard," he said.

"A year is a long time, Jake," I said. "People change. It's just easier this way."

"I don't want it easy," he said. "I want you."

Jake's unwavering conviction pulled me up like a drunk man yanked to his feet—within ten minutes we were both promising abstinence for the next year and a half.

In three short months, his unit was to mobilize out of Fort Carson, Colorado. During that time, I felt like I was in suspended animation—unable to move forward, incapable of turning back. Jake, the war, the military, the carnage in Iraq consumed my thoughts. I flew out to Colorado to spend Thanksgiving with him while he and his unit prepared to go. At night, I made him show me the "kill moves" he had learned that day—a rehearsed sequence of lethal blows for hand-to-hand combat that looked like something out of a Chuck Norris movie. I wanted to know more about this strange new world. It was the first time in my life I'd ever been on an army base and hung around army people. The officers I met, including Jake, seemed like a very sober, intelligent and steely bunch, which provided some comfort. I flew out one last time the final weekend he was in the United States. His father and brother drove out west and took Cowboy back to Baltimore. The morning of Jake's deployment, he and I stood outside the barracks in the frigid February wind. My nose was red from the icy chill and I could not for the life of me stop crying. He and his unit were to board a C-17 Globe Master cargo jet for a twenty-seven hour direct flight to Kuwait. He was dressed in pixelated desert fatigues, the pants tucked into tall canvas boots. A fully loaded backpack and a heavy Kevlar helmet lay at his feet. Into my palm he placed his long silver chain with the cross on it, a gesture that made one fat solitary tear drop into my open palm. I wrapped my arms around his waist and lay my head against his chest, squeezing tightly as though to prevent my own life from slipping away. I told him I loved him, and with that, a burden lifted. I loved him. I wasn't vacillating between infatuation and devotion anymore. He warmed all my chilly spots and filled my dark spaces with sunlight. He took my shoulders and looked at me.

"Have you ever heard the expression 'burn the ships'?"

I shook my head and sniffled.

"After landing on enemy shores, a famous Spanish conquistador instructed his men to conquer the enemy or die trying. He burned all the ships to prevent his soldiers from fleeing."

He smiled and then kissed me. "I'm like that Spanish conquistador—failure is not an option."

Nine

War Bride

As soon as Jake left for Iraq, that's when I realized, ironically, I never wanted to leave his side. I started saving all my money. I stopped going out. I threw myself into work with a fervor I didn't know I had; anything to distract myself from the ache of missing him. I took another permalance assignment—which seemed the way the entire economy was going—at a new tabloid spin-off devoted to the homes and hobbies of celebrities. But the only celebrities willing to grant me a peek inside their sumptuous interiors, invariably bedecked with chenille sofas and thick vanilla-scented candles of varying heights, were D-list reality TV stars. I spent my days writing about reality TV rejects with stripper poles in their home gyms while sporadically checking the Internet for news of Iraq. I scanned stories about suicide bombers and dead soldiers, making sure the bloodshed was still contained in and around Baghdad and Fallujah and hadn't seeped south to Nasiriya, where Jake was stationed. That I usually did this while making calls to starlets' publicists, inquiring whether they wanted to respond to criticism their client was too fat for high-waisted jeans, added a level of surrealism to my situation. Colleagues knew my predicament—it was all I talked about—and often asked me how Jake was doing. For a long time, I answered the questions truthfully and thoughtfully: He wasn't sleeping well, there was an outbreak of dysentery at the base, he had inexplicably started a strenuous program of power-lifting. But the questions began to feel perfunctory, a way for people to make idle chitchat with me as they watched their frozen burritos rotate inside the office microwave at lunchtime. My stock answer became "he's fine." To many Manhattanites, the war was an abstraction. A headline. The news crawl on CNN. It wasn't real. It was "out there," fought by people who expressed their emotions through the lyrics of a Nickelback power ballad.

I knew this because up until three months ago I had thought the same thing. My heightened sensitivity made me wonder if some of my colleagues questioned my decision to commit to a soldier not because Jake might be killed or maimed, but because the military, God and country, patriotism, yellow ribbons, the War on Terror, were so far outside the cushy confines of Manhattan's media world that there was simply no frame of reference. It did not compute. Even my own friends began to feel distant to me, as if I had one foot out of New York already. Over the summer, Maria invited me and a bunch of friends to a bull-riding championship. But I knew that to go would invite patronizing comments from my well-meaning but otherwise droll friends as they made a spectacle of scoping competitors' chaps-clad asses. I didn't want my pain cheapened, so I stayed home.

I stayed home a lot that year. I read books about metaphysics and yogic philosophy. I watched a lot of *Law & Order*. I did brainteasers. I became an expert in Sudoku Level I. When I did venture out, I sought enlightenment by attending a lot of yoga workshops, an experience that taught me that for all the ego-shedding properties and inner-connectedness yoga is supposed to bring, it sure attracted a lot of sanctimonious jerks. Yoga had made me more aware of the self, *myself*— I was more up my own ass (both figuratively and literally; I could almost wrap both legs around my head) than ever. For every fixed opinion I thought I had about the world—"I'm a progressive liberal"—I was assailed with another point of view that was equally true—"*I'm a progressive liberal who's never done one thing for my country.*" It was a mental hall of mirrors that rendered me incapable of making even the slightest decision.

This is what a year and a half apart during a war does to you. It plays tricks on your mind—white becomes black and black becomes white. My angst, my lack of faith, returned like an old, familiar friend. What the hell was I doing? We barely knew each other. Yet the love I felt for him was so all consuming and so overpowering that it was all but impossible to resist the pull. I lay awake for hours at night agonizing over what he was going through and ruminating over what future we might have together. I clung to his cross. I needed something to hold on to—

to convince me my sacrifice was worth it. My relief came from letters, beautiful handwritten letters posted from his army base, up to twelve a week, which occasionally included a CD mix of his favorite country songs. Packets of white legal-size envelopes spilled out of my mailbox like dominos on the floor. I scooped them up and ripped open the one with the oldest postmark on the way up the stairs to my apartment. I popped in his mix, sprawled on the floor where I read his words over and over. Email was available (Skype at that time was not), but we gravitated toward pen and paper. Something about the rush of words scampering down each page (often accompanied by funny stick drawings of us in some old-fashioned display of courtship) offered a more visceral expression, and the sheer volume of handwriting that passed between us was affirmation that our sacrifice, our fidelity was worth it. Our relationship took on the air of a grand romance. I felt like a war bride, an antiquated archetype suddenly made relevant. I searched out books about World War II soldiers and their lovers back home, feeling a rousing solidarity with their struggles. Unlike my friends who had to search for meaning in some guy's acronym-heavy text (WTF LOL NSFW STFU LMAO!!!), my heartache felt more overwhelming, more real. I wallowed in Jake's words, by turns goofy and sad, funny and sweet, and written in a small, precise, rightward-slanting print that I followed like a lifeline.

Hey, baby, baby, baby. I was born lucky, I guess. Nobody is shooting at me. I'm alive. I've got a new CD to send you. What else could go my way? If you were here, that's what. If you came and brushed open the door of my tent, you and Cowboy . . . I'd fall right out of this chair, good golly.

The most important thing in my life is my relationship to God. You are a close second, you and me. I want to love you as much as I can, more than I can . . . you are a bonfire among candles, a tiger among barn cats, a firework among sparklers.

Every once in a while, though, some of his letters gave me pause.

I can't wait to show you some of my hillbilly friends in their environment. You would be up for that, wouldn't you? Or would that be like mixing fire and gasoline? Some of the best moments of my life have been spent in a cow field in the middle of nowhere while people sit around on the back of trucks and guys give girls rides on ATVs on warm summer nights. There's a fire going and guitars playing, there's dogs and beer . . .

I laughed uncomfortably. I had zero aptitude for fields and hillbillies. I thought ATVs were on par with aboveground pools.

I couldn't reconcile that Jake's spirit was more familiar to me than anyone, yet his interests and passions were so opposite mine. As the days turned to weeks and the weeks into months, I wondered again if I was more in love with the idea of Jake, the cowboy fantasy, than the man himself. He mentioned moving to Lexington together upon his return. "I think of it as my town," he wrote. "My favorite place in the whole world." But he insisted he'd move to New York for me if that's what I needed. I was touched, but couldn't quite picture him ordering the Tuscan roast chicken at West Village restaurants or shopping for juicers together at Bed Bath & Beyond. Bougie urban living would make jerky of his soul. And what would a ranch hand do for work in Manhattan anyway—make furniture out of driftwood for hot Tribeca moms?

So I did what many Manhattan women do when they are crippled by confusion: I went to a psychic. A woman named Glenda from Barbados who lived in a fifth-floor walk-up in Bay Ridge. I took a seat at a table opposite a window overlooking Brooklyn's Fifth Avenue. Glenda sat facing me with the window behind her. Her posture was stick straight and she probed deep into my eyes. I tried to speak or move as little as possible during our introductory chat so as not to betray anything about myself. Within forty-five seconds, Glenda informed me that I was in love with a man from across the miles, and that he'd be gone for more than a year in a dangerous place. I tried to remain blasé. She took my palm and closely inspected its lines and crevices, turning it this way and that to better catch the light. She picked up a small Chinese teacup containing a scattering of leaves and shook it. After inspecting the position of the leaves, she confirmed that this love runs deep, the deepest of my life. She shook the cup once more and studied the contents closely. When she spoke, it was the same tone you'd use to confirm a dental appointment: "But it won't last."

She said a bunch of other stuff but I stopped listening. I staggered down the stairs. When I reached the street, I felt like I had been punched in the chest. I felt dizzy. I fumbled for my DJ headphones and punched the volume on my iPod. I fought tears as I almost ran to the subway, accompanied by Kenny Rogers's "Coward of the County." When the R train finally came, I slumped in a seat. Passengers eyed me indifferently as I dug in my bag searching for Jake's most recent letter.

You'll never guess what I wished for on my birthday. Well, you might be able to. It did involve you and life's simple pleasures, the little ones that are really the big things. You are my desire, my pleasure. My laugh, my smile. You are my good mood, my high five when the game is over, the spring in my step on cool mornings. I'm loving you like my life depends on it. And it feels so right, so complete sometimes, like right now, in this sea of heartbreak, tears and fears. I want to be good for you, and I will be.

By the time I emerged from the subway at Union Square, I was angry at myself for having gone to the psychic. I was upset for allowing my worst fears to be confirmed. I had betrayed Jake. I had cursed what we had and now it really wouldn't last.

As the year dragged on, I flipped through so many assumptions and judgments about myself, about us, that I decided the psychic was wrong. She had to be wrong. She had simply picked up on doubts I myself had projected. My quivering mindset was the only thing capable of dooming our relationship. But how could I steady the mental ebbs and flows? We were leading three separate lives, Jake and I: The life he lived in Iraq, the life I lived in New York and the mysterious, blurry fantasy life we had each carved in our heads of how we might one day live together.

Hush was a ballast during moments of insecurity. One night at a bar on the Lower East Side I met up with her and a funny, stubbly, handsome photographer named Mike who shot for *Outdoor Adventure*. He was tall and muscular with a shaved head and studs in his ears and he wore a large black backpack loaded with camera equipment. A tribal tattoo peeked from beneath his gray T-shirt. There was an easy rapport between us. When he retired to the men's room, I gave Hush a look that elicited the response, "Jessie, don't even think about it."

I shrugged petulantly. "How do I know Jake's not hooking up with female soldiers over there?"

Hush set down her drink and shook her head like I had insulted her. "Because he won't. He wouldn't."

"How do you know?"

"I just know. Jake wouldn't do something like that. He's not like that. Have some faith."

I looked into the bottom of my glass, feeling tremendously sorry for myself but also relieved and emboldened to know that Hush rooted for me—there are some sacrifices worth making.

Mike came back to the table. He wore premium washed jeans and action sneakers. Over a round of drinks, we chitchatted in the smooth vernacular of downtown—our travels, Queens of the Stone Age, good falafel, our quiet yearning for verisimilitude. As he reached his arm across the table for a napkin, I caught a whiff of his body wash—a mélange of ginger and sandalwood—

probably selected by a cool ex-girlfriend. How easy it would be to date a guy like Mike. We spoke the same language, he and I. We caught the same references, told the same jokes, wore the same damn body wash. Jake wore Old Spice. He didn't know what "street cred" meant. He set a broken finger with a Popsicle stick and a sanitary napkin. He said "Turn that frown upside down, silly clown" with a straight face.

The very idea of Jake made me drunk. So what if our story was straight out of a G-rated romantic comedy starring a princess and a white knight serenading each other in a magical field? I loved Jake. He loved me. End of psychoanalysis. I tried to conceal my smile as I finished my cocktail, paid my tab and walked back to my apartment alone, listening to the same Chris LeDoux song, "Millionaire," on repeat the whole way.

Somewhere around the sixteenth month, two months before Jake was due to come home, the tone of his letters changed. Where he once was emotional and effusive, a subtle trepidation took hold, as if the war had finally started to wear him down. He remained maddeningly oblique—he never mentioned what he witnessed or experienced, never articulated what exactly troubled him—but an emerging thread in his letters was the need for space. He was confused, he said. Not like himself. Things he thought were important didn't mean so much anymore. He wanted to take it nice and slow. Logically, I understood this, but emotionally, it was a death knell. I was crushed. He had given me the rope to hold, had asked me to hold the rope in the first place, and now wanted to loosen his grip. I felt the strands unraveling in my hands as I dropped his letters to the floor.

"Time alone?" I wanted to scribble back. "Isn't that all we've had?" But I wrote nothing. I couldn't think of a single thoughtful, mature response. My words were churlish. Maria chalked it up to battle fatigue. Hush said give him time. I was exhausted, wary; I felt cheated. I took more Ambien, drank more wine, threw myself into a whirling dervish of Kundalini until blue exploded from behind my closed lids. But nothing would erase the growing suspicion that I had wasted more than a year of my life on a dream.

And then he came home. I met him halfway up a flight of stairs at the Baltimore train station, a full year and a half after we'd kissed good-bye in Fort Carson. I had ridden the train down from New York. He grabbed me and awkwardly swung me around, nearly dropping me down a flight of concrete stairs. He was bigger, a lot bigger, owing to the months of power-lifting and creatine weight-gainer shakes. His Wranglers hugged his buttocks aggressively. Slivers of skin showed between each snap button on his shirt. His teeth were blindingly white. He craved fresh pineapple, berries, and juicy oranges, having subsisted so long on the army's MREs, powdered eggs and variations on "shit on a shingle." But he had the same smooth, tanned skin, the same high and tight haircut, the same gentle eyes. I looked into those eyes for the truth and saw only sincerity with flashes of guarded fatigue. I had no choice but to acquiesce to his request for space. I had nothing to lose, having given up so much already. All we'd ever known was distance and separation, funny stick drawings, CD mixes, words on paper—what was another gulf to bridge?

When I needed reassurance, I returned to his letters, I splurged on a weekend trip to Iceland with Maria. Jake drove out to Montana with Cowboy and two buddies to collect his stuff. He eventually settled into a new job training race horses outside of Washington D.C., the closest place he could find that allowed him to still be a cowboy and close to me. With Cowboy by his side, horses, green grass and open fields, he found his bearings. He returned to his normal, lithe weight. We began spending weekends together. I wondered if he'd killed anybody in Iraq but didn't want to ask, so I asked him to rate the difficulty of his deployment—10 being *Full Metal Jacket*, 1 being *Private Benjamin*. Jake looked up from horseshoeing a fidgety mare and squinted. "Maybe a two?"

I gasped. Perhaps he was exaggerating for my benefit, but the admission was like a slap in the face, a rebuke of my self-imposed misery agonizing over his safety and mental state in a war zone. All I could think was, if it was so easy, why did he need to take it slow upon his return? I realized his hesitation had less to do with Iraq and everything to do with me, with us. He wanted to make sure he too hadn't succumbed to fantasy.

Say what you will about war, but it has a way of making big decisions very easy: Five months later, we decided to marry.

But where would we live? I was ready to leave New York, but wasn't ready to abandon culture and decent dining options. I insisted upon a university town. Jake suggested the home of his alma mater, Lexington, Virginia, which boasted two colleges. He had many friends there, he said, including many female friends he thought I would like. I resisted. Virginia sounded so antebellum. His female friends were probably a bunch of truck-driving cowgirls. He suggested we check out Lexington anyway so we could definitively cross it off the list. I reluctantly agreed. We searched for houses for sale online and, stacked with a pile of real estate listings, took off in his big white truck, heading south.

Ten

The War of Northern Aggression

The day was strong and bright and the sky a cerulean blue as we traversed the interstate through the Shenandoah Valley into Virginia where we saw a trio of domineering white crosses on a hilltop overlooking the highway. The crosses, to me, signaled the vast gateway to the true South, the God-fearing South, bounded by the soft curves of the Blue Ridge mountains. The mountains out my window weren't at all dour and majestic like out West, but pleasant and unostentatiously feminine, as though they didn't resent civilization at all but welcomed it. It's no wonder much of the Civil War was fought there—the valley was so flat and expansive, checkered with freshly plowed brown fields and green new pastures, that it probably seemed unnecessary to push God-fearing Confederate soldiers into less cooperative country.

The interstate was two lanes each way and jammed with nearly bumper-to-bumper tractor trailers. Every awful-looking truck caused Jake to whip his head around with such focused intensity that he spent much of the drive with his eyes conspicuously off the road. After hitting the rumble strip for what seemed the twentieth time I accused him of loving trucks more than life itself. "No, hon," he yelled over Garth Brooks on the radio. "I *understand* trucks. I *love* you."

We exited the interstate onto an old highway that offered a more up close and personal view of the landscape heading into Lexington. We passed drowsy old farmhouses—cozy two-story abodes with shady porches—farms, deserted motor lodges, the occasional vegetable stand, barns and tidy board fences confining cows and horses. A truck hauling live chickens trundled sedately in front of us. The birds were in stacked cages, so cramped and zombie-like, their hollow eyes staring vacantly into our windshield, that I asked Jake to pass but he couldn't because the road was too twisty. I shrank in my seat as hundreds of soft white feathers fluttered into the windshield, like so many scraps of paper scrawled with messages pleading for escape.

We drove through an old village where the buildings were set back about five feet from the road. I noticed a large sign for a travel agency that read, "We'd love to see you go away!" In front of us at a stoplight, an old Honda Civic wore a Confederate flag bumper sticker with the words, "If you don't like what you're seein', stop lookin'!" I glanced at Jake; he shrugged and said that for a lot of Southerners the Civil War—rather, the War of Northern Aggression—had never ended, and that plenty of them were proud of their Confederate heritage. I noticed more than a few rebel flags hanging from porches, waving from brawny trucks and taped discreetly into small bedroom windows, and I wondered aloud if we might come across a Ku Klux Klan rally around the next corner.

"Do black people even live around here?" I asked after we passed a truck stop called White's and then a highway sign for a town called Lynchburg.

"Oh yeah, plenty of black people live here," Jake said. "You just don't see them that often because they don't live in the same neighborhoods as whites." I was about to take offense when I realized most of America was like that. Maybe the North and South weren't so different after all.

We cruised the eight or so streets of downtown Lexington, which, on first glance, looked like a shoot location for a Lands' End catalog populated by happy citizens dressed in light fleece and roomy walking shorts. There were a handful of bakeries, two bookstores, a few art galleries, a wine shop, mortgage lenders, clothing stores selling either preppy or outdoorsy attire and a movie theater. Conspicuously absent were any bars, which Jake said was because of a state law that any place serving alcohol had to derive a certain percentage of its revenue from food. The shops along Main Street sold mostly ephemera for the home and Civil War memorabilia to tourists and history buffs. We actually saw a woman wearing a frilly bustle skirt and holding a parasol go into the Stonewall Jackson Museum, and I realized this trip to Lexington was the longest I'd ever thought about the Civil War—I mean, the War of Northern Aggression—in my entire life.

The military academy looked like a prison, which Jake said it basically was. It resembled a vast Civil War–era fortress (it was bombarded by the Union army during the war), a collection of stolid buildings with crenellations and painted a sickly blend of wheat and mustard. A large statue of the school's most famous alumni, Stonewall Jackson, guarded the entrance to the school. I stopped to read the inscription as Jake ambled ahead of me. Behind the statue, just inside an airy vestibule leading to a courtyard surrounded by barracks, the general's most famous quote was visible to all: "YOU MAY BE WHATEVER YOU RESOLVE TO BE."

I squinted in the sunlight and thought about that. How nice. How simple. I can be whatever I resolve to be. And what did I resolve to be? I looked at Jake, body contorted, digging dog poo out of the treads of his boot with a small stick. My heart gushed with love. I resolve to be the best woman, the best wife for that man right there . . . even if it means moving to the middle of nowhere.

Four male cadets emerged from the barracks and walked toward me. They wore white uniforms, the pants of which were so voluminous they could have been used to traffic dwarves. The cadets walked briskly and with much purpose, hands clenched tightly at their sides, each being pulled along by an invisible fishing lure stuck in their cheeks. I seized up slightly at the display of such traditional masculinity.

"Good afternoon, ma'am," one said. "How you doing, ma'am?" said another. "Beautiful day, ma'am." "Need any help, ma'am?" My face soured as they strode by. "Ma'am." What a bunch of jerks.

Adjacent to the military academy was Washington and Lee, a small private college that Jake said was regarded locally as something of a finishing school for privileged Southern "haves." Its stately white pillars, quaint red cobblestone paths and immaculately sprayed lawns where dandelions dared not grow perfectly suited a college that predated the United States. Jake said 80 percent of the student body was Greek and from what I saw during our walk around campus, dressed accordingly—attractive, healthy girls wore Barbour coats and carried Coach bags; guys dressed in khaki shorts, flip-flops and polo shirts with the collars unironically popped. It was as though the entire student body eagerly awaited a successful future administering the nation's tax code.

We walked by an ice cream parlor just off campus and inside its windows I could make out one of these dewy debutantes from the private college and her uniformed beau from the military academy sharing a milkshake, slurping side by side through two straws. The cadet's hat rested politely on his knee while she lightly grasped her straw with delicate fingers—like Archie and Betty on a date in the 1950s.

"You gotta be kidding me," I gasped. "Is Jughead going to invite us to the cotillion? There's no way I can live here."

"Yeah, they make really good ice cream," Jake answered, apparently not listening to what I'd said.

We spent the night with some of Jake's old friends who had a sheep farm. The following morning, Jake wanted to make a pit stop at the bank where he used to have an account so he could say hi to the tellers. Cowboy strode in with him—without a leash, as Jake always said his dog was too proud and too well trained to wear one. The trio of female tellers recognized "Cowboy Jake," as he was known, and his dog instantly. Jake and the tellers caught up on old times for what seemed an eternity. After we got back in the truck, Jake said he wanted to introduce me to another friend of his—a woman named Miranda he had mentioned on various occasions who he thought I might like. The way took us through Lexington's horse country. The left side of the highway was bordered by a sturdy four-board fence and a rolling green pasture that seemed to extend to the mountains. A woman on horseback came into view. She galloped expertly across the field, making a wide arc so that the horse ran in the same direction as our truck. She rode just ahead of us, her long wavy black hair catching the sunlight. Jake slowed the truck. "There she is," he said, sounding just a little in awe. He turned the truck into the long driveway. The woman reined the horse to a stop and turned as we slowly drove by, trailing dust. Jake honked and laughed. She beamed and waved.

Jake parked the truck near the barn and jumped out to meet her as she trotted the horse toward the nearest gate. I shuffled over to meet them.

"Hey Miranda!" he called. She laughed as she dismounted. Jake enveloped her in a bear hug that lasted approximately one second too long. There was a frisson of warmth between them— or was it something more?— and as they parted, every hair on my body stood on end. They were both six feet tall and saw precisely eye to eye. She didn't look anything like I'd imagined. Jake had mentioned her plenty of times before. He brought her up whenever he was on his "You'll *love* Lexington!" campaign. And I easily dismissed her, deciding she had to be an unpolished, unattractive rube—a mental image I'd crafted to make myself feel better. What she actually looked like was a Victoria Secret's supermodel turned horsewoman. Svelte and healthy, she was dressed in a slouchy tank top and skintight riding pants tucked into tall dusty riding boots. Her jet black hair, wild and free and ever so slightly snarled, was in the perfect bed head configuration. Her sinewy arms showed not a trace of body fat. A handful of freckles scattered across her nose and cheeks. Thin, chapped lips encased large front teeth. I felt squat and Rumpelstiltskin-like by comparison. My oversized celebrity sunglasses, gold-flecked jazz shoes and a romper—a romper!—made me look like I'd been hatched from some Urban Outfitters fashion victim trend pod. I kicked at the dirt with my jazz shoe and smiled through gritted teeth as they caught up on old times. I was deaf to the conversation because of the white noise hammering between my ears, though I did catch snippets: "You've always been the strongest woman I know!" "I don't know anyone who works harder than you." "Remember when we said if we couldn't find anyone else to marry we'd marry each other? That's a joke, hon!"

By the time we left, I was very quiet and reserved, cursing the very existence of a romper. On the ride home, I stared blankly out the passenger window trying to make sense of the exchange. *You're the strongest, hardest-working woman I know. Remember we said we'd get married?* Oblivious to my turmoil, Jake placed his hand on my knee and commented on a shiny green John Deere tractor puttering across a field. I wanted to say something but I couldn't. It felt beneath me somehow, like it would sully the grand romance. I had been guilty of the worst kind of vanity by assuming someone as gee-whiz wholesome as Jake *couldn't* have had a life before *me*, a life that included women—glamorous, sexy horsewomen. I burned with jealousy but was chastened for my hubris, for my stupidity. *Must beat that bitch at her own game. Must learn to ride like the wind.* I willed myself to bury what I'd witnessed and tried to concentrate on the love letters divided among five stuffed shoeboxes at home.

Many roads cut across the county. Armed with our listings of homes for sale, we chose a country run that wended along a river toward a canyon. This particular road carved through gently rolling hills and was so full of hairpin turns that the legal speed limit of 55 seemed more like a dare than law. We somehow managed not to hit a bearded red-haired man pedaling furiously ahead of us on a ten-speed bike. Even though it was a perfectly warm day in May, and the road cut up and down a series of frightening hills, the man was wearing a dirty ski jacket and flip-flops. As we drove past him, Jake leaned across me and offered him a ride. The man didn't so much as acknowledge our presence; he just kept his eyes fixed on the road. That suited me, because I got the distinct whiff of old ham when our truck idled alongside.

We finally slowed down when we came upon the address with the "For Sale" sign in the yard. Jake pulled into the short gravel driveway. On first sight, the house looked like a dull white box set on an unimpressive rise of grass situated way too close to the road. The paper in my hand said the property was on eight acres, but from the front it looked like it belonged on a quarter-acre lot in some nondescript lower income cul-de-sac. "Nope, can't move here," I said. "It's not safe for Cowboy." To the right of the house opposite the driveway, a white potting shed covered in Virginia creeper sagged uncomfortably. We walked up a small rise toward the back of the house and were greeted by a charming rough-hewn gazebo hugged by trees and wild flowers. The property suddenly lost its uninviting look. The beds surrounding the gazebo were lush and well-tended. To the right of the gazebo, the land sloped gently down to an acre or two of level green grass bounded on one side by woods and wildflowers as tall as me. In the center of this low-lying patch of yard was a dilapidated though picturesque barn. Fifty feet or so across from it the land dropped precipitously to expose a deep sinkhole that looked like it had been carved by a meteorite in the shape of a shoe. But the chasm was so overgrown with foliage—walnut trees, wildflowers, shrubs, raspberry and blackberry bushes—that it seemed more part of an ambitious landscape project than a geologic mistake. In fact, the more we looked around, the more the property began to resemble a well-thought-out park. Every turn revealed something new and beautiful. We walked up through a heavily wooded area to a tangled barbwire fence that marked the rear of the property. The land leveled off and the trees opened up to a gorgeous pasture where the roof of a house was just visible between two gentle hills in the distance. Beyond the house, there was nothing but forest (and the tip-top of a power station) for as far as we could see. We walked back through an orchard of peach, pear and apple trees, as well as a nectarine, Asian pear, persimmon and what Jake identified as a mulberry tree—as evidenced by its dangling crimson berries. I'd never tasted a mulberry, and wasn't entirely convinced of Jake's botany skills when he popped one into his mouth.

"Don't!" I cried. "That could be poisonous!" He smiled.

"Mmm!" he said, offering me one. I bit into it. The taste of blackberries, raspberries and tart green apples spread over my tongue. We stayed under the tree until every low-hanging berry had been eaten and our fingertips were stained purple.

Between the mulberry tree and the road there were another three to four acres of grass, spacious enough for the mother of all gardens, a shop, even another house or two. A tangle of bramble lined the road. On the north side of the sinkhole, the land dropped again to reveal a shady grove encircled by towering walnut trees. In the middle of the grove was a fire pit. A hammock was slung dreamily between two trees.

"I want that," I said to Jake, pointing to the hammock and the carefree, self-reflective lifestyle it spoke of.

To my delight, the inside of house had been recently renovated to feature a modern, open floor plan with new cherry cabinetry, bamboo floors, recessed bookcases and Arts and Crafts–style stained glass. There was even a cheerful white propane stove in the kitchen that the owner said kept the house toasty warm. What the house lacked in space—twelve hundred square feet, two bedrooms, one bathroom—and amenities—no central heat, no air-conditioning, no dishwasher, no washer and dryer—it more than made up for in style. As we stepped out onto the front porch, I thought that with the right trim treatment, a bit of paint and more stained glass, this modest little house could be turned into a Frank Lloyd Wright–like country abode, the kind that a stylish New Yorker might call home.

"I'll take it!" I heard myself say.

We placed a bid on it—less five thousand dollars after the owner found out Jake was a veteran—which was still probably a hundred thousand less than the bathroom in my West Chelsea hampster hole. The offer was accepted and the next thing I knew, I was moving to Lexington, Virginia.

Now, this might seem like a strange thing to do for someone who has spent a considerable number of pages describing the extent to which rural living was not for her, combined with her aversion to the suffocating Normal Rockwell–like atmosphere of the town and a county full of equestrian supermodels. But standing in the yard as the sun nestled into the hills and seeing the first fireflies of the evening flutter up from the grass like tiny beads of light, I succumbed to a romance that was almost poetic: delirium for the simple life. The *authentic* life. Here was a chance to escape into a whole new persona, a whole new way of life. I was through with neuroses and uncertainty and ambition. I wanted to drift back to a quieter, more wholesome way of life. Everything would be fine—*more* than fine as long as we had each other. We could each live the life we'd always imagined for ourselves; Jake, working with his hands in the great outdoors while I continued to write for publications in New York—independent and free, successful on our own terms.

We drove his horse trailer back to Manhattan. There, to the gapes of dog walkers not used to seeing a long horse trailer idling on a city street, we packed up the contents of my life, and literally drove off into the sunset in bumper to bumper traffic on I-95.

Many months later, I married my cowboy in our backyard surrounded by loved ones from New York, Montana, Baltimore and Virginia; all the people who knew and loved us in our myriad walks and guises. I wore a silk, backless gown made from a vintage pattern, which sounds so elegant, but the dress fit like the case for a body pillow—a belted rectangle with holes for the arms and neck. In my eagerness to adopt the mores of the country, I had hired a local seamstress-slash-hairdresser to sew the dress, but realized after she'd been avoiding my phone calls for two months that she was better at administering home perms than fashioning do-it-yourself haute couture. And Jake couldn't be bothered to go to a barber, not even for his own wedding, and gave himself one of his signature sadomasochistic buzz cuts, which I thought made him look like a prisoner of war in a tuxedo. These style transgressions aside, the reception turned out to be quite the party, complete with a full moon and square dancing, flaming torches and moonshine. It's still talked about to this day. Years later, I came to see the day as a snapshot of our entire marriage—energetic, individual, a tiny bit nuts. Especially when family members stood up during the reception wearing overalls and straw hats, sunglasses and fur wraps, and sang us the theme song from *Green Acres*.

Part Three

Eleven

Go Big or Go Home

"Get ready to get bored," the junior Walmart pharmacist snorted as she handed what I had decided would be my last prescription of antidepressants.

Since moving to Lexington, my dependence on happy pills had begun to fade faster than a face full of makeup down a coal mine—they made no sense. I'd like to say this was because I experienced a natural high just wandering into my orchard and seeing all the peaches the size of baseballs, or sitting in the gazebo at twilight and marveling at how much property I owned. That was part of it, of course, but the real reason for stopping the meds was that I didn't want Jake to know. I was too embarrassed. Besides, I had no legitimate explanation for them, except that a man who reminded me of a garden gnome had once told me to take them.

The gimlet-eyed girl behind the counter blew a lock of purple-streaked hair from her round face. Underneath her white smock were subtle indicators of a Goth girl stuck in a small town—two chunky chains around her neck, a thick leather wrist cuff, a hole through her lip where a ring normally fit, Kelly green eyeliner apparently applied in a darkened bedroom with no mirror. She was responding to my unsolicited admission that "I had just moved to Lexington from New York City! I'm still learning the country ropes—hee, hee!" I believe those were my exact words. I'm surprised she didn't bury the row of mystical pagan rings on her fingers in my face.

I couldn't help myself. I was genuinely happy. I loved being married. I loved being married to a man like Jake. He brought out the best in me by inspiring me to be better, to be less cynical. I loved the novelty of being a "country person" and I was having fun trying to define what that meant. There was no way I was going to get bored here. There was too much to do, too many new things to experience, too many country skills to acquire that, incidentally, were experiencing something of a resurgence among trendy urbanites: gardening, sewing, home brewing, pickling, butchering. I had visions of myself strumming Creedence Clearwater Revival songs in the gazebo with a sprightly red cardinal on my shoulder. I wouldn't have time to get bored.

No, the junior pharmacist's remark was more a reflection of her own lack of imagination and an inability to see beyond the sale rack at Hot Topic.

The first step in my new country transformation: Get a motorcycle license and buy a used motorbike—a 250R Kawasaki Ninja (aka, a crotch rocket), on which to navigate the twisty back roads and old highways that curved and looped across the county like a bowl of spilled spaghetti noodles. (This is a benefit of a Montana upbringing, raised by parents who grew up on cattle ranches. My brother, sister and I all learned to ride a motorcycle—more like a scooter but with five gears and a clutch—by the age of ten, tearing up and down the long gravel driveway without helmets on my grandparents' farm.) Jake was impressed by my riding skills when he took me to test-drive a variety of bikes at the local farm of a friend, who happened to own a motorcycle shop in another county. The first bike I test rode was a scooter, and I was surprised by how small and puny it felt despite my twenty-two-year hiatus from bikes. I quickly upgraded to the 250, considered the smallest of the "big" bikes. I paid two thousand dollars for it, borrowed a helmet and drove my new purchase nearly all the way home, jostling over hills and jerking around bends, followed closely by Jake and Cowboy in the big white truck. I was flummoxed when the motorcycle ran out of gas by the side of the road, until Jake jumped out and showed me how to switch on the reserve tank. "There you go," he said, looking up at me with pride tinged with just a bit of envy, so I let him cruise the rest of the way home while Cowboy and I followed behind. A couple of weeks later, Jake bought his own secondhand bike, concluding it was no fun at all for his wife to traverse the back roads of Rockbridge County alone. Many weekends that first year were spent tooling from one end of the county to the other together, and if there's a prettier county in America, I don't know where it is.

Those rides sometimes concluded at the Walmart Supercenter on the outskirts of town. It was an appropriate introduction to life outside of Manhattan—that is, life in America. I quickly learned that a Walmart Supercenter was not to be confused with a mere Walmart, because a Supercenter sold groceries and was open twenty-four hours. I'd also heard that the best time to catch a glimpse of the county's most exquisite hillbillies was around three thirty in the morning, when it wasn't uncommon to find some lady with buckteeth growing sideways, pushing a cart full of Crisco near the cereal aisle hollering at her son or lover—maybe one and the same—that, "Damn you, Dale. You know we can't afford no Puffed Wheat!" while reaching for the less expensive house brand.

I would be lying if I said I wasn't having a serious love affair with the Walmart. I loved that I could throw on a backpack, hop on my motorcycle and squeal into its expansive parking lot in fifteen minutes if I pushed the speed limit the entire way. I experienced a subtle thrill bidding a cheerful hello to the greeter lady with the beehive hairdo just inside the front door. I got a kick out of being called "ma'am" by the cashiers once Jake placated my age insecurity by informing me that in the South the label applied to any woman over the age of twenty-three—which meant I probably looked twenty-four.

Granted, my love affair with the store was more of an ironic infatuation. I amused myself by calling it "the Walmart," the way an old person might refer to "the Facebook." This hinted that shopping at a box store was such a strange and foreign custom to me (Walmart didn't exist in Montana in the early nineties, right about the time I moved to New York) that I had no grasp of the lexicon.

But there was nothing ironic about my love for the store's low, low prices. Many times I found myself strolling the store's spacious, fluorescent-lit aisles tossing into my cart $2.50 pints of ice cream that went for six dollars in New York. An entire *barrel* of pretzels for $3.49! Greek yogurt, organic milk, toothpaste, yams, a book for holding recipe cards, Miley Cyrus leggings on clearance for a dollar, charcoal briquettes, a shovel, lingerie, a deck chair, a birdcage and a seventy-two-inch plasma HDTV—though we didn't own birds and Jake didn't watch TV. I took a step back and stared at the teetering avalanche of merchandise in my cart, gripped by a kind of hyper-consumerist paralysis. I left it all, except for the recipe book and the shovel, stranded somewhere near the arts and crafts section while I walked briskly through checkout and out the door.

I needed the recipe card book because I had recently become intrigued with the idea of cooking food in a kitchen larger than a dish sponge, which is how I prepared meals in New York.

Hush: How's it going down there????? I miss you!!!

Me: I miss you too!! I love it here!! I love farm life!

Hush: does 8 acres really = farm? I know I'm from Jersey and all but I thought you needed "a back 40" to be a farmer.

Me: semantics. you should see all the meals I've made that come from our backyard!

I felt the need to become proficient in more rustic fare that could be sourced to my own backyard—things like Asian pear tarts from my own trees, handmade ice cream topped with fresh mulberries, ratatouille made from eggplant, tomatoes, peppers, garlic and basil planted and picked from my own plot of fertility. Jake was an eager accomplice in my "back to the land" cooking adventures, though he personally had no special commitment to organic, locally produced food. For him, food was simply a source of fuel, a way to make the engine go, and he didn't particularly care whether calories came from a Snickers bar or a garden potato (when you burn eight thousand calories a day like he did, you can afford to be flip about diet). He was more interested in food production—the process of sowing and growing, the system of harvesting and making, which dovetailed nicely into my desire to eat from scratch, so we were simpatico on this front. Though I'd have to laugh at the sight of him kneading dough for some hopelessly complicated artisan bread recipe while casually munching a Pop-Tart. He saw no contradiction in this, and even bought me an ice cream maker so I could perfect my "artisan" ice cream. We realized the black orbs littering our yard were black walnuts. Jake wasn't one to let food go to waste—no matter how labor intensive—so we gathered buckets of the nuts, let them dry in the basement for a couple of weeks, then smashed them to smithereens with small sledgehammers, painstakingly extracting the meaty bits locked within, to be turned into a black walnut cake and fig and walnut tapenade with goat cheese. He gobbled up my cooking like a starving man and never once complained about the dearth of animal protein on his plate (I was still intimidated by meat). My goal was to rate and catalog each of our handwritten DIY treasures and keep a record of them in my very own special recipe book. It seemed like something a pioneering country woman might do.

As for the Walmart shovel, Jake had asked me to pick one up because he had recently gone on a tree-planting bender and needed another shovel to add to his collection of seventeen similar instruments. He had more tools than a construction company, yet he needed more in order to "improve efficiency." (I think he wanted one from a box store to round out the lower end of his shovel spectrum.)

I'd noticed since marrying him that Jake's fondness for pithy one-liners wasn't limited to lofty, feel-good expressions of the "I'm alive and I'm free" variety. They now included more grounded, task-oriented maxims such as "improve efficiency." This was one of the biggest things I was learning about my husband—just how insanely productive he was. I saw glimmers of this from the beginning, of course—the meticulous hand-crafted bar stools, the hundreds of handwritten love letters—and it was one of the things I loved about him most, but it wasn't until he became my husband that I realized the premium he placed on work. Jake didn't have an idle or procrastinating bone in his body. If he thought it, he did it. I wanted to emulate this quality, even though at times I was afraid of it. Take chores. The word "chore" to me has become synonymous with Jake—when I think of some unbearably dull and tedious task, I think of my husband, performing it with gusto. He had a knack for deconstructing chores, breaking that chore into specific steps and reorganizing those steps into The Most Efficient Sequence so that not one movement, one breath, one k-calorie of energy was wasted. What took normal people twenty minutes to accomplish he finished in the blink of an eye. (It was because of Jake that I learned the proper sequence for washing dishes by hand—glasses and silverware *before* greasy frying pans.)

I could already see it on his headstone: "May Jake rest in peace, efficiently."

Who knew shovels came in such a wide variety of shapes and sizes? I didn't until he gave me a walk-through, with commentary, of the awesome collection that lined one wall in his workshop; long handle, short handle, angled tip, straight-edge, varying thicknesses of metal. Turns out there's a specific shovel for planting trees. To get the most use out of this particular shovel, he had recently joined the Arbor Day Foundation to receive the complimentary seedlings, saplings, shrubs and bushes the organization frequently mailed to members. He purchased seven more fruit trees. He pulled eight sugar maple saplings from the woods to transplant along the road near my future garden. But the first time he plunged the new shovel into the soil, the metal head shattered as if it had been dropped from a five-story building.

The shovel-shattering incident underscored the passion Jake had for digging holes. He dug holes for trees. He dug holes for fencing posts. When we first arrived in Lexington, he set about looking for work that suited this odd talent. He learned that decent fencing contractors were few and far between—there was a "hole" in the market, you might say—so he got his contractor license and with the money he'd saved in Iraq, invested in a skid steer and a hydraulic post pounder and began installing fancy four-board agricultural fence "systems" for ranchers, farmers and horse people around the county. If there's a more labor-intensive, arduous and backbreaking profession, I don't know what it is, but for Jake going to work was like a child going to Six Flags—he loved it. Fencing was in his blood and whenever I'd assist him on jobs, he'd spread his arms before a beautiful pasture offering 360-degree views of surrounding mountains and say something like, "This is *my* office!" From the moment we moved to Lexington, he was pretty much booked solid, owing to his already established reputation and his unparalleled capacity for hard work.

Did I mention Jake liked to work? The man worked twelve hours a day building fences, then came home and worked some more. Whether it was making a pile of tortillas for tacos from scratch or installing a new culvert in the driveway, it made no difference to him. I got tired just looking at him.

"Where do you get all your energy?" I asked him one day while watching him carefully stack large rocks until it transformed into an actual stone wall.

"You."

I snorted. "That sounds like cheap flattery."

He smiled. "Would you rather I watched TV?"

"We don't have TV." This wasn't technically true—we had a TV, a faux-wood-paneled cube from the 1980s given to us by Jake's grandmom. We didn't have *cable*.

He stood up, breathing heavily, to inspect his handiwork. "You gotta admit, this wall looks a lot better than no wall, right?"

The low stone wall framing my front beds did give our place a tidier, cleaner appearance, though I can't say I would have noticed much of a difference without it. "Yeah, it looks nice."

"I want to do you proud, babe."

I couldn't tell if that was more cheap flattery or if he really, really, really felt compelled to build walls, but there was a reason I'd found Jake on a Montana cattle ranch. It wasn't just the romanticism of the rugged West that lured him out there. It was the physical labor that had so captured his imagination and made the tiniest of dents in satisfying his need for making and producing and landscaping.

I had married a farmer, a true farmer.

The downside to his ceaseless productivity was my concern it left less time for me, which Jake made up for by encouraging me to join him in all his chores and tasks. He summed up his Herculean work ethic thusly:

"Gotta get after it, hon."

I felt this most keenly on Sunday mornings. Before I got married, I had visions that weekends would be spent relaxing from the week's labor *with* my spouse. I blame women's magazines for spouting this fallacy. I'd had in my head that Sundays would be spent lolling in bed together until ten; then we'd drive into town for a coffee and the *Times* followed by a trip to a neighboring village for maybe a maple festival or an annual gourd toss—a leisurely schedule that allowed us to explore our feelings while throwing miniature pumpkins at each other. This was not to be. On more than a few occasions, I'd roll over to Jake's side of the bed for an early morning cuddle and he'd all but leap from the sheets, fully dressed with boots on, already holding a shovel and out the door by 7:04. I wouldn't hear from him again until two hours later when I was just drifting back to sleep and my cell phone blew up with orders to come help him with some hellish task for which I was woefully unprepared.

"Hon, why are you wearing flip-flops? Can you grab me another nail? That's it, now push the throttle forward. Go ahead and raise the bucket. You're doing great. Did you ever think you'd drive a bulldozer? It's fun, right? Now jump into that tree."

As much as I wanted to bury my cell phone in the bottom of my sock drawer on those painful mornings, I felt compelled to lend a hand, not only because assisting my husband seemed like one of those marital duties that can't be avoided and I enjoyed spending time with him, but doing chores seemed like the *country* thing to do. What kind of country person would I be if I didn't do chores?

Besides, he made everything look so easy, so effortless. He had a way of harnessing a meditative, utterly focused unselfconsciousness to chores that would have landed someone like me in the hospital. He was meticulous. He was fast. He was thorough. He spread compost over the newly dug vegetable garden like someone doing tai chi. He built an addition onto the gazebo before breakfast, whistling merrily throughout. He mowed our four acres of lawn in two hours flat approximately three times a week (for fun) with the precision of a golf course groundskeeper—perfectly diagonal, alternating strips of Kelly green and sage over a sloping topography. I, on the other hand, quickly learned not to bother cutting the grass at all since I could barely figure out how to turn on his new eight–thousand-dollar, zero-radius turn, commercial riding mower capable of reaching fifteen miles per hour on the highway (we know this because Jake occasionally opened 'er up on the highway for kicks). He couldn't resist re-mowing my drunken attempts at stripes anyway. When it came to hammering, he sunk nails with precisely two powerful strokes each, while mine punctured a millimeter or so into the wood before I'd violently imbed them at mangled angles somewhere on the outside of the board. When cutting lumber for a new woodshed, Jake's edges were smooth like soap whereas mine looked like they'd been torn apart by a kung fu reject. He encouraged me to move faster and talk less while working, or, as he had a tendency to say in the middle of some throat-clearing proclamation I was about to make during a brief respite from carrying lumber:

"Talk and work, hon, talk and work."

Unlike walking and chewing gum, at which I somewhat excel, talking and working with Jake is actually harder than it sounds. I compare it to juggling and riding a bicycle blindfolded on a freeway. It required the total and complete engagement of all my senses—or I might risk accidentally shooting myself in the heart with a pneumatic nail gun while attempting to verbalize my most recent adventure at the Walmart. Needless to say, I learned to work in silence or risk hurting myself.

All I had going for me on the manual labor front was a piddling competitiveness to keep up and a keen desire to fit into my new surroundings.

We had recently decided that to better acclimate myself to life in the country, we would get chickens. I thought this was a grand idea. Since moving to Lexington, I harbored a vision of myself standing outside an airy chicken coop with a shawl wrapped suggestively around my shoulders, tossing cracked corn to a flock of four, maybe six, happy hens. Jake squashed this pleasant daydream by ordering thirty-two laying hens and another fifty chicks to be raised for meat, thus demonstrating his most oft-repeated maxim that would gnaw at me throughout our marriage:

"Go big or go home, hon."

Jake was a "maximalist," which isn't even a word, but if it was, the dictionary entry would include a picture of a skinny, grinning cowboy clutching a handful of shovels amidst hundreds of yeeping chicks. Jake did everything in extremes. If a handful of chickens would have sufficed, he became a four-star general of his own chicken army. If a recipe called for a teaspoon of cumin, he dumped in half a cup, figuring that more of the spice must make the dish taste better. He thought following recipes was for the faint of heart and abhorred waste of any kind, so he added anything and everything he could lay his hands on when baking—candy bars, peanut butter, maple syrup, coconut flakes, leftover bread, frosting, cognac, a handful of cereal. His desserts were laden with fat and calories but he ate them like popcorn.

"Correct me if I'm wrong, but eighty-two birds sounds like *chicken farming*, not *raising chickens*," I said one morning as he handed me a shovel.

"Well, we don't have enough land to raise cattle so we may as well farm chickens," he said, then turned to walk to the other side of the yard to get his skid steer.

"What do we know about farming chickens?" I called after him.

"How hard can it be?" he yelled back. "Feed, water, slaughter, repeat. What's hard about that?"

"The word 'slaughter' calls up some pretty vivid images!" I shouted.

"There's money to be made in birds, hon, I'm telling ya'!"

"No, there's money to be made in Google stock. Not chickens."

"Positive mental attitude, hon. Now can you help me run a water line?"

"Positive mental attitude, hon."

If I had a nickel for every time I heard that one.

In order to prepare the old barn for its new occupants, we had to run electricity and water from the house to the barn two hundred and fifty feet away, which necessitated digging a trench with Jake's skid steer. I stood by wearing a T-shirt under a pair of big boy work overalls as Jake rumbled across the property in his skid steer. To the front of the machine he'd attached a device called a trencher. It resembled the blade of a chainsaw, only much bigger and deadlier; sharp, claw-like blades designed to carve into the earth. The roar of the machine was so loud I covered my ears. He sunk the trencher about a foot from the back of the house and plunged it deeper and deeper into the ground. Heaps of clay-rich soil mounded up around the edge of the trench, as he inched the machine backward to the barn. The machine moved in small increments and I realized this task would take all day. It was only eleven thirty. I very much wanted to sit down and stare up at the shapes in the clouds but I didn't want to come across as lazy. So I stood there holding my shovel, smiling feebly, trying to focus on the novelty aspect of the task.

After awhile, Jake had dug a line about forty feet. He decreased the throttle and made an obtuse hand signal in my direction.

"What?" I called out.

He made the gesture again.

"What!?!"

He decreased the throttle and called out, "Can you get in the trench and make sure it's level?"

"Oh."

The skid steer started up again. I stepped over to the trench and peered into it. I looked back to Jake for guidance, but he had resumed digging and couldn't hear over the din of the engine.

I stepped into the three-foot deep trench, figuring this was as good a place to start as any and scraped the shovel across the bottom of it, loosely filling the spade with a handful of dirt and flinging it over my shoulder in the way I imagined a lonely but hard-working prisoner on a chain gang might. The trench was too narrow for the head of the shovel, so I had to rotate it, causing me to spill half of every paltry load. I continued digging and flinging, digging and flinging as I inched my way forward. After fifteen minutes, I was breathing heavily. A thin layer of dirt coated my skin.

"You missed a spot," Jake's voice said from overhead.

I looked up to see his kneecaps in front of me. He had cut the engine of the skid steer and come over to inspect my work. "Back here," he said, pointing. "There's a mound of dirt that didn't get leveled out."

"Oh."

"If the ground isn't level, the water won't flow right in the pipe." He took the shovel, and hopped in the trench. "See, if you do it like this," he said, deftly swirling the shovel like a longtime dance partner, then flinging a large mound of dirt from the pit, "you can get more dirt onto the spade. Saves more time over the course of the day. Here, now you try."

I forced the tool into a clumsy pirouette and flung the dirt with an exaggerated flourish. "Ta-dah!"

"See, it's not so bad." He smiled. "It's kinda fun, right?"

"Like Christmas."

We were interrupted by the sound of an ATV motoring across the grass toward the barn. It was our sixty-one-year-old neighbor Jim, who lived on top of the hill across the road with his wife, Roberta.

Jim pulled up to the trench and cut the engine. His big brown eyes squinted against the smoke from the cigarette—one of about a thousand he smoked daily—dangling from his lower lip. He wore a lime green, short-sleeve shirt, blue jeans and thick-soled brown shoes with white socks. His black hair was in a spiky crew cut. Strapped to the front of his ATV was a small cooler containing his life's sweet nectar: Miller Genuine Draft, the "champagne of beers." Jim never went anywhere without his cooler of beer; he even mowed his lawn with it. He scanned our project momentarily before releasing a short, wet belch.

"Thought I heard something goin' on over here," he said as he twitched a fresh cigarette out of the packet.

Jim and his cousin Mel, who occupied a trailer just over the hill, had lived across the road from our house their entire lives. They had hunted in the forest surrounding our house so long that they knew every deer stand, every spring, every wild mushroom and watercress patch. Therefore, they had no hesitation whatsoever about driving their vehicles—truck, tractor, ATV—into our yard, over the grass, to wherever we happened to be standing at the time. At first, I was a little taken aback. Once I looked up during breakfast to see Jim puttering around my raised beds just outside the kitchen window on his ATV, cigarette slumbering on his lower lip, beer in hand. But Jake said that asking Mel or Jim to do otherwise would come across as the height of rudeness, since in the country, our neighbors were our closest—and really, only—allies.

True enough, Mel and Jim were the best of neighbors. They were always on hand to offer assistance and advice, share gardening wisdom, cooking tips and local gossip, watch over our place, and keep us stocked with the most delicious homegrown food. I realized after about a week of living in Lexington that "Southern hospitality" wasn't just a cliché, it was true. Every other day we found bags of bell peppers, heirloom tomatoes and cucumbers from Roberta's garden on our front porch. Roberta, who was in her early sixties, was the type of no-nonsense Southern gal who rose at four thirty in the morning to watch reruns of Paula Deen on the Food Network, bake a few hams and make a couple of pints of pineapple jelly before heading into her job as executive administrator of a prominent law office in town, a position she'd held for forty years. Roberta was incapable of idle behavior. "Oh, I would just go cr-aa-zy if I had to sit around," she'd say in her lilting Southern drawl, shaking her head disgustedly while firing up the lawn mower for a third trim of the morning. She frequently brought us warmed dinner plates wrapped in plastic of the most succulent steaks, chops or smoked turkey I'd ever eaten, steamed green beans with bacon, buttery mashed potatoes and fluffy homemade dinner rolls, plus a container or two of rich dessert. Her cooking rivaled anything I'd eaten at trendy homespun restaurants in New York. Jake and I eagerly looked forward to Jim and Roberta's frequent invitations to dinner.

As for Mel and his wife, Melinda, I never did learn what they did for money, but the procurement of food was their primary occupation—they were both avid fishermen and hunters (mahi mahi, deer, tortoise, even the occasional squirrel) who loved to forage and eat. They, like Jim and Roberta, were exceptionally generous. They gave us homemade apple butter, foraged ramps, foraged morels the size of my fist and wild asparagus so crisp and juicy it required no cooking. Mel delivered pounds of tuna steaks caught by him and Melinda off the coast of Virginia. In the fall, we looked forward to a minimum of two deer, butchered and packaged (and possibly shot from Mel's living room window, but no mind), apples, chestnuts and lots of homemade jerky. In December, they indulged us with so many bags of winter greens— kale, mustard greens, collards—I didn't have to buy a leafy vegetables until March.

"Looks like ya'll making a big mess a things," said Jim as he surveyed the deep gash in our yard.

"We're getting the barn ready for eighty-two birds," said Jake.

"Mm-mm," said Jim. He turned to me. "Looks like haws betcha oobledy workin' so hard."

I knew he was addressing me but I often had trouble deciphering his drawl. I turned to Jake for translation.

"Yeah, she likes digging a trench!" Jake said.

"Uh, yeah, it's a heck of a way to spend the afternoon," I said. My voice sounded strange to me; tinny in my throat, like I was lapsing into some strange country character. "How about one of those champagnes?"

Jim tossed me a beer that I caught with one hand, thus completing my transformation to gnarly longshoreman.

Jim drained his beer and flicked the butt of his cigarette into the grass. I wondered if saying something about his wayward butt would also be a violation of the country code. I kept quiet. One of the first things Jake told me upon moving to Lexington— other than not broadcasting I was from New York—was that I should go out of my way to get along with everyone, since gossip in a small town went around the hills and valleys and back again and I was bound to bump into enemies at the Walmart or an ice cream social, so I was better off making nice and keeping my mouth shut.

Accordingly, I listened to Jim and Jake talk about chickens and nails, trenches and lug nuts. Jake's drawl became meatier the longer he talked. He was going native—laying on the country charm with a trowel, which I'd heard him do in Montana when talking to farmers and cowboys. I tried to interject, but they were deeply immersed in Man Talk, that mysterious language of farming minutiae that seemed to go on for hours, and one thing I had learned was that Man Talk was as impenetrable as a Chinese/Taiwanese trade summit. I eventually put down my shovel and caught Jake's eye. I made my own version of a cryptic hand signal to signify I was taking a break.

I walked around to the front of the house and laid down in the scratchy grass. The sun warmed my bare arms and I knew I'd have to slather on a fresh coat of sunscreen to avoid the dreaded farmer's tan. I rolled my head to the side and spotted something red in the gravel driveway. I walked over to pick it up. It was a small cellophane sandwich baggie containing a red business card and a handful of rocks. The baggie was stapled shut. The business card belonged to one Tyler Sissly, "professional painter with 20+ years of experience." After puzzling over it for a few moments, I realized I held in my hands an exquisite example of hillbilly marketing; instead of going through the hassle of mailing his materials or enduring the drudgery of walking up our front steps and inserting a business card into our screen door, Mr. Sissly drove by our place and threw his business card, helpfully weighted down by a handful of gravel, into our driveway. The overall presentation spoke to me. It said, "I'm fast, I'm resourceful. I will make a mess of your walls."

I jostled the package in my hand, eager to show it to Jake later. People, strangers, were always dropping by, coming over, throwing parcels out the window. The first few months after moving in, our doorstep became a veritable shrine of wildflower bouquets, Pyrex dishes containing tater-tot casseroles, three-bean salads and fruit pies, and six packs of beer—agrarian tokens of friendship not only from Jim and Roberta, Mel and Melinda, but from old acquaintances of Jake's as well as neighbors who lived farther up the road. We hadn't lived in Lexington a year before we were the proud recipients of a friend's cast-off king-size bed and another's walnut dining table with six matching chairs.

Women in particular seemed to take a keen interest in me. I think those who already knew "Cowboy Jake" took a perverse interest in knowing more about the city chick he ended up with. Other ladies around town just felt sorry for me, I think—whether it was from my questionable decision to ditch Manhattan for the sticks or my status as a Yankee, I'm not sure.

I'd noticed the women of Rockbridge County (and by extension, everyone) fell into one of three types. There were the Southern Belles, the shiny blond Lily Pulitzer wearers who looked like they graduated from the elite private college and stuck around to marry one of the pillars of the community and raise children with names like Walker and Sheldon. They lived in grand Victorian homes in town or McMansions a stone's throw from the city limits. They voted Republican, went to church and said "y'all." Then there was the farmer/horsewoman contingent, the ones I called Horse People. Horse People were all a bit deranged because they cared more about their Black Beauties, Seabiscuits and My Pretty Ponies than they did humans. Some Horse People had barns more deluxe than their homes. They drove monstrous, almost obscene trucks and discussed hay at dinner parties. They said "y'all" but didn't necessarily vote or go to church because they worshiped at the altar of Sparkle Wind Racer. And finally, there was a third type—the group that eventually came to comprise my own social group—The Earth Mothers. The Yoga Moms. The organic farming, La Leche League, attachment parent subscribers who ended up in Rockbridge County as refugees of some northern city and, it dawned on me months later, were not unlike any progressive procreator in Park Slope. Only these ladies tended to live in log homes, cabins, converted milk parlors and yurts heated by wood and featuring dial-up connections. They didn't vote Republican, go to church or say "y'all." They ate soy nuts.

Jake's friends tended to come from the first two groups, so that's who I ended up hanging out with the first years we were there. And I couldn't help but notice that some of these ladies took an interest in my spiritual salvation. I'd been asked to join three ladies Bible clubs within the first months of moving here.

My foray into the world of ladies Bible clubs began, coincidentally enough, right after I'd slipped Tyler Sissly's business card into the bib pocket of my overalls, and a Volvo SUV pulled into the driveway. Out the door stepped a delicate slipper-clad foot belonging to another of Jake's old drop-dead gorgeous friends from college. (Were there any women in this town who weren't drop-dead gorgeous??) Her name was Katrina. Katrina was a graduate of the elite private college, who had gone on to marry one of the pillars of the community. With her white-blond bob, coral nails, chunky wristwatch and fitted navy blazer rolled to the elbows over a pair of tailored knee shorts, it was a no-brainer to identify her tribe. Indeed, she had a First Lady quality about her, grace born from impeccable breeding, with perfect posture and great manners, which she demonstrated by presenting me with a bouquet of flowers from her garden. Then casually, almost like an afterthought, but not, she handed me a pamphlet that said "God Is Here for You" on the front. As I looked it over, she told me about the great friendships she'd made over the years as a result of belonging to a Bible club, and how membership in the sacred circle had given her a deeper understanding of the Scriptures, and of life in general. Her Bible club, she pointed out, "is not like *that*," as if to imply I probably wouldn't witness any exorcisms.

"No pressure," she concluded in her soft, friendly drawl. "But I think you might like it. We're an interesting bunch."

"It *does* sound interesting," I said.

After she drove off, I settled into the wicker loveseat on the front porch and opened the pamphlet. It read:

Are you pining to be cleansed of life-accumulated insecurity? Are you cloaked in a heavy dirt-shawl of anger? Do you yearn to break free from years of mind-numbing dissatisfaction?

Mmm. Yes. But that could also be from low blood sugar.

On the inside of the pamphlet was a color photograph of a woman I shall refer to as Anna Bundance. She was dressed in loose-fitting slacks, a sleeveless shell top and a minimum of tasteful gold jewelry. Her teeth were a dazzling shade of white and she had a confection of hair held aloft by an invisible web of hair spritzer. She looked hysterically happy. I scanned her bio. Anna Bundance was a phenomenon in the Christian world. She'd written multiple books specializing in Christian women's issues. Her base of operations was something called Open Arms Open Hearts—which I took to mean a sprawling mega church— somewhere outside Atlanta. For fun, she taught Christian aerobics. It was Anna Bundance's trademarked Bible study group, complete with DVDs and workbooks, that I was being asked to join.

I wondered if it was the time to embark upon my serious spiritual quest. Declining such an invitation, multiple invitations, was probably the biggest violation of the country code of all. Besides, religion had become somewhat of a tender topic between Jake and me. I know this because I'd asked him about it one night while we sat in the gazebo eating his handmade fettuccine tossed with morels and wild asparagus foraged by Mel.

"Are you okay with the idea that I may . . ." I groped for the nicest way to say "die an unbeliever." "May never play for the Christian team?"

"I know where I'm going when I die," Jake said slowly, reaching across the table to daub a bit of cream from the corner of my mouth with his thumb. "I hope you go there with me."

Such a comment from anyone other than my husband probably wouldn't have sat well, but from Jake, it made me wonder what exactly was so great about my beliefs, or lack thereof. All I knew is that I wanted to be better. I wanted to live in a better way. I wasn't even sure what that meant exactly, but through him I might be able to figure it out. As Shakespeare put it in *Othello*, Jake had a lightness that sometimes made me feel dark.

I closed the pamphlet.

"Jessie K!" Jake's voice echoed from the backyard, interrupting the memory. "C'mon! We gotta lay more pipe!"

By late afternoon, after many more hours of awkward shovel-dancing, we fit the trench with two long pipes, one for water and one for electric. We then refilled the entire trench with dirt, tamped it down with the skid steer and planted the whole thing over with grass seed. With the last remaining hours of daylight, we hooked up a new water hydrant a foot from the front door of the barn.

"I give you—water!" I cried as I pulled the lever of the hydrant to release a cold spray that splashed all over my overalls and boots. I washed the grime from my face and hands. I felt dog-tired yet invigorated from having helped build something with my own hands. Funny, digging the trench *was* a type of choreography, requiring the learning of steps and movements. My shoveling had become stronger and more precise by the end of the day. I began to understand the importance of refining and perfecting physical movements in order to conserve energy and accomplish more in less time. I looked back at the dirt path that stretched like a river all the way to the house, and was amazed that we had managed to accomplish so much in a single day. But that's the way it was with Jake. Talk and work, indeed.

That evening, every muscle in my body felt loose and warm from the day's efforts. I tacked Tyler Sissly's red business card to the bulletin board near the refrigerator and noticed that my pasty shoulders clashed with my ruddy forearms. I put the back of my hand to my nose and could still smell the sun, dirt and grass in my pores, even after a hot shower. My skin smelled like Jake's. I busied about the kitchen, putting the final touches on my greatest culinary meat masterpiece to date, Coca-Cola Ham. It was nine o'clock by the time I pulled the five-pound brick of protein, its skin a crackly glaze of jalapenos and caramelized soda, from the oven. Cowboy was outside checking the perimeter, a nightly ritual of trying to scare up any "critters"—one of my new Lexington words—who tried to bed down on his property for the night. Jake, still dressed in his dirty work clothes, scrubbed his blackened hands under the faucet. He sat down at the table. I slid before him a plate of thinly sliced ham drizzled with a spicy glaze, nestled by a pillow of mashed potatoes and stalks of greener-than-green asparagus. I sat down as he grasped my hand and bowed his head.

"Dear Heavenly Father, thank you for this beautiful day and for helping us be good stewards of your land," he said. "Thank you, God, for my wife's adventurous spirit, for her sense of humor and for her hard work. Please watch over her as she makes her way in a new place. May we grow closer together as we grow closer to you, Lord. Amen."

I looked up, misty-eyed—not from the steam of hot ham

wafting up in my face, but from his words. Spirit. Jake thought I had spirit. No one had ever made that observation about me before. I leaned over to kiss him and tasted salty perspiration and a bit of sweet jalapeno glaze on his upper lip. I thought of Katrina's invitation to join the Ladies Bible Club and thought, *Why not? A little soul searching will do me good.* Besides, I wanted to be closer to my husband, who in that moment seemed finer than Jesus.

Twelve

Dive into The Word

There's nothing like riding a motorcycle in Rockbridge County in the spring, near sunset. The horizon glows orange and pink above silhouetted mountains and the landscape all but throbs with color and fertility. The very air seems to shimmer.

I sped down old highways fringed with redbud and sun-drenched forsythia under a canopy of towering oak trees, past fields dotted with round bales, trailing farmers in battered pickups who gave a two-finger wave when I passed, my face hidden behind the blackened shield of my helmet. Sometimes a horse broke into a gallop at the sound of my engine and we raced to the end of a fence line, nothing between me and the pavement except a pair of tires and my own abilities.

Concentration is crucial when riding a motorcycle. Maybe it

was because I was a relatively new at riding a big bike, but I was incapable of thinking of anything other than the road ahead. I rode as if invisible to other motorists—defensively, a little twitchy. I carefully negotiated each bend and turn, and avoided looking at the pavement directly in front of me, where every pebble seemed like a boulder, every divot in the road a yawning chasm. I learned to keep my gaze fixed two car lengths ahead, my eyes taking corners before the machine, and exhaling slowly and deeply throughout to maintain calm control.

Tonight I wore a messenger bag strapped to my back. It contained a bottle of Yellow Tail and one of Jake's many monogrammed Bibles. I was on my way to Katrina's house for the inaugural Bible club. Truth be told, I was a bit relieved to finally abandon the charade of pretending I knew the first thing about wine, something I sometimes did in New York. I secretly believed that as long as wine cost more than ten dollars and didn't depict a hot-dog cart on the label, it was worthy of my discerning palate.

On my ride through town, motorists glimpsed the long ponytail flapping below my helmet and looked twice, which thrilled me. I turned onto one of Lexington's more flawless, sun-dappled residential streets, where old homes had windows made of warped vintage glass and flower boxes were a profusion of flowers and hanging vines. I parked my bike in front of one such picturesque place, envying the front porch where four matching rocking chairs swayed in the breeze.

Katrina opened the door. She gave me a radiant smile, lightly touching the small gold cross at her pale throat. Her hazel eyes sparkled. She wore an ice-blue twin set, blue jeans and flats. We hugged lightly and I gave her the Yellow Tail.

"Oh," she said. "Wine."

She ushered me into the living room, decorated in tasteful pastels. A print of Van Gogh's *Sunflowers* hung on the wall. A "shabby chic" couch and two plump chairs surrounded a coffee table laden with an intriguing cheese plate, brownies and other assorted snacks. Facing the seating arrangement was a large flat-screen TV. Decorative suitcases were stacked in order of size on top of a nearby bookcase. Two women, both in their late twenties and also blond, sat in the easy chairs. One wore her short hair tucked beneath an eye-catching headband. She sat with her legs crossed and offered the woman next to her a brownie. The brownies must have come from a box mix because the woman offering was on the tail end of remarking "I don't *do* homemade . . ." when Katrina interrupted and introduced them as Amber and Megan. They smiled.

"Did you ride a motorcycle over here?" asked Amber, covering her mouth as she spoke. "That is so rebellious. You're like Angelina Jolie!" Her tone was cheerful, but I was unsure whether she was complimenting me or mocking me.

"Jessie, would you like some of this wine?" Katrina asked.

I weighed the offer. "Mmm. Yes. A drop of wine might be nice." I thought it sounded like something Southern belles might say.

Katrina left the room. Amber and I made small talk while Megan reached for a piece of cheese.

"New York! That is so exciting! This must be such a huge change for you!" Amber remarked. I briefly considered telling her I originally hailed from Montana but decided that would have muddled my theme. I'd long believed it was important to have a story I could tell about myself to help cement my identity in other people's minds. When I lived in New York, I was Jessie Montana. Now that I lived in Lexington, I was Jessie the New Yorker. I found I got more mileage trading on "city girl goes country" tropes than admitting I had essentially swapped one rural place for another with a fourteen-year detour in Manhattan.

"Yes, it's a huge change—a big adventure."

"Do you currently belong to a church?"

"Yes, Jake and I go to services at the VMI chapel."

"Oh, I love the pastor there!"

"Yes, he's really great. His sermons are . . ."

"Electric, I know. Katrina says this is your first Bible study group?"

"Yep, first one."

"Well, Anna Bundance is amazing. I've been studying on and off with her for years."

I nodded, wide-eyed and close-lipped.

"It's very exciting to have you here."

"Yes, I am excited."

We shifted in our seats.

"You will love Anna Bundance," Amber finally repeated. "She is . . . the best." She closed her eyes when she said "the best."

"Can you hand me the mint water?" Megan asked.

Katrina returned with my glass of wine. The ladies sipped ice water infused with lemon and mint. Katrina nestled into the couch and folded her palms between her crossed legs. Eyes moved from face to face. The ticking of the clock became louder, and I was overcome with the urge to do jumping jacks. Finally, Katrina cleared her throat and spoke. Her tone was soft and melodic, almost a whisper.

"The new workbooks have come in. Since Jessie is new to the group, I thought we'd start fresh with those since we're almost done with the last series. Is that okay with everyone?"

Amber and Megan gave their assent. Katrina reached into a small shipping box on the floor near the couch and handed each of us a thick workbook featuring a bewildered cartoon queen on the cover. Her eyes were wide and she nervously bit a finger, like she wasn't sure what to do. Behind her was a content and happy king, looking upon his queen with satisfaction. The title read, *Strong Queens, Tough Choices.* I flipped through the pages, scanning passages like ". . . life isn't a beauty pageant . . . we aren't plastic dolls and this isn't pretend . . ." and highlighted questions such as, "Do you know a woman who makes you feel scarily insecure?" and Mad Libs–style fill-in-the-blanks: "It's not easy being a lady in a world where love is _____."

I took a large swig of wine. More chitchat eventually ascertained the depth of our respective religious beliefs: Katrina, Megan and Amber—aboard the bullet train to heaven. Jessie—wandering aimlessly around the station in search of a vending machine. Near the end, there was a lapse in conversation as we all deduced that one of us was not like the others.

"Well, shall we watch the DVD?" asked Amber.

The DVD.

Katrina inserted the disc into the player. She turned off the lights and pulled the shades. I got up and moved closer to the TV in order to convey rapt attention, which I thought might ingratiate myself more to my hostess—and conceal my facial contortions in the event the DVD turned out to be a sermon of crazy.

The DVD opened with a long shot of a big, beautiful home in what looked like a forest glen. Red and golden leaves swirled across the shot, accompanied by a dreamy jazz score. The camera pulled in to the wraparound front porch, decorated with the accoutrements of fall: gourds, pumpkins, smiling miniature scarecrows, wreaths made of straw and decorated with crimson bows edged in a glinty copper. Out of the front door stepped Anna Bundance. She wore a kicky tan cloche and a matching shearling coat. She leaned her elbows on the railing, closed her eyes and inhaled the crisp autumn air. Then she looked deep into the camera—she was in her early to mid fifties, attractive with twinkling eyes. Her expression was warm, inviting, a bit mischievous. Her makeup palette—coppers and burnished crimson—matched the season. She spoke about the special love Jesus holds for all women and invited us, the viewers, to join her on this spiritual journey.

"Come on in." She beckoned the camera toward the front door with an Isotoner-gloved hand. "We're waiting for you."

The scene faded to black and reopened inside a very large theater awash in peach tones. It was packed with hundreds, perhaps thousands, of women—young, old, fat, thin, all predominantly white and blond. Fancy flower arrangements, large plants and more gourds filled the stage while plump candles burned in large glass votives along the front edge. You could almost smell the peaches and cream wafting through the theater, aromas held aloft by Kenny G notes.

Anna Bundance took the stage amid thunderous applause. She wore an almost-invisible headset and strode energetically back and forth across the stage. A bulky brown sweater, embroidered with an overflowing cornucopia, hung on her thin frame. She wrung her hands and spoke quickly, almost frenetically, ending most sentences with, "Amen." As in, "Jesus doesn't *care* how much money you have, amen? He doesn't *care* what kind of car you drive, amen? He doesn't *care* if Neiman's is having a blowout sale on St. John cocktail dresses, *amen*?" The audience roared with laughter at this last question, and shouted "Amen!" back to her. Rapport thus established, the discussion turned serious.

"Have you noticed that one of the most common human experiences is the inability to be completely satisfied?" She asked. "We look to idols to fulfill us. We look to something outside of ourselves to worship."

I helped myself to another "Montana pour" of wine—to the brim.

"Instead of beseeching God and soaring to a place of freedom, we conceal ourselves," she said. "We hide behind our jobs. We busy ourselves at church. We hide behind activities. We end up playing a role that is inauthentic to our divine selves.

"Beloved, whatever or whomever you cling to to bring you satisfaction is a lie—unless it is the source." In a powerful whisper, she asked, "Who is the source?"

"Jesus," the congregation responded in unison.

"Who is the source, amen?" She practically hurled her body to the front of the stage and raised her eyes and palms to heaven.

"Jesus!" everyone cried.

The DVD eventually ended. Katrina switched on the light. I glanced furtively around the room.

"So . . . what did you guys think?" asked Katrina.

"Amazing," said Amber. "The lady knows how to dive into The Word, and I mean *dive in* to The Word."

"What did you think, Jessie?" Katrina asked.

"I . . . Did she really teach Christian aerobics?"

Katrina cleared her throat. "I believe she did, yes."

For homework, we were required to read the story of Esther and answer questions in the workbook pertaining to the sermon we just watched.

As I gathered my things to leave, Katrina came over and handed me the half-empty wine bottle and gave me a hug. "I'm so glad you could come," she said. "It's so interesting to have a different perspective. Will you come again next week?"

"Oh, yes," I gushed.

"Are you okay to ride at night?"

"Yes, quite."

I slid the helmet over my face and walked out with a sense of deliverance, as if Jake's optimistic nature radiated from my every pore. I had made it through my first Bible club meeting without reverting to cynicism or disdain. *Ha! Who's armored in serenity?* I pushed the cork deeper into the half empty—half full, *half full*—bottle of Yellow Tail and tucked it into my messenger bag. I started up the bike and motored down the street.

Thirteen

I, Chicken Farmer

I continued to throw myself into my new rural identity with gusto. Because that is what people of strength do—they adapt; they bend and sway in the breeze while more intractable sorts snap in two the moment they step outside their comfort zone.

Which is to say, I studiously read the assigned Bible passages, I jubilantly sang the hymnals at church. I scribbled in the blanks of my *Strong Queens, Tough Choices* workbook.

I also joined the YMCA, a no-frills exercise facility housed in an old auto body shop located in a strip mall. The first time I went to the Y, I was greeted by the sight of a fifty-something woman running really fast on the treadmill in her jeans and I realized I had moved to a place with no cult of fitness. This was absolutely shocking, I know, but I gritted my teeth and became a devotee of the Y's Body Blaster class anyway. Body Blaster was a strength-training class taught by a joyful older woman who said things like, "Okay, peeps! Who's ready to sweat out the jams?" Whereupon she would pop in a cassette tape of early '80s remixes ("Yamo Be There! Up and Over!") and direct the class in a series of weight lifting and toning exercises. Cursing at the YMCA was very much frowned upon. The gym's older clientele would complain to the front desk at the mere suggestion of racy language. Instead of "butt," the instructors called it "tail feathers." The predominantly middle-aged ladies in the class all laughed and chatted throughout—catching up on last night's *Idol*, talking about kids' T-ball—like it was some sort of fizzy cocktail party, a stark contrast to the poker-faced women who dared not look at each other during Introductory Hip-Hop at Chelsea Piers. During squats, the joyful Body Blaster instructor would look right at me and say, "Go lower! *Lower*! Imagine you're hovering over a truck-stop toilet! That's it. Now *smile*!"

When I wasn't pretending to hover over truck-stop toilets or immersing myself in the Bible, I was in my home office trying to come up with story ideas for various magazines, a somewhat tedious exercise since high speed Internet wasn't available to us, only a clunky satellite connection—and the economy had entered a deep contraction by that point. Editors weren't returning my emails, let alone phone calls. It was clear more stories were being produced in-house, so freelance work was becoming a lot more competitive. But instead of pitching more stories to make up for this new world order, I found myself becoming more listless and disconnected, like New York City was this great dark planet in a faraway galaxy that had no bearing or relevance on my new life whatsoever.

My attention was turned to more pleasant distractions: my cute little house, my gorgeous property and my marriage. Because I was having a hard time ginning up work, we agreed that Jake ought to work more hours to make up for my faltering income. This was something of a conceit since Jake already worked a lot of hours—he and Cowboy usually left the house at seven and returned by seven—but now he left earlier and returned later and worked either Saturday or Sunday. He was also still very active in the Army Reserve. He had recently been promoted to captain and company commander so he was gone at least one weekend every month for army duties, leaving me and Cowboy a lot of time to figure out what outlandish meal to prepare for dinner. Granted, I was thankful Jake had so much work and opportunity when so many others did not, but the yawning days without much company made me realize the extent to which I lacked skills. I didn't know how to *do* anything in the country other than dabble in the kitchen and wander around my property. It was during those slow, meandering turns that it occurred to me the characteristics that had made me successful in New York—surfing the Internet, imbibing, downward dogging—had no currency here. What's more, in New York, that was enough. Life came at *me*, not the other way around. I was propped up by the energy of the street, the caustic wit of my friends, the dysfunction of the workplace. Hitting enter, ordering the right selection of cheese for a cheese plate and reading the *New Yorker* were the extent of my qualifications for living. But in a rural environment, where cows counted as my closest neighbors and long hikes in the woods were considered the wildest part of my weekend, I began to feel handicapped, like my hands were stumps—useless appendages at my sides.

Faced with this realization, I left the house and fired up my motorcycle and rode toward town. I wasn't sure where I was going—I couldn't really think of anywhere to go—so I ended up at the Walmart, so filled with people and sounds and light and color that maybe if I half shut my eyes it would feel like wandering through Times Square, but not. I found myself in the fabric section of the store, my helmet tucked under my arm, when I noticed a collection of *Project Runway* sewing patterns—mod-inspired shift dresses that looked relatively easy to make. A lightbulb went off: Must learn to sew. I purchased a few of the easiest looking patterns. Over the next month, I managed to track down a sewing teacher—a young New York transplant in Charlottesville—who taught me about bobbin threading and backstitching, and eventually steered me toward a deluxe, secondhand sewing machine. I couldn't really afford it, but I figured it was a hedge against the junior pharmacist's prophecy, and charged it anyway. And it was a great hedge—sewing was tactile, it was precise, it required full concentration. I could get lost in it, in the same way a craftsman gets lost in a building project. I started out making aprons; kitschy reversible aprons with ribbon, pockets and fanciful buttons that I made for every remotely domesticated female I could think of—myself, my mom, some more for me, my mother-in-law, even Hush and Maria (though I knew theirs would be worn about as often as they used an Easy-Bake Oven).

I began scouring yard sales on Saturday mornings while Jake built fences, and was delighted to discover that mint condition vintage sewing patterns from the '70s that would cost thirty dollars on Etsy.com could be had for as little as fifty cents. I found Halston and Pucci patterns and even scored a rare Sonia Rykiel tunic dress with bell-bottom slacks. I made special trips to fabric stores in neighboring counties and bought yards of funky, colorful cottons and wools and stretch jersey. Jake encouraged my new hobby by giving me one of his old canvas construction totes to hold all my new sewing supplies. I'd sit at the dining table, surrounded by colorful fabric and printed tissue paper, sipping yerba mate tea and struggling to sew a collar big enough to sail a boat with onto an A-line dress with mutton sleeves. If that sounds less than exquisite, it was, but I didn't want to waste my time making anything that looked like it came from Ann Taylor Loft, which I felt defeated the purpose of making clothes from scratch. My prêt-à-porter was all about maximum style and high drama (and it took me awhile to admit that '70s patterns in wild prints were more Halloween than haute couture).

Jake looked at the small stack of aprons next to my sewing machine. "I was thinking—maybe we should get you a dog. Someone to keep you company during the day. What do you think?"

I thought a nice, gentle house dog might nice, so we visited the local SPCA. I'd never been to a dog pound before and was therefore emotionally unprepared for the sight of so many desperate little creatures flinging themselves against their cages, clamoring to be freed, while the smell of urine and ammonia burned my nostrils.

Four dogs looked promising, so we took each out for a trial walk to see how they'd respond to the leash. I had zero dog sense—Cowboy was one of only a handful of pets I'd ever spent time with, and the only one I really cared about since he was basically human. But Jake the dog whisperer was looking for very specific traits. He said to look for one that took greater interest in us than their surroundings. Three of the dogs kept their noses to the ground the entire time, frantically sniffing and pulling, which is to be expected from animals confined to small spaces all day, but could also be a sign of indifference, or a complete lack of training. The fourth dog we walked was a dainty, carefree black mutt with white feet who scampered ahead then frequently turned to look at us with utter adoration. "*That's* the dog we want," Jake said. "Someone who's eager to please."

We brought her home and named her Sunshine. Sunny was the beta to Cowboy's alpha—she was sweetly submissive, totally lovable but lacking confidence. She loved staying home with me. As I prepared to become a chicken farmer by reading books like *Pastured Poultry Profit$*, Sunny would stare adoringly up at me, paw resting on my thigh, and in those wet, limpid eyes I saw a Victorian romance novelist reincarnated as a dog.

On the week the laying hens were due to arrive, Sunny and I drove to the post office in the next county to pick them up. When I arrived, there was a line of ten people in front of me. I heard a faint chirping sound. At first it sounded like an infestation of pigeons on the outside of the building. But as the line inched forward, the chirping became quite loud and I realized it was the sound of chicks. My chicks. The line suddenly seemed excruciatingly long. A sole disgruntled postal worker manned the counter while an elderly woman at the head of the line fished five dimes individually from the bowels of her purse for one measly stamp.

"That chirping sound," I said to the grim employee once I reached the counter. "Are those chicks?"

He nodded. "Yeah, got a shipment in today."

He shuffled to the back and a few moments later emerged with a perforated, covered cardboard box that read, "Caution. Live chicks. Please handle carefully." I peaked inside. Thirty-two chicks squeezed together like miniature brown and yellow swirls of cotton candy with eyes and beaks, each one trying to out-chirp the chick next to it. It was a melodious racket. I felt every eye in the post office on me. I closed the box and turned around. I sheepishly blurted, "Happy farming!" on my way out the door.

I drove home quickly because I was afraid the chicks might die before I got there. Chicks naturally do not eat or drink the first few days of life, which is why it's safe to mail them right after hatching, but I didn't want to delay their relief longer than necessary.

As I entered Rockbridge County, I passed Miranda's farm, the sexy horsewoman I'd met on my first visit to Lexington. I craned my head to have a look in spite of myself. There she was, near the riding ring, brushing the long, swishy black tail of a thoroughbred. Her own ebony tresses extended nearly to her bottom. *Two asses with split ends,* I thought as I floored the accelerator.

When I got home, I rushed the box of yeeping chicks down to the barn, which we had retrofitted into a spacious coop divided into two sections. In one section, Jake had built a brooder—a three foot by three foot open-top box over which we hung two heat lamps—in order to keep the chicks confined to toasty warm space until they sprouted feathers. I climbed into the brooder and knelt into the mattress of wood chips. I opened the chick box. The concentration of birds gave off a sweet vinegary smell—the muskiness of new life mixed with earthy old barns—that tickled the inside of my nose. I carefully lifted each peeping bird out of the box, downy puffballs in both my hands, and dipped each beak into the trough to familiarize it with the taste of water. Some chicks recoiled, but I baptized them anyway, then released them in the brooder where they swayed and struggled to find their sea legs before breaking into a happy jog. After nearly all the chicks had been removed, I noticed one had died in transit—its body had been trampled and was as flat as a floor rug, a somewhat jarring introduction to chicken farming.

I lowered the heat lamps a bit to ensure the brooder temperature was toasty enough, then climbed out and watched the chicks play. They looked vibrant and healthy, except for one who swayed uncomfortably.

I heard a diesel truck pull up outside the barn. One of the truck doors squeaked open. There was a short rap on the barn door. Melinda poked her head inside.

"How's them new babies?"

Melinda was in her sixties and looked a bit like her husband, Mel. Both were powerfully built and stocky with prominent bellies and a gait like a football player's. She had crinkly skin and soft, friendly eyes, and usually wore her mouth in a lopsided smile or a mischievous pucker. She wore glasses and today had on a cap advertising the services of a local excavator. Her oversized T-shirt extended nearly to her knees and read "Hillbilly Drag Racer!" The couple had been married a handful of years. To hear Mel tell it, the courtship consisted of the following exchange:

MEL: "You hunt?"

MELINDA: "Yeah."

MEL: "Wanna get married?"

MELINDA: "Okay."

They'd been making sweet venison sausage ever since.

"Oh, aren't they just the most precious little babies!" she said. She pushed her glasses farther up her nose to prevent them from falling in the brooder. Her voice was high and tightly strung, like an out-of-tune banjo. "Now you make sure, Jessa, you don't go feedin' them any bread cause that'll keel 'em dead. I done fed a chicken a half a piece of bread and I come out the next morning and it was keeled dead. The bread stuck in its froat."

"Oh?" I said.

We watched the chicks in silence. Two chicks began to peck at the weaker one who swayed uncomfortably, demonstrating the species' most disturbing characteristic—an appalling brutality toward one another.

"What should I do?" I asked. "Should I separate her?"

Melinda sniffed. "Nah, them G.D. chicks will just peck someone else, Jessa. Always gotta be someone on the bottom."

Melinda was the type of good-hearted country lady who would never dream of using the blasphemy "God damn." Among most of the older folks around our little neighborhood, the G.D. euphemism was firmly entrenched.

The majority of the flock was now facedown and spread-eagled, wings extended, as though a miniature bomb had gone off in the brooder.

"They look . . . dead."

"No, them babies just sleepin'," said Melinda. "They fall over like that when they tired."

The truck continued to idle outside. Melinda asked me to come out and talk to Mel, who typically didn't leave the driver's seat during pilgrimages to our place. This was due partly to his girth—his rotund belly was usually constrained in an ill-fitting T-shirt that exposed a large slice of flesh above his belt—and Melinda's willingness to act as his personal emissary-slash-step-and-fetch. I got the feeling the couple's foraging expeditions in the woods consisted of Mel trailing Melinda in the truck while she stumbled through the undergrowth, brambles stuck in her hair, blindly searching for a single stalk of asparagus. Not that she seemed to mind the arrangement.

Mel had one hand draped over the steering wheel and the other slung across the top of the passenger seat, smiling like a beneficent rural king. He was a heavier, puffier version of his cousin Jim, only with a thick black pompadour and mustache, and a fifth-grade education.

"Whare's Jake?" he asked.

"At work."

A brief look of agitation crossed his face—I think Mel felt

more comfortable conversing with Jake than with me—before his smile returned and he thrust a plastic bag at me. "Here."

I opened the bag and took out a glass jar of strawberries soaking in a crimson liquid.

"What is it?"

"Take a sip," he chuckled. "You'll see."

"Now Jessa, make sure you got something in yo' tummy before you go drinking that," Melinda chimed in.

I unscrewed the lid and sniffed. It smelled like rubbing alcohol, corn and strawberries—moonshine. White lightning. Grandpa's cough syrup. Pappy's drank.

I hadn't tasted moonshine since Mel and Melinda had given us some for our wedding. They both looked at me expectantly.

"Go ahead," Mel urged.

"Have a little nip," said Melinda.

I raised the jar to my lips and nipped. The sensation in my throat was like a lit flamethrower dipped in liquid nitrogen. My eyes watered. I gagged. Mel roared. Melinda giggled.

"Aaarrgh!" I coughed. "Where did you get it?"

"Can't say," said Mel.

"Franklin County," said Melinda. "But that's all I'm gonna say 'bout that."

"Here." Mel thrust another bag at me, this one containing a glass jar of a gelatinous beige meat substance streaked with gray.

"It's chicken," he said. "Canned it up this morning. To cook it, add a little flour, a little salt and pepper and a little Crisco to the pan. It's real good."

"Canned" and "chicken"—two words I never thought belonged together.

I waved good-bye as Mel nearly backed over one of our new apple trees. I went back into the barn to retrieve the box containing the dead chick and unceremoniously flung its lifeless body into the sinkhole. The brutal ease with which I did this surprised me, but I wasn't sure what else to do with the body—flush it? A proper burial with last rites seemed over the top. I was a farmer now. A chicken farmer. Farmers had to be unemotional in the face of death, since death was part of the equation, particularly with a creature so low on the food chain. That's what Jake said, anyway.

I placed the moonshine in the liquor cabinet, next to all the other similar jars we had collected since settling in to Rockbridge County. Our road, we had learned, was something of a "moonshine alley"—plenty of folks tucked back in the hills either distilled their own spirits, or knew a guy who knew a guy who did. I didn't particularly care for the taste—jelly beans soaked in battery acid came to mind—but having a connection to this rare and precious commodity helped bolster my country identity, solidify my country theme. I couldn't wait to sip Pappy's drank with Hush and Maria.

The fifty meat birds arrived a few weeks later. Each flock required separate housing. The books I had read advocated housing birds in mobile structures that could be easily transported around the yard, giving the birds constant access to fresh forage; stationary coops, the book said, confined birds to a too small area they'd quickly defoliate, which then became a breeding ground for disease. We were determined to raise happy, healthy birds, so Jake designed the mother of all mobile coops that was literally a small house on a trailer—it looked like something the Beverly Hillbillies might pull in lieu of a Winnebago. Originally intended as something I could pull around the yard myself, the Hen Hut, as it became known, featured an A-frame roof with a skylight and a weather vane, two windows, nine laying boxes, four roosting bars, a ramp and two doors. Metal grate flooring allowed droppings to fall through onto the grass below. The best part was it hardly cost a thing. With the exception of the five-hundred-dollar trailer on which the house was mounted, Jake had built the Hen Hut from scavenged parts—lumber from old job sites, windows picked up from the dump, a weather vane found in a field, metal grating given to him by one of his Man Talk friends. I no longer questioned the piles of scrap metal and old parts and broken down furniture he'd occasionally haul home from job sites; it all had a purpose. Sooner or later, he'd put it to good use. That was the other thing I was learning about my husband: He had a knack for making due with what was at hand. Where others (I) saw trash, he saw opportunity. Indeed, the Hen Hut was a thing of beauty. Absolutely one of a kind. We proudly displayed it in full view of the road so passersby could honk in admiration at our tidy little farming operation. The only down-side was that at some point during its construction, Jake's maxi-malist tendencies took over; the finished Hen Hut was so heavy and huge there was no way to haul it without a machine. He ended up installing a hitch to the front of it for pulling it around the yard with the commercial lawn mower.

For the broilers, he built two heavy open-bottom sleds that could be pulled around the yard with a rope. One warm morning in early summer, Jake handed me the rope for a test pull. Facing the coop, I grasped the rope with both hands and pulled as hard as I could until my heels were the only part of my foot on the grass and my body angled forty-five degrees from the ground. The coop didn't budge.

"C'mon, hon," Jake said. "Put a little muscle into it."

"I *am* putting a little muscle in it."

"It's not that heavy," he said. "Here, give it to me." He took the rope and with a momentous heave, the coop slid forward. "Don't just lean back. You gotta put your legs into it."

I tried again and pulled as hard as I could but the coop didn't budge. I dropped the rope. Jake walked toward me and picked it up.

"I don't think you were pulling as hard as you can."

"Oh no?" I said, lightly touching my rib cage. "My hernia suggests otherwise."

He dragged the coop to a level patch of ground. "Just keep practicing since you're the one who has to pull it while I'm at work."

I felt oddly guilty, as if I *should* be able to pull this behemoth across the yard. "And you're the one who neglected to put wheels on this contraption."

"Wheels lift it up too high and make room for critters to squeeze through."

"That sounds like an excuse for a design flaw."

Jake laughed and unclipped the birds' water trough. "No design flaw here, babe. You just need to do a few more push-ups."

I gave a limp salute. "Aye-aye, Cap'n."

He left to go fill up the chickens' trough and I considered this retrograde notion—that conquering my new environment depended in no small part on my ability to pull and lift and carry things, a yardstick by which I never dreamed I'd be measured (was I being measured?) but was in a very real way the currency of success in such a back-to-the-land milieu—the currency of men. My gym muscles, sculpted and toned by years of yoga, Pilates and now Body Blaster, had no real use here.

While the broilers fattened and the hens began to lay, Jake and I prepared the garden for an onslaught of vegetables. We tilled the soil until it was loose and loamy enough to punch my arm into up to the shoulder. I succumbed to the disease that afflicts every gardener by buying more plants and seeds than I could possibly eat myself or give away: sugar snap and snow peas, eight varieties of heirloom tomatoes, eggplant, cantaloupe, broccoli, five different kinds of chili peppers, beets, radishes, cilantro, dill, chard, kale, turnips, rutabagas and bok choy. A fifty-pound bag of purple potatoes caught Jake's eye—it was on clearance—and he proceeded to plant almost every one, which necessitated digging an extension onto the existing garden. Each potato had to be painstakingly cut into golf-ball size chunks with a paring knife, each chunk containing one eye. It was tedious and hard work especially considering there was no way we would ever be able to eat what would turn out to be hundreds of purple potatoes. But we did it anyway because it was time spent together—talking and laughing and planting as the sun set and the dogs snoozed at the garden's perimeter. I could tell Jake was pleased with my newfound abilities even though vegetables planted by me looked like someone had thrown a packet of seeds in a strong wind—eggplant cozied up to chili peppers, tomatillos grew amidst watermelons—while those planted by him were orderly and well spaced, like perfect little soldiers. He was concerned my haphazard plantings might hurt business (he being a builder of straight lines and all) but it was too late to do anything about it because the plants, feasting on virgin, nutrient-rich soil and blessed with plenty of rain and sunshine, practically shot up in the span of an afternoon. Eggplants toppled over from the weight of their own fruit, pea vines bulged with pods, a bush was dotted with so many tomatillos I realized I had no idea what to do with them. One afternoon in late July, I picked fifty-four cucumbers in a single day, which required the wheelbarrow to haul them all back to the house.

We ate cucumbers for breakfast and lunch. I sautéed them for dinner. I mixed them with yogurt, with vinegar; I froze a gallon of gazpacho. I tossed them in salads by the handfuls; I tucked several into Jake's lunchbox before he left for work each morning. But still, there was no end to them. As we stared at the wheelbarrow brimming with cukes, it dawned on us I'd have to do something I never thought in a million years I'd do—I'd have to learn to can.

I went to the local library and checked out several eighties-era cookbooks on the subject (the most recent titles available). The

Lexington library was the kind of place where townsfolk—young, retired, the unemployed, the crazy and dispossessed, me—would come to loiter for lack of anywhere better to go (I sometimes wrote freelance articles from there). A row of complimentary computers were available to patrons, but these were so heavily filtered with porn guards and smut nets it was impossible to research anything racier than "chicken breast recipes," let alone navigate to my own email account. I had to rely on what was on the shelves. The canning recipes had a similar vintage quality, but I didn't care. I was determined to win the cucumber war. I checked out several cookbooks, all bearing a variation of the title *Saving the Season* or *Preserving the Harvest* or *Maniacally Preserving the Seasonal Harvest in a Jar* on the cover. I tied on one of my fancy new aprons and proceeded to make just about every pickle in the canon of rural housewifery.

I made bread and butters, dill pickles, lemon cucumber pickles. I pickled eggplant. I made habanero hot sauce. I canned five varieties of bell pepper relish, including one audaciously called Tropical Island Thunder. By then, the peaches were ripe and begging to be picked, prompting me to make peach jam, butter, sauce, pie filling and salsa. I canned whole peaches. I canned half peaches. I dreamt about quarter peaches. Then the tomatoes, rosy red and dribbling with juice, cried out for attention, and the pores in my face opened to the size of saucers as I stood over the boiling cauldron processing quarts of tomato sauce, ketchup and salsa. The temperature inside my un-air-conditioned house hit ninety degrees, the windows steamed up and my couch still harbors an omnipresent pickle smell, but by the time the first leaf fell in late September, I had canned fifty-four jars of food, spent hundreds of dollars on jars, ingredients and equipment, and suffered from a kind of post-traumatic canning disorder in which every food item I looked at, I wanted to stuff and seal in a canning jar.

One day Jake came home with thirty pounds of tomatoes, another food gift from Mel, and announced he was going to make wine out of it.

"Why do I feel like I'm living an episode of *Hee Haw*?" I said as he began washing the produce in the industrial sink. He'd recently scavenged the sink from a store that had gone out of business and installed it in our mudroom.

"What else am I going to do with them?" He nodded toward the row upon row of gleaming canning jars filled with every shade of red lining the pantry. "You've canned enough tomatoes to last us a lifetime."

"Give them to the chickens?"

"No way," he said. "Besides, I've been wanting to get into wine making. And home brewing. Just think how much money we'll save not having to buy wine or beer."

"Right, just like all the money I've saved by canning."

After we washed all the tomatoes, we blended them in batches in the food processor. The pulp was then transferred to a large piece of cheese cloth, which was tied off and lowered into a fermentation container filled with water, where it soaked with a precise amount of sugar, grape tannin, raisins and yeast for twenty-four hours. Over the next five days the soaking liquid was repeatedly strained to remove any floaty bits. Once clear enough, we transferred the wine to glass carboys, and finally, 750 milliliter bottles Jake had pulled from the recycling center, each one soaked and sterilized and scraped. Once all twenty-five bottles had been corked, we stowed them in an old cistern Jake had somehow transformed into a grotto underneath the house, complete with stainless steel shelves (another scavenged find) where they would ferment for the next three to five months.

Hush and Maria came down for a visit around that time and it seemed like a technological revolution had taken place since I'd left New York. No sooner had they arrived, Maria bellowing, "You have lost your mind!" (for moving to the rural South), than they were jacked into their various devices, emailing, texting, wi-fi-ing, uploading and gigabyting themselves into a glorious network of white noise. Meanwhile, I stood off to the side trying to interest them with jars of my homemade pickles. I wondered if I'd ever been that plugged in. I must have been. I had to have been. I just noticed it more now that my life was so wholesome and serene.

In October, Jake and I got together with friends who owned an old cider press and gathered buckets of apples and pears and squashed them into cider. Jake reserved half our haul for fermentation. He wasn't kidding about wanting to make his own alcohol. The mudroom, and soon the kitchen, began to resemble a microbrewery, featuring tools like hydrometers and copper coils. Carboys bubbled with hard pear cider, habanero beer, IPA, chocolate stout, Pilsner, rhubarb wine, peach wine and mead. The entire room smelled like stinky cheese. Then it was time to make homemade venison jerky using my brand new deluxe dehydrating machine—I was officially a country woman now!

That night, as I dumped a jar of Mel's canned chicken topped with charred tomatoes and chile salsa in a skillet, and Jake thumbed through the latest issue of *Commercial Truck Trader*, I thought about all the new skills I'd acquired to widely disparate degrees of success since moving to the country. I rode a motorcycle. I read Scripture. I sewed, sang, played the guitar, raised chickens, amassed moonshine, gardened, canned vegetables and bottled tomato wine. I was determined to master the horse. And I did it all with an open mind (mostly) and an open heart (generally).

That was one epiphany. That same night, when I spooned a mouthful of the fiery chicken mash into my mouth and felt a tiny, almost imperceptible chicken feather brush my tongue, I had another: The only difference between do-it-yourself living and living like a hillbilly was one's perception.

Fourteen

Horse People

Is it possible to be jealous of a man's love for his horse?

Yes, I'm afraid it is. This realization came to me after Jake began spending more time on his horse, a quarter horse mare named Yamaha—yet another thing to compete for his time. I can't claim to be surprised by my husband's close bond with animals. He and Cowboy were inseparable and I'd met him at a rodeo, after all. It was one of the things I loved about him. But time with Yamaha meant less time with me, so I keenly felt it was time for me to learn to ride, not only to conquer my fear of large, unpredictable animals that spook easily, but so that Jake and I might increase our time together and I might fit more seamlessly in my new world. There was just one problem: Horses still scared the crap out of me. Jake must have picked up on my inner turmoil when he arose one Saturday morning in early autumn to go for a ride and I flopped back into the pillows in an agitated sulk.

"Well, why don't you come with me, hon?" he asked.

"Because you know I don't know how to ride."

"I'll teach you. C'mon, let's go. The day's a-wasting."

I donned a pair of his old Wranglers and my new cowboy boots, threw on a T-shirt and a baseball cap and met him in the driveway as he loaded tack into the back of our pickup. He whistled when he saw me.

"You sure do look hot, babe," he said.

I looked down at my redneck ensemble. "And you think I look like an absolute sex goddess in a pair of overalls and welding gloves."

"Heck yeah!" he said.

We drove over to the neighbors' barn, where Jim and Roberta generously allowed Jake to board his horse for free. Cowboy, Sunny and I followed Jake into the barn, where he set about readying Yamaha for a ride. He fed her, brushed her and petted her. He spoke to her in such a gentle and loving manner, the bond between them was so palpable, I almost felt small. I couldn't help but ask what it was about horses he liked so much.

He heaved a saddle atop a square of blanket on the animal's back and cinched it tightly. "A horse is the most pure, honest creature on God's earth," he answered, as though he'd pondered the question before.

"Like you?" I wasn't sure if I was trying to flatter him or understand him.

"I wouldn't say that," he said. "But there's no faking it with a horse. With a dog or a person, you can pretend to be someone you're not for a little while before they eventually figure you out. But a horse can see right down to the core of your being. If you treat them with kindness and respect, there's no end to how deep the relationship can go."

"Hm."

Yamaha evidently found my depth lacking. She refused to follow my physical cues or verbal commands once I sat on top of her. My body became stiff and rigid as I tried to make her turn 360 degrees one way, then 360 degrees the other way, while Jake stood off to the side issuing directives.

"Don't let her toss her head, hon," he called. "Don't let her eat grass. C'mon, hon, control your horse or she won't respect you."

"How do I 'control my horse' if I don't know how to ride one?"

"Not so hard, hon!" he called. "Loosen your grasp! Pull up! Now pull down! Relax, babe. Control her, hon!"

"Alright. I've had enough. I want off."

"You can't end a riding lesson on a bad note, hon. You have to finish positively."

I was so agitated my hands trembled as I tried to grasp the reins, but the image of Miranda, the sexy horsewoman, popped into my mind. She had actually become a permanent fixture of my brain, mentally taunting me in her contour-hugging riding pants, bed head and effortless equestrian skills. Everything about her was just so gosh darn natural and free I wanted to punch her in the face, except she'd probably hit me back twice as hard. I pulled up on Yamaha's reigns as hard as I could, causing her to violently jerk her head.

"Whoa, whoa, whoa," Jake called. "Calm down, hon. Easy, easy." He strode over and put a hand on Yamaha's bridle. "You okay?"

"Great. I am having a fun time."

"Take a few deep breaths and relax," he said, inhaling by example.

I breathed in. Once my nerves had steadied, Jake asked that I walk her into the barn and calmly dismount her, in order to end the lesson on a positive note. To drive this point home, he asked that I also remove her saddle and brush her mane.

"Good job, babe," he said as I cautiously brushed. "I'm proud of you. You hung in there."

"Uh-huh," I said, silently cringing.

That afternoon, we were invited to a potluck, which I'd begun to realize was the defining social event in all of Rockbridge County. To not own a Pyrex platter in Rockbridge County was like not owning a vehicle—it meant social Siberia. It seemed like every other weekend right up until the first snowfall we were invited to one G.D. potluck after another—potluck dinners, potluck bluegrass jams, potluck canning parties, potluck weddings. I'm surprised I was never invited to a potluck home birth in someone's backyard. But I didn't mind. On the contrary, I actually enjoyed trying to crush the other wives with my potluck pleasers, like tonight's creation: Super Nachos.

It wasn't until Jake backed his truck up to his horse trailer I realized today's potluck theme would be horse-related: Potluck team penning. It was hosted by a couple who were as nutty for the equine arts as Jake and who lived on a seventy-five-acre farm just outside of town featuring a large riding ring. (In Rockbridge County, the mark of comfortable living was not a swimming pool but a riding ring.) As expected, there were a lot of Horse People present. Men, dressed in plaid snap-front shirts, Wranglers, boots and caps, congregated in the backyard holding paper plates stacked a foot high with food, discussing hay, horseshoeing and barns. Women, wearing jeans and T-shirts, assembled in the kitchen to catch up on gossip, swap mothering stories and probably talk hay.

As I walked around the buffet table, helping myself to crackers and various iterations of quickly coagulating cheese, I considered that most potlucks we attended seemed to segregate along gender lines. I didn't know if this was because we lived in a place where a masculine, conservative, blue-collar ethos held sway, or if this really was the natural order of things once children entered the picture, regardless of one's location—women discussing kids in one room, men discussing gadgets in another. Maybe it was like this in New York too—I left before any of my friends started having kids—but I bristled at the separation and walked outside into the sunshine, a last gasp of a long Indian summer, to join the menfolk where I was quickly bored silly by the discussion of chain saws.

A few of the other women had drifted out of the house by that point. One of them bantered with a guy who looked a little more rough around the edges than the others. He was in his late thirties, tall and thin with copper hair and a beard. He wore a voluminous plaid shirt tucked into jeans, hiking boots and a cap. As he sipped from an open bottle of Jack Daniel's—which seemed a tad extreme for four o'clock in the afternoon—I overheard him make a sudden belittling remark to one of the women, loud enough for everyone to hear. The yard got quiet. The woman tried to play it off like it was a continuation of their banter, but her downcast expression conveyed she had been humiliated. I disliked him instantly. Rather, it was the *idea* of him I found unappealing (plus he answered to the name of "Scratch" or "Skitch" or "Skatch"). I guess by moving to the country, I had all but invited the Scratches of the world into my life, but I couldn't disguise my antipathy when I bumped into Scratch on my way to the bathroom. I think the look on my face made him dislike me too. We were from opposite worlds, Scratch and me—not so much men are from Mars and women are from Venus; more like I was from Venus and he was a total Uranus.

When I walked back into the kitchen, the party seemed more stifling than before. I walked outside and followed a group to the barn. The hosts had set up a mobile chute in the ring. A steer was loaded into the chute. Each time the chute was opened, the steer ran into the ring, chased by riders on horseback as they attempted to lasso the animal. It was decided I wasn't ready to participate so I was offered "to sit" (nonsensical Horse People slang for "to sit on") a tired old speckled beast named Gus.

"Gus is real safe," the couple's seven-year-old son, Huck, said. Wearing a cowboy hat and boots, Huck straddled the top of the chute, preparing to pull the lever to release the steer into the ring for each rider's turn. "Dad says he's pretty much retarded."

"That's great," I said.

"He says some dead horses have bigger brains than Gus."

"Why don't you go get a popsicle, Huck?"

I "sat" Gus conspicuously off to the side behind the chute while several other riders whooped and hollered and threw nooses around the poor steer's neck and yanked really hard. They all seemed perfectly in their element, effortlessly galloping and lassoing, chatting amiably about their technique between each turn. It was a language I didn't understand, a problem exacerbated from my perch atop a stuffed animal.

Jake rode up to me, smiling brightly. "Hey, baby, baby! Wanna turn?"

"Yes, I mean, no—I don't know?" I huffed, yanking at the reins. "Why does this dumb horse keep lowering his head?"

"Because you're not controlling your horse," he said.

I smiled reluctantly. Then there was a crack—the lever jammed, the steer stepped on something, I'm not sure—and Gus, brain-dead Gus, the horse I'd been told was too dumb to move, took off at a full gallop across the ring. I screamed in terror, like a nine-year-old girl on a roller coaster after too many Nerds and cotton candy. Gus began bucking in time to my wails, clumsy and unsure of himself at first, then increasing in power and malevolence. Next thing I knew, I was aloft, floating in space as if in slow motion, my arms and legs in a sort of desperate dance before crashing on my back on the gravel ground.

I saw the sky, a blue so faint it was almost white. I was alive. Or was this heaven? I blinked my eyes and gasped. Jake's face, then Cowboy's tongue, appeared over me.

"Hon, are you okay?"

And then I saw it. On Jake's mouth. He wore a slight smile. No, not a smile. A smirk. He smirked at me! He was trying not to laugh! I squeezed my eyes shut.

"You're laughing at me!" I screamed. He stumbled backward as I leapt to my feet and ran toward the fence, a tight ball squeezing the inside of my throat. As I dashed toward the house, past Scratch, past kids, past women, I was aware of being stared at by everyone at the party. I dashed upstairs to the bathroom where I stood over the sink extracting microscopic pebbles that had become embedded in my bloody elbows and palms. I had never felt so dumb, so humiliated. I looked in the mirror. My eyes were as red as my face. Why am I riding horses when I don't even like horses? Because that's what everyone here does. And I wanted to fit in, to make Jake proud. So I guess I did it for my husband. And he laughed at me? He *laughed* at me? Why did I even bother?

I heard footsteps on the stairs. I quickly doused my face with water. There was a short rap on the door, with Jake standing on the other side looking sheepish. I sniffled.

"Hon, are you okay?" He inspected my bloody palm. "You got pretty banged up out there. You know what that means, right? You're a real horsewoman now."

"Jake, you laughed at me."

"No, hon," he said as he picked another pebble out of my hand. "I didn't laugh at you."

"Yes. You did."

"No, I did not."

"You did. I saw you."

"Hon, if I did make a face—which I did not—it was an innocent nervous reaction and I'm sorry." He took both my hands and turned my body to face him. "But getting bucked off is part of the deal, Jessie. You know how many times I've been tossed off a horse? You know how many times everyone out there has been tossed off a horse? Too many times to count. You don't quit when something gets hard. You get right back out there and ride."

I looked at the floor. I was trying so hard and all he could see was me not trying hard enough.

We left for home not long after.

Fifteen

The Cheese Incident

Many strange thoughts go through your mind when your hand is shoved inside the warm cavity of a freshly slaughtered chicken, and the thought that kept drifting through mine one brisk Sunday in late November two years after moving to the country was, "I'm flying. I'm really flying." I couldn't help but laugh. Jake eyed me from the kill cones near the woodshed, his jeans dotted with fresh blood. "You okay over there?"

"Couldn't be better!" I cried, even as I groped deeper into the slippery cavern, my fingers deftly detaching organs from parts unknown. I had been trying to master a new disemboweling technique taught to me by one of our more experienced poultry farming friends in which the hand takes the shape of an arthritic claw. If the claw rotates just so, it's possible to extract all the organs and entrails in one squishy handful. If the fingers of the claw miss even one extraction point, the organs must be sloughed out individually, a surprisingly more disgusting alternative that is also less efficient. *Efficiency. Talk and work. Gotta get after it, hon.* I had developed a begrudging respect for these old saws now that I spent many weekends with my hand inside the hot pocket of a chicken. Let me be clear: Somewhere between my tenth and twentieth disembowelment, I stopped seeing my birds as fluffy pets, friendly nibblers of cracked corn. I saw them as units of production. Dollar signs with wings. Oh sure, our chickens lived a grand chicken life: free range but confined to a portable electric mesh fence, plenty of exercise and sunshine, unfettered access to fresh forage, their own luxurious Hen Hut, but at some point in my transformation to chicken farmer these conditions ceased being in support of the birds' comfort and became only about making them taste yummy.

Jake walked behind his truck to fetch another bird from its holding cage. We kept the cage concealed from the kill cones so as not to stress the birds about their impending doom. He returned with a spastically flapping chicken, held upside by the legs. We'd learned that holding chickens like this just before slaughter induced a dopey, trance-like state that made for easier handling. Sure enough, the inverted bird suddenly quieted and became very still. Jake lowered the upturned body into one of the cones, and the chicken's head poked through a small opening at the bottom. Jake gave a slight tug on the chicken's wattle to pull the head lower, fully exposing the throat. He picked up his small, sharp, Army-issue "kill knife" and made a swift vertical slash in the throat. The legs jerked violently as a thin stream of blood poured to the ground. While the bird bled out, Jake leaned against the wall and casually crossed his ankles, like a man waiting for a bus. He caught my eye and grinned. Sunny gingerly approached for a nuzzle but he shooed her away from the blood and feathers. Cowboy napped underneath a nearby bush.

An icy chill stung my ears but I was warmed by my work. As I dug and pulled and sliced, Jake fetched and slit and bled out. It was monotonous, icky work, but strangely meditative. It served a simple purpose. We raised chickens, slaughtered chickens, sold chickens. Actions followed by results. Sweat transformed to money; a clear, concise loop of productivity.

After each bird's throat had been cut, the bodies were dunked into "the scalder," a large portable tub of boiling water to loosen the feathers. The carcasses were then transferred to "the featherman," which resembled a giant, top-loading washing machine with sides and a bottom affixed with long, thick rubber fingers that spun around really fast to remove the feathers in thirty seconds.

I had somewhat mixed feelings about Jake's purchase of the featherman and the scalder. I equated these purchases with my lack of warmth. Lately I'd noticed our cozy little abode felt about ten degrees colder than the outside temperature. This was because of all the cold air that infiltrated our unfinished basement (really more of a crawl space tall enough to stand in) and rose up through the uninsulated floor boards to caress my ankles like an Arctic breeze. Even wearing a ponytail inside my own house was like draping a cold, wet towel across my neck, and I realized the previous owners' claim that the "cheerful" white propane stove in the kitchen was enough to keep the house warm was only true if their previous lodgings had been a cardboard box heated by a candle. No, the stove, which looked so cute and inviting and rustic when I first saw it, put out about as much heat as a fireplace—it only heated the side of me standing two feet in front of it. With winter bearing down, I thought we might want to invest in a legitimate heating system. Jake opted for the featherman and the scalder instead.

"Trust me, hon, you do not want to pluck a chicken by hand," he said. "That is not how you make money in the chicken business. And I can install a wood stove for free in the basement."

And he did eventually install a wood stove for free (another scavenged find) in the basement. And the house *was* a bit warmer. But the purchase of the featherman and the scalder underscored the growing economic disparity in our household. My freelance had slowed to a crawl. I was for all intents and purposes a chicken farmer, dependent on what money I could scrounge up selling eggs and plump broilers. Jake was the primary breadwinner, and therefore had more leverage with which to make the case for high-tech chicken processing equipment over a twenty-first-century heating system.

A ninetenth-century heating system, as any pioneering homesteader will tell you, must be stocked several times a day, twenty-four hours a day, seven days a week from the end of October to early April, which required a small forest of trees to keep going.

This raw material was abundant and free, since Jake regularly knocked down rows of trees with the skid steer to make way for fence lines. At least three weekends in the autumn were spent cutting the trees into segments with a whiny chain saw, then splitting them with a noisy gas-powered wood splitter. Each piece was then flung by me into a dump trailer, whereupon Jake offered pointers on how I might refine my technique.

"Cut the wood three-quarters of the way through *then* flip it," was a typical suggestion. "And when you throw, roll your wrist just a bit before you release." I would grunt and point at my earplugs. It seemed that by choosing to live a hand-made life, I had inadvertently cast myself as perpetual student, requiring instruction and advice for how I might flesh out my new role more completely. Once the wood in the trailer resembled a small mountain, we would drive it back to the house and dump it in front of the woodshed, where we would spend several more hours stacking it in tall, Jenga-esque structures.

I bagged and weighed the last four chickens, recorded their weights, and deposited them in the "chicken freezer" that we kept in the woodshed. We spent the rest of the afternoon scrubbing and sanitizing the kill site. The offal and feathers were loaded into the bucket of the skid steer and dropped in a hole on the far side of the property. While Jake buried the blood and guts, I rummaged around the woodshed for logs of oak and locust, hard woods that burned more slowly than soft varieties like pine and poplar. My house was freezing either way, but at least I could now identify the optimum burning woods.

*   *   *

As January came to a close, I realized I hadn't had an assignment in four months. Yet it seemed every time I turned on the computer, another spastic government official was quoted as saying, "Looks like the end of the recession is near, everybody! Get out your checkbooks!" But from where I was standing—on top of those noninsulated floorboards that occasionally seeped smoke from the wood stove downstairs, I'd say the recession was just getting comfortable. I'd say it was just hunkering down for a nice long visit, like the houseguest who takes a while to loosen up but once he does, eats all your food, makes a mess, leaves the seat up, then asks if he can borrow your long underwear because your house is cold and . . . are you going to finishing eating that?

It was Monday and Jake had left for work a few hours ago. I walked into the living room, followed by Sunny, and stared at the thermostat Jake had installed, teeth chattering, debating how to keep warm. Dressing in the morning had become a farce. I no longer bothered with the snug, formfitting sweaters and tops, skinny jeans—vestiges of my life in New York—or the shoe caddies stuffed with stilettos, strappy sandals, and spike boots that hung pointlessly from every bedroom door. Because, really, what did it matter what I wore on a chicken farm? My daytime attire boiled down to a pair of ratty old fleece pants over long johns, a green puff vest, and a pair of shearling boots I'd had so long they were always sort of damp inside. For variety, I succumbed to purchasing a pair of black Dansko clogs—arguably the most unflattering, asexual foot coffins in history that had somehow become the unofficial footwear of modern motherhood—after several Horse People and Earth Moms kept telling me how comfortable they were. "You can go from the barn to Body Blaster to a potluck in them!" they said. "Without ever again thinking about what to put on your feet!" I hated myself for this style betrayal, this acknowledgment of how frumpy and sensible my life was becoming, but the clogs *were* really comfortable and I could wear them down to the Hen Hut and to Walmart with equal *je ne sais quoi*. The finishing touch on spectacularly cold days like this one was a spongy thick, wheat-colored knit cap featuring a small, sculpted protrusion at the top that resembled the tip of a condom and did in fact come to serve as a kind of birth control: When the hat came out, Jake knew not to bother.

It was one o'clock, time to abandon the pretense of writing for dollars. Sunny and I wandered into the mudroom where I slipped on Jake's canvas Carhartt coat and a pair of his muck boots then ventured down to the Hen Hut clutching my wire egg basket. It was bitterly cold. A dusting of crunchy snow covered the yellowish grass like a layer of cheesecloth. As I approached the Hen Hut, the entire flock of layers seemed to ignore me except for Mrs. Knadler, a gentle black Australorp with glinty green feathers. She ran toward the fence surrounding the Hen Hut. I unclipped the metal prong on the fence so I could enter the chicken yard without getting shocked, followed closely by Mrs. Knadler. I scooped her up and she cooed in my arms. I checked the laying boxes for eggs and found at least seven broken shells and frozen yolks. Ungrateful savages. Some of the chickens had discovered the joys of eating their own eggs. As I deposited the twenty or so remaining eggs into my basket, I heard the sound of heavy feet on the metal grate inside the Hen Hut. Rooster feet. I eased down the lid of the boxes and slowly backed away. He emerged from the chicken door and craned his head around. His high red comb, the tips tinged with frostbite, sagged between his eyes, like a spiked Nazi helmet worn too low. A wide strip of black—another vestige of winter's bite—bisected both sides of his wattle. It looked like scars from a knife fight. Adolph hopped to the ground. I picked up a stick with one hand, the other grasping the egg basket, and held the stick toward him. Unimpressed, he chest-bumped it.

"Stay away from me," I warned. The rooster half circled away from me and lunged for my legs, but I intercepted him with my stick. "Stay away!" I thrust him away and backed toward the fence. I no longer bothered to swat Adolph in the chest after I realized there was too much padding in the breast area to be a deterrent. It was an *anti*-deterrent. Chest blows emboldened him. Suddenly, Adolph flew at my rubber boots, his talons bared like knives. I felt a hot prick of pain and looked down. "You punctured my boot, you little bastard!" I swung the stick. He hopped up and over it, like we were playing a game of jump rope. His fearlessness enraged me. I swung again, harder this time. He tumbled, but regained his footing within a second. With a brisk ruffle of his feathers, he strutted forward, ready for another lunge.

"No! Crap!" I stumbled through the fence opening and fastened it shut. Sunny bounded over. "Thanks for the backup," I said. Adolph turned and dropped his head in a charade of peck-ing. He knew I'd be back. So did I. He had won this round, but I had the eggs.

I brought the eggs back to the house and carefully washed and dried them. I wondered what to make for dinner. My cooking had become increasingly complex after I read somewhere that a cook's proficiency lay in her mastery of the egg, it being the pro-tein that binds everything together. I found myself searching for recipes, from perfect hard-boiled eggs to deep-fried poached. I discovered vintage cookbooks were a mother lode of rich eggy recipes, created during a time when it was assumed womenfolk had piles of eggs laying around and the inclination to beat every last one into submission. Old-fashioned recipes along the lines of Spaghetti Souffle with Creamed Ham caught my eye, less for their maddeningly vague cooking instructions ("lash the egg ball with a flagon of butter, place in a warmed oven and cook until done") than for what was involved: "creaming ham."

I carried several cartons of eggs and bags of frozen chicken out to the car to be delivered to clients around town. I dropped car-tons off at one of the dance studios, the mortgage lenders, a couple of restaurants and the frat house. As I sauntered across the crowded dining hall of the fraternity house on my way to the kitchen, pass-ing young guys munching yogurt granola parfaits and leafing through the latest issue of *Inside Lacrosse*, some of these hunky specimens looked up at me with a mixture of indifference and dis-dain, like I was a fleece pant, clog wearing, egg delivering townie. If it looks like a duck, and quacks like a duck . . .

My final out stop of the afternoon was the home of my friend

Jenny, who lived outside the town of Natural Bridge. Jenny had invited me and three moms over for a midday potluck. Jenny, who was tall and fit with short dark hair and glasses, was a farmer. She had three young children, the youngest of whom was usually strapped to her chest. Jenny's husband, Lance, was a craftsman who had built their rustic, eco-friendly home and every piece of furniture in it—two beds, one table, four chairs, one island, one vanity, one bench—by hand. Everyone's husband, including mine, worked in agriculture or construction—mainstays of the local economy outside of academia. Satisfying careers for women (outside of academia), on the other hand, were a little harder to come by. Many of my friends opted to stay home, whether by choice to raise children, or out of frustration over earning eighteen thousand a year in the local job market.

The purpose of the potluck was to discuss spring planting—already around the corner. Spring planting was sacrosanct among this group, though a few of us were still learning the language. The five of us poured over a stack of organic seed catalogs while several young children played underfoot. My friend Carrie, a cheerful but sarcastic mom of two, ladled five bowls of her homemade sunchoke soup while we lusted over pictures of burdock root, celeriac and bok choy. I brought my homemade hummus and cartons of eggs for all. Jenny pulled two homemade pizzas topped with marinated fiddleheads from the oven.

I looked around the home and was struck by its sparse simplicity. The furniture was in a sturdy, un-fussy Mission style, which reflected the couple's preference for minimalism and craftsmanship over a bunch of shoddily made, mass-produced goods. The walls were mostly bare. There wasn't a protrusion of plastic toys overflowing from bins. The pantry was lined with Jenny's canning jars. Against one wall in the kitchen, garlic tied together hung like a braid from the ceiling to floor. The toilet was affixed with a hose for blasting poop out of cloth diapers. Out the front door and across a brook was Jenny's massive vegetable garden, which she tended by herself in the summer with three kids to mind. Jenny was the ultimate modern homesteader, though I doubt she thought of herself as such. For her, living close to the land was a way of life that simply made sense—without labels, without moral superiority, without proselytizing over the sanctity of the locally grown. And she never raised her voice around her kids. I was sort of in awe of her.

My friend Alice helped herself to a pile of greens drizzled with homemade ginger dressing. Of all the ladies, I was probably closest to Alice, a petite caramel-skinned massage therapist in her early thirties who had long, glossy black hair and expressive hands. Alice ended up in Rockbridge County after falling for a man from the area who she met while they were both students at the University of Idaho. At the time, her husband—a handsome, soft-spoken loner with dreadlocks and little need for possessions—had been living on top of a mountain in a teepee. As in, he used to live on top of a mountain in a teepee. She had to hike an hour just to bring him lunch. Now he worked as a timber framer (sans dreadlocks) while Alice raised their two daughters and performed shiatsu and deep tissue massage out of her house.

"Mmm, this dressing is so good," Alice said between bites.

The woman who brought the dressing nodded sweetly. Her

name was Lucy. Lucy's tiny frame, short bob and adorable splash of freckles across her nose gave her the appearance of a precocious sixteen-year-old, definitely not a mom of two in her early thirties. Despite the small, delicate packaging, Lucy was a powerhouse of will and strength, which manifested itself in a keen observance of surface details, particularly related to food—organic food. She read ingredient labels like a neurologist studying brain waves and carefully scrutinized her children's diets, from ingestion to elimination.

"Who wants eggs?" I asked the group.

"I know I do," Carrie responded. Carrie ran a small sewing company out of her house.

"They're three dollars a carton," I said. "I had to raise the price." The egg business was, in a strange way, not a bad business to be in during a recession—eggs, like butter and salt, were an essential. People needed them. No one cut back on eggs like they did fancy cheese or expensive wine.

The ladies looked at each other.

"Oh, you're *selling* them," said Alice, reaching for her wallet. Bartering was big among this group, and I think my friends thought I'd be willing to trade eggs to put toward a shiatsu or a pair of homemade pillowcases. But I was like Donald Trump that way—my brain processed nothing but cold, hard egg cash. The ladies each passed me their wadded up dollar bills.

Lucy knelt down to pick up her ten-month-old daughter, who whimpered at her feet.

"Oh, sweetie!" said Alice, addressing Lucy's other child, a precocious four-year-old girl with long dark hair. The child grasped a chunky candy necklace around her neck. "Where did you get your pretty candy necklace?"

The little girl looked incredulous. "This is not candy."

"That's right, sweetie," Lucy chimed, trying to hold on to the baby who wriggled in her arms. "It's plastic. A pretty *plastic* necklace."

The little girl wandered off, inspecting the jewelry more closely. Alice gaped at Lucy. "You didn't tell her it's candy?"

"They gave it to her at preschool," Lucy sighed. "Hard candy contains Red 40, a food dye made from petroleum that's linked to hyperactivity and severe allergic reactions." She looked toward her daughter busying herself in a corner. "Sweetie! Sweetie, honey, don't eat that, it's poison." With a resigned, cherubic smile Lucy said to me, "Parenthood! See what you have to look forward to?"

I must have made the smallest face because she smiled slyly. "Oh, you know you'll love it. Being a mom is your true calling! You're more domestic than all of us, with your homemade dresses and your canned goods."

That wasn't true. All the women at the table were as domestic as me, all ruled by goodness, yet I seemed to pursue it with a bit more fevered intensity, a bit more focus. And wasn't parenthood the inevitable end point of all this feverish domesticity? But I couldn't think of a clever comeback so I turned my attention to my egg bag loaded with full cartons, which I parceled out to the ladies.

Lucy's daughter began to gnaw in earnest on the necklace. "I should probably go grab some kale chips from the car." Lucy sighed. "Here, hold her." She plopped the baby girl in my arms, almost as a dare, before throwing on her coat and dashing outside. I stiffened. The baby felt like a bag of potatoes in my hands. She looked at me like she was going to cry.

"Good baby," I said in a creepy whisper. "Nice baby."

A cell phone on the table chirped. Carrie glanced at the screen and picked it up. "Lucy's cell phone, may I help you?" she asked. "Hi, Ed! Yes. Your wife's outside rummaging for kale chips."

"Jessie, do you think you and Jake will have a baby one of these days?" asked Alice.

I impatiently thumped the baby on my knee. "Mmm, I . . . I'm not so sure."

Jake, the eldest of six, couldn't wait to have kids. He loved children. He looked forward to fatherhood, which I found both refreshing and absolutely terrifying. Since lately I had begun to wonder if it was possible to be a mom in the country without abandoning the notion I was an independent, sophisticated woman. *Independent woman.* It sounded so anachronistic to even use the phrase, evoking some first wave feminist, fighting for her rights while tossing her bra into a burning barrel. But there it was.

"Uh, okay, Ed." Carrie cocked an eyebrow. "And how exactly do you want me to convey that information? Right, okay, buh-bye."

Lucy came back inside holding a bag of crisped roughage. "Here you go, sweetie," she said. "Try these. Mmm! Aren't they tasty? Yum! Good!" The child cried at the switch.

Carrie spoke: "That was your loving husband calling from the job site. He wanted me to tell you . . . that, um, you forgot to put cheese on his sandwich."

We turned to Carrie.

Lucy looked up from her little girl. "What?"

"And he wanted me to tell you 'in the nicest way possible.'"

"Did you tell him to go screw himself?"

"Yeah, we . . . didn't get into that."

"Did you tell him he's a baby who cries too much?" Lucy masticated a kale chip. "Did you remind him I cook, I clean, I raise both kids. Did you mention I'm totally *f-ing* overwhelmed? He spends every weekend hunting and he has the nerve to complain he doesn't have enough cheese on his sandwich?"

"It was no cheese, actually," said Carrie.

"Lucy," Jenny said. "Why are you making his sandwiches?"

"Because if I didn't, he would eat processed food all day." Lucy said this as if it was the most obvious thing in the world.

I sat back, vaguely alarmed by the extent a woman as badass as Lucy had to fight to retain a sense of purpose around here. It was as if by choosing to live the life, we had all somehow condoned taking a few steps back as women as well.

I turned to Alice. "Yeah, I'm actually not so sure I want kids."

sixteen

Osmond Family
Sing-along

A couple of weeks later, Jake and I drove home from playing Biblical Trivial Pursuit with members of our church after services.

"You okay, babe?" Jake asked. "You seem a little quiet today."

"Oh, it's nothing," I said. "I think I just woke up on the wrong side of the bed is all."

Truthfully, I hadn't wanted to go to the potluck Biblical bonanza. I wasn't in the mood. Something about the episode at Jenny's house a few weeks back struck in my craw, bringing up apprehensions I had about my place here, and the subject of having children. Theoretically, I guess I always figured one day I'd have kids, though I wouldn't say I was one of those women who stared longingly at babies modeling monogrammed bath wraps in Pottery Barn catalogs. If anything, having children seemed more like an obligation or a duty, like setting up a will or having wisdom teeth pulled—not exactly a thrill in the moment but a blessing down the road . . . when I was old and gray and had no one to spend Thanksgiving with because my husband was gone because he had worked himself to death. For me, that was the essence of motherhood: A bet against future loneliness. So freaking touching.

Still, I was in my mid-thirties. My uterus, that old monthly workhorse, probably wasn't as spry as she once was, and I knew I probably shouldn't ignore the biological clock much longer. And Jake wanted kids. He wanted his own child army. But I was having a hard time reconciling my own modern misgivings about motherhood with this old-fashioned life I was living. Throw in a game of Biblical Trivial Pursuit, and I was feeling a bit testy, you might say.

But Jake had wanted to go to show support for the congregation. He did not disappoint. He turned on a full hundred and fifty watts of charm. He fetched sweet tea for little old ladies and talked cattle with local farmers. He cheerfully shouted out answers to the questions, his mouth full of banana bread, while I knew the answer to only one—which I didn't bother to vocalize—despite my months of Bible schooling. But there was another reason I was taciturn. I was stoned. Well, not much. Just a little. Mildly, at most. But enough to render me mute. That morning, while rummaging through my dresser drawer looking for a pair of tights, I stumbled upon a film canister containing a small bud of marijuana—no bigger than a fava bean or two. It had been a gift from Hush during her last visit.

"Well, what do we have here?" I cackled mischievously. I tucked the crumb into the pocket of my skirt and hummed a happy tune while Jake came into the bedroom to lace up his boots.

"What are you so happy about?"

"Oh, just saw my first blue jay of the season and it was marvelous!" I said it with just enough pep to hide the bitter sarcasm in my voice. Once the game commenced after church, I snuck outside in the cold for a small puff—my rebellion against the cabbage patch of wholesomeness within. But as soon as I stepped back in the living room and was met by a thousand blinding smiles worthy of an Osmond family sing-along, I was seized by a paranoia so overpowering I could barely find my chair, let alone speak or risk betraying my sin. I said nothing and smiled tightly until we left.

As we neared home, the last vestiges of the THC had receded, making me feel more or less lucid, but still hypersensitive and groggy. Jake waited as I got out of the car. He put my hand in his as we ambled toward the front door.

"You hungry?" he asked.

"Starving."

"You want me to make you a deer neck taco?"

The deer neck taco. This was one of those culinary creations sparked after money had become so tight we opted to eat our way through our freezer, containing many off-cuts of venison, remnants of deer given to us every fall by Mel and Jim. I had pulled one such five-pound hunk of meat from the bottom of the freezer, read the label and asked, "The heck do you do with deer neck?"

Jake, who stood behind me, shrugged and said, "Put it in a taco?" And we did. We put every questionable meat stuff in a taco since it is an acknowledged fact that everything tastes better in a taco. We discovered that deer neck, in particular, if slow cooked with canned tomatoes, chipotle powder, and other spices long enough, then pureed in a food processor, had the finished consistency and flavor of any fast food taco—tasty, economical, and certain to give you gas.

I retrieved the leftover taco filling from the refrigerator while Jake queued up a country CD on the stereo. Something about the sudsy twang and the lyrics about waitresses and prison made me want to stab myself with the fork in my hand.

"What are you doing tomorrow?" Jake asked while quickly rolling out a small batch of dough then flattening them into disks in a tortilla press.

"Oh, loads," I yawned. "Collect the mail, collect the eggs, *wash* the eggs. And there's Body Blaster at four thirty."

"Think you can come to work with me?" He placed a tortilla on a hot griddle and flipped it with a spatula.

"Um, yeah, I guess."

I wasn't wild about going to work with Jake, but I found myself doing it at least a couple times a week to stave off feeling like I was turning into a house ornament. It wasn't so much the physical labor I found punishing, it was his tendency to morph into a drill sergeant on the job. Generally sweet and considerate as a husband, he was the type of boss who could barely contain his annoyance when employees assumed they were allowed to sit down for lunch; the unwritten rule on one of his job sites was that food should be eaten with one hand while the other grasped a nail gun.

But money was a real issue. We were effectively a one-income household. Turns out I couldn't maintain my own socioeconomic course or live life on my own terms in Lexington the way I had fantasized. Besides, to turn down Jake's request for help when he needed it most seemed almost selfish and indulgent, like nibbling bon-bons in my fuzzy mules at home while he worked his butt off to keep the bills paid.

He slapped a spoonful of reheated deer neck on a warm corn tortilla and slid it on a plate before me. "There you go, honey bun. Eat up."

I topped the pureed deer meat with some of my homemade salsa and a handful of grated cheese. Jake took a seat next to me. He reached for my hand and said a small prayer, something about being thankful for the life we had chosen—I was distracted by the tortured mewling on the stereo. After we ate, Jake washed the dishes while I dried.

"Hey, do you mind if I go finish up that job on Palmer's farm?" he asked.

"Jake, it's Sunday."

"I know, but the mortgage is due and I gotta get paid. It shouldn't take more than a couple of hours." He patted his hands dry on a dish towel.

"I guess." How could I argue? The mortgage *was* due and our bank account was in the double digits. Yet I resented the idea he might rather be working than home with me. I could already feel the deer neck taco working its way through my system. "I'll probably spend the rest of the afternoon in the bathroom anyway."

Jake laughed as I returned the leftover meat to the refrigerator, realizing we'd be eating this stuff again tomorrow night. He came up behind me and clasped his arms around my waist, digging his hands into the front pockets of my skirt. "I love you, hon," he said. "You're the best thing that ever happened to me. I just want you to know how much I appreciate everything you do for us."

His right fingers touched something metal. I squirmed as he pulled the artifact from my pocket. It was my Lancôme lipstick lady pipe. He opened the tube to expose a small red bowl, sticky with pot residue. He took a step back.

"It's not what you think," I stammered, turning to face him, even though it was exactly what he thought.

He looked at me, disappointed. My pulse raced. His face slackened as he deposited the pipe in my hand.

"You do what you need to do, hon."

He turned and walked into the bathroom, closing the door behind him. I slumped onto the coffee table and looked at the pipe, which seemed like a desperate, idiotic little toy in my hand. In my old life, when we first met, this transgression would have barely registered. I would have waved it away with a "What? It's just pot" and "It's not even addictive." But in my marriage, "just pot" and "not even addictive" was to speak in the language of stoners. I fished the crumb of weed from my other pocket, and went outside into the cold. I walked down to the sinkhole, still bare and raw and cavernous from the season's long pause, and tossed the pipe into it. As it sailed through the air and landed with a delicate ping on the bottom, reminiscent of the sound a canning jar makes as it seals, I realized there went the last vestige of my old life. I flicked the crumb of weed in behind it but it was so light it blew back toward my feet . . . where Mrs. Knadler, who had scampered up behind me, pounced on it before I could react.

Seventeen

❧

200 Hammers

We barely said a word to each other the following morning. I was tired and chastened. Jake was glum. The day's forecast called for cold and more cold. I suited up in my dirty worker wear—insulated overalls, three socks, boots, my jaunty condom chapeau pulled lower than my eyebrows—and strapped Jake's deluxe nylon lunchbox filled with his 'n' hers working-man lunch: peanut butter sandwiches, apples, oranges, Pop Tarts, and one bag of soy nuts across my chest, which bounced off my leg with each step. I fed the chickens and the fire while he loaded the truck with the necessary tools. The four of us, Jake, me, Cowboy and Sunny, loaded up in the cramped cab together and pulled out of the driveway.

We didn't speak much during the forty-five-minute drive to

the job site, located in a neighboring county. My stomach already growled in protest over what was sure to be a nutrient-deprived day. Jake cranked up the cheerful charm during an early morning call from one of his buddies. "Shoot, Shelby, them tires don't do nuthin' when you're pullin.'" Under normal circumstances, I would have shot him a horrified sidelong glance for using such hickish locutions but I just closed my eyes. I had no leverage today.

The job site was far from any town, accessed by a dirt road that ran between two hills before turning up the side of a mountain. As the truck inched up a series of switchbacks, the tops of pine trees at the summit came into view, their furry needles tossed back and forth in the whining wind while great black clouds surged angrily around the mountaintops. What looked like miles upon miles of new fence—some four-board, some woven wire, some high tensile—crisscrossed up and down the endless terrain, demarcating nine separate pastures. All nine pastures contained a large freeze-proof water trough bolted onto a square concrete pad. To close one eye and look down one of Jake's fence lines was like following an arrow shot to the horizon.

The land leveled off at the top, where his skid steer, post pounder and other equipment was parked.

"Wow, did you do all this yourself?" I asked as I hopped out of the truck and took a slow 360-degree turn.

"Yup. Well, me and Andrew."

Andrew was the retired British Special Forces soldier and sometimes employee who was the only one who could keep up with Jake for long. I was Andrew's stand-in.

"Wow. I'm impressed." I *was* impressed. My husband had built a mountaintop of fence, a metropolis of fence, tangible proof of the man's relentless productivity.

The day's tasks consisted of hanging twenty-five farm gates. Each gate weighed roughly 125 pounds. The gates had to be hung between various openings in the fence line. We also had to pound a line of treated pine posts into the ground using the post pounder attached to the front of the skid steer. Jake used the skid steer to load the gates onto his truck, which we drove from site to site. Jake would jump up on the flatbed and heave a gate off the back, where we would each grab an end and lug it to the necessary position. I'd stand on tiptoe straining to hold my end as Jake drilled large holes into the top and bottom of each post. As he drilled, tufts of wood shavings sprayed out the back end. I struggled to maintain my hold. My eyes followed Cowboy as he ran up a steep incline and disappeared into a wall of pine trees, followed closely by Sunny, both in pursuit of some invisible creature. They would eventually return, both panting, tongues lolling, covered in burrs and reeking of deer poop. I'd never seen more blissful, free, energetic dogs. I was proud to call them mine.

"Um, about yesterday," I said as Jake maneuvered the top end of the gate onto the pin.

"Hon, you don't have to tell me," he sighed. "It's your life."

"I just want you to know that stuff isn't important to me," I said, releasing my grip once the gate was secured. *That stuff.* I couldn't even call it by its real name.

"Hon, it's okay," he said. He swung the gate open and closed to make sure the bottom didn't touch the ground.

"No, it's not okay," I said. "I don't want something as dumb as pot to come between us. If you don't want me to smoke it, I won't smoke it."

"Don't put it on me." He gave an astonished laugh as he collected his tools. "I just wish I knew why you felt the need to use drugs in the first place. I mean, do you sit around the house getting high all day?"

"No, of course not."

"I hope you know it doesn't make you any more fun to be around, or clever or interesting," he said. "It makes you seem kind of . . . dumb, actually."

"Right. I should be high on life. Like you."

He took a swig of coffee from a battered thermos. "Well, it might sound dumb to you, but you should try it sometime."

"Jake, what do you think that knee-high stack of aprons in the closet is all about? And the canned goods? And the creamed ham?"

I suddenly regretted apologizing for the pot. I had thrown my pot pipe away for him . . . my one and only pot pipe, my only crumb of weed (damn it! My weed!), the last, pitiful holdouts of my old, messy life. I threw them away to hold on to the gee-whiz purity of this marriage, and all he did was judge me. And I couldn't even yell at him for guilting me into tossing the pot pipe because it was a pot pipe! Griping about it would probably confirm every low opinion he already had of me.

And when I wasn't sewing aprons or creaming ham, I was building a farm fence with him, an activity I disliked, but did it anyway. Why? To demonstrate once again the bottomless pit of my "adventurous spirit"? Or to rationalize having moved here? Whatever the motivation, it all suppressed a creeping, niggling purposelessness that was threatening to overtake me. Suddenly my rib cage felt like it was squeezed in a vise; I could barely breath at the recognition of what was happening to me.

"Next you'll be telling me I forgot to put cheese on your sandwich," I said.

"Cheese on my *what*?" He cocked an eyebrow before turning back toward the truck. "Ya lost me, babe. C'mon, next gate."

As the morning dragged on, my mood went from gray to gunmetal to black. The job sucked. My muscles ached. I was starving. While my humor flatlined, Jake's mood—whether to gird himself from me or help pull me out of my funk—slowly, triumphantly soared like a mighty eagle over the trees. I found it just short of unbearable.

"A little higher, hon," Jake said. "You're doing great, hang in there."

I gripped the horizontal bar tighter and tried standing *en pointe* to raise the last gate up. My shoulder muscles bulged like they might detach from my back. How far New York seemed. Even in the midst of the Great Recession, so many of my peers up North had managed to shift their careers into high gear—helming magazines, running popular web sites, producing television shows—in all ways moving mountains. I, meanwhile, hung farm gates *on top* of a mountain. There had to be an inherent integrity in what I was doing to make up for its lack of glamour.

"C'mon, higher, hon!"

I grunted.

"We gotta finish this," he said. "And hon, don't get mad but we'd move a lot faster if you would try to anticipate my next move. By the time I get to the next step, you should already be there handing me the right tool."

I looked down at the pile of dirty, smudged pieces of metal at my feet, forgetting which one was the 1 1/8 inch wrench, even though Jake had shown me twice already. When I didn't retrieve it fast enough, he walked over with a bracing Boy Scout smile and picked it up himself.

"I'm sorry!" I cried. "I forgot!"

"You're doing fine, babe."

As we collected the tools to bring to the next gate opening, the dogs bounded over to us. Sunny rolled onto her back, a show of doggie submission and an invitation to rub her belly. Cowboy dropped a large stick at Jake's feet. Jake picked it up and threw it hard. Cowboy tore after it, disappeared into the trees, while Sunny just lay there with her paws in the air.

"That dog." Jake shook his head and chuckled. "Sunshine, you're not good for much, you know that?"

"Why? Because she doesn't chase sticks?"

"Well, she's not much of a working dog, you gotta admit."

"Who says she has to be a working dog?" I cried. "You honestly think Sunshine has less value because she's not a working dog! Not everyone wants to be a working dog, Jake! You can be so black and white!"

"Okay . . ." he said slowly, like a question.

When the time came to drive the posts several hours later, I had already eaten my allotted crackers and carrots but my stomach groaned for attention. Jake threw me a can of Beefaroni. A corpulent chef in a toque winked suggestively at me from the label. I could handle a lot of abuse in this life, but as I spooned the cold pasta into my mouth, I realized Beefaroni might just break me. It was getting colder. There was no feeling in my toes. I threw the empty can onto the flatbed. I desperately had to pee. I leaned over and tried to blast one nostril like Jake had taught me, but failed—half the contents stuck to my cheek, riding dangerously close to my lip. I wailed. There was no tissue. There was no toilet paper. Jake told me to use leaves. I grabbed a handful of the moist plant matter, walked down a steep hill and disappeared behind a tree, quietly sobbing into the wind. From my feral lady squat, I saw the skid steer in silhouette on top of the hill, waiting for me, taunting me.

Inside the cockpit of the skid steer, I felt like a small child locked inside a metal cage. My ears were encased in a pair of soundproof earmuffs. The fence line cut through precarious terrain, down a steep hill and over rocks jutting from the ground. Sitting in the cockpit at such a steep angle was like sitting in a roller coaster car at the precipice. Jake stood in front of the skid steer and steadied an eight-foot post to be hammered into the ground with the post pounder. Without taking his eyes off the post, he began making the dreaded hand signals.

I cautiously pressed forward on the hand levers. The machine inched forward. He scowled and made a sharp, slashing motion with his hand and gestured for me to back up. I pressed my right heel down and the post pounder tilted forward. "No, babe, reverse, reverse!" I pressed my left heel down and the bottom of the post pounder slammed into the ground. "Hon!" he yelled over the sound of the engine. "Back up on the levers! *The levers*!" I slammed the levers into reverse, scraping the bottom of the post pounder on rock—*Crack!* I couldn't reverse any farther. I tried again. *Grind! Griiiiind!* Nothing.

"Stop! Stop!" he shouted. I threw up my palms like an apprehended burglar. He walked around to inspect. I craned my head around. Somehow the track had slipped off the drive sprocket. The skid steer was broken. I broke the skid steer! I made a car-crash face. Jake spun around on his boots and threw his cowboy hat into the woods, cursing wildly.

I squeezed my eyes shut, willing the world to become subsumed by the sound of the engine.

The workday ended not long after. We left the skid steer at the job site to be tended to in the morning, presumably without me. As we made the long drive back to Lexington, I gazed out the passenger side window, trying to resist the urge to slam my fist into the radio to silence Carrie Underwood's plea to "Jesus, Take the Wheel."

"I gotta go to Walmart," I grumbled.

We drove through town and pulled into the store's sprawling parking lot, the hub of social activity in Rockbridge County. Old men, young families, teenagers, county people, and the occasional VMI cadet filed in and out. Jake's truck idled loudly right outside the front doors. I checked my wallet: three dollars.

"Can I have some money, please?" I asked, still looking out the passenger-side window.

"Sure thing, babe," he said, reaching into his wallet. "You

earned it. You did a good job today. I'm sorry I cursed earlier." He handed me four new twenty-dollar bills. I was struck by how crisp they felt.

"Jake," I said as calmly as I could, slipping the money into the bib of my overalls. "I didn't *earn* your walking-around money. I helped you because I am your wife. You give me money because you are my husband." The retro-regressiveness of this statement infuriated me.

"Oh, okay," he said, leaning over the two dogs to kiss me. "Consider it a present then. A present for helping me out and being a great wife. I know it's not always easy coming to work with me."

I jumped out of the truck, suffocating on my husband's relentless optimism, and shut the door harder than necessary.

I strode into the store, pulling my condom hat lower on my eyes and shoving my hands deeper into the pockets of my overalls in an attempt to disappear into the folds of my Carhartts.

I made a beeline through the store, picking up my usual sundries. I had over the months become a reluctant connoisseur of Walmart's house brand—those plain, white packages labeled with utilitarian variations on popular name brands: Bran Flakes with Raisins, Crackers of Graham, Wheat that Is Puffed. Sadly, there was no Wine in a Box, just the fancy twenty-dollar boxed wine, which I hungrily deposited in my basket.

I turned to see Alice standing right in front me, wearing fleece pants, a fleece vest, a long-sleeve fleece crew neck and a hat made of fleece. We looked like two wooly mammoths meeting around the watering hole. She deposited a case of beer into her cart while her two daughters loitered behind.

"Oh my gosh, Jessie!" she said. "I didn't even recognize you. What brings you to ol' Wally World?"

"Tragedy," I said hoarsely.

She looked confused then broke into a forced laugh. I forced-laughed back at her, which became too uncomfortable for both of us. I excused myself and headed for the self-checkout area. All four kiosks were taken. I positioned myself between the four stations, figuring whichever opened first was the one I would use. With this strategy I rarely got stuck behind some poor schlub who took twenty minutes trying to find the bar code on the back of a can of Tang. Several people lined up behind me. A fit, weathered fifty-something woman, a frenetic ADD Horse Person sort wearing a thick knit headband, fleece jacket, scuffed riding pants and boots, marched up to one of the stations holding a bag of dog food.

"Excuse me," I said. "The line is back here."

"What line? I don't see a line."

I could tell she was from the North, a retiree from D.C. or Boston or Baltimore who now devoted her life to her trusty steeds. She blinked rapidly, like she had no eyelashes.

"See all the people behind me in a string? That's a line."

"Well, then line up behind one of the machines!" she yelled. "You can't stand all the way back here"—indicating the four-foot distance between me and the machines—"and call it being in a line."

Already defeated by the day, I assumed an air of stolid calm. "Why?" I asked. "Who says?"

"Because it's not fair, that's why."

"What makes you an authority on the fairness of the Walmart line system?" I laughed and turned to gauge the reaction of the guy behind me, but he stared straight ahead like a deer about to be flattened by an oncoming semi on I-81. Wimp.

She stepped toward me. A pocket of spittle had collected in the corner of her mouth. "Oh, I'm not even going to get into this with you." She turned to walk away, but not before looking me up and down, itemizing the unrefined contents of my basket, and mumbling, "Redneck."

I casually chuckled in an attempt to hide my rage as she stomped away. "Yeah! Sure! Good one! *I'm* a redneck. That's rich!"

I turned in the vain hope of sharing a laugh with the wimp behind me, but his lifeless carcass was already strewn across I-81. I closed my eyes and tried to tune into my third-eye point, but saw only black. I paid for my items and skulked out of the store.

"Did you get everything you need?" Jake asked as I climbed into the truck.

"Just drive."

When we got home, Jake asked me to help him unload. As I replaced the nail guns and air hoses in the shop, I heard gravel crunching under tires in the driveway. Outside, Mel sat on his four-wheeler. He and Jake were talking tools and moonshine. Mel brought out four mason jars of a yellow liquid, which Jake deposited in his lunchbox. As they talked, I noticed Jim high up on the hill across the road puttering down his long driveway on his own four-wheeler. He eventually turned into our driveway.

He cut his engine and cracked open an MGD, tossing one to Jake.

"What're all doin'?" Jim asked, taking a drag off his cigarette. He nodded toward me. "Looks like you had some help today."

"Yeah, she's been coming to work with me a lot here lately," said Jake, stealing a glance in my direction—"she," the woman with no name. Wordlessly, I retrieved my groceries from the truck.

"Let me see that there hammer," I heard Jim say.

Jake tossed it to him.

"She's a beauty." Jim flipped it in his hand. "What is it—titanium?"

"Yep, titanium."

Jim chewed his cigarette. "I got me a buncha hammers but they all as useless as a fart in a whirlwind. This one here musta costa pretty penny, mm-mmm."

"Shoot. Two hundred dollars," said Jake. "I got three of them."

I couldn't help doing the math. Two hundred times three equals . . . equals . . . Hold on . . . six hundred dollars! Six hundred dollars worth of hammers—*one* type of hammer! Jake must have owned two hundred hammers, to say nothing of the thousands and thousands of dollars worth of other equipment hanging in his shop.

"Shelby says he's never seen anyone with more tools," said Jim. "Says you got the finest collection in the whole county."

"Shoot, I don't spare no expense," Jake said, unconsciously thickening his accent. I could almost see his chest puff up. "If I need something, I buy it. In multiples. Got to. Nothing is worse when equipment breaks on a job and you don't have the right tool to fix it."

I looked down at the plastic Walmart bag in my hand. The words "Excaliber Estates Boxed Chablis" were just visible. I pushed the hat away from my eyes. So, Jake *was* under the yoke of money and status, just like I was, just like we all were. He hadn't transcended anything. His craving for status was just another kind—a kind that had been invisible to me in New York, a status defined by power tools and titanium hammers. I had projected my dreams of the simple life onto him, but he was no more unalloyed than anybody else.

I looked at the titanium hammer as Jim tossed it in his hand. It seemed to flip in slow motion, as if suspended in midair. I looked at the truck, which Jake had customized with a dazzling array of shiny aluminum toolboxes and more LED lights than a Christmas tree. A formidable deer catcher hugged the grill, the center of which showcased a plaque in the shape of Texas Longhorns. The muffler had been replaced (by the previous owner, but still) for an even louder version that sounded like a thousand Hell's Angels driving by on a fleet of choppers. Everything about the truck was unequivocally redneck, right down to the shiny chrome strips adorning the bottom of each mud flap, which flirtatiously caught the sunlight as the vehicle hauled ass down the highway. It was a working man's Ferrari, that truck. I looked at the little house. The featherman and scalder tucked in the woodshed. The smoke coughing anemically from the chimney. I took in all the trappings of my raw country life—a life I had traded New York City for—and realized all that was missing was a turkey fryer on my front porch. There was nothing romantic or authentic or pure about any of it. I shuddered over how little control I seemed to have of my own life . . . how dependent I'd become. Holy shit. I am dependent on my husband and his eighty dollars' worth of "walking-around money." I am dependent like a 1950s housewife. No, not like a 1950s housewife—that comparison was too modern. My dependence went further back into the annals of housewifery. My dependence was more along the lines of Ma in *The Waltons*, a woman with two inches of flour and bacon grease fermenting in the furrows of her face, whose arms dragged on the ground from lugging water to chickens and whose hair held the permanent stench of smoke from sticking her head in a fireplace all day.

I leaned against the truck and massaged my temples with my fingertips, eliciting a concerned look from Jake as he concluded his hammer clinic with Jim and Mel. The cousins puttered off on their four-wheelers in opposite directions. I let out a melancholy sigh. Jake placed a hand on my shoulder, trying to catch my eye.

"Hey?"

I cleared my throat and assumed my most polished, corporate tone. "Question: Why is there money available for two hundred hammers while I am relegated to drinking Excaliber Estates Boxed Chablis?"

Jake smiled cautiously. "Answer: Because having the right tool at the right time improves efficiency and efficiency in the fencing business means more money. And I don't know what relegate means."

"Exactly."

I walked quickly into the house, where I changed my clothes and barricaded my ears behind the padded walls of my noise-canceling headphones. The exotic, foreign sounds of trip hop, a gift from Hush, who tried to keep me abreast of new music, crashed over my ears. In the kitchen, I tore at the perforated cardboard square on the side of the boxed wine and yanked the spout from its hiding place. I ripped the tiny sticker that sealed the spout and filled a cup with the fruity liquid.

Spirit. So this is where my adventurous spirit gets me—drinking boxed Chablis from a plastic cup, made possible by the benefaction of my hammer-hoarding husband.

I raised the cup to my lips and drank, efficiently.

❧

Eighteen

Genesis 3:16

Spring eventually rolled around but a chill had settled inside our house. I couldn't stop thinking about the hammers, and Jake was too busy to notice. We didn't have dramatic arguments where we yelled and screamed at each other and stormed out of the house, followed by passionate make-up sessions. That wasn't our way. We weren't tempestuous types, nor had we many arguments, in fact. Tension in our marriage was suppressed through humor or work—when feelings became uncomfortable, we usually made a joke or busied ourselves with tasks. But somewhere along the line the humor and the chores became masks for my growing loneliness.

So I rode my motorcycle. Even though it was April and still too cold to be gunning up and down the highways, riding my motor bike fostered the illusion that I wasn't stuck in a small town. I wasn't one half of a traditional Ma and Pa marriage. I could roll out at any moment—unanchored, untethered, bugs splattering off my helmet.

The issue of money bore down on me because it was the first time in my adult life I did not have any of it or, crucially, the means to earn it beyond what I could make as a chicken farmer and assistant fence builder. I found it deeply distressing (though not entirely surprising given my impetuous track record) that I had willingly moved to a place I *knew,* before I had even set foot in Lexington, had such limited opportunity for working women. It was a trade made for love, a most romantic gamble, that I now saw came with a price. I toyed with the idea of going back to school to earn a master's degree so I could teach, but after crunching the numbers it became clear the cost of tuition for a fancy writing program outweighed whatever paltry salary I might earn as an adjunct professor (adjunct professor = ramen noodle eater = freelance writer). My other option, the prospect of memorizing PLU codes on bananas (#4011, in case you're wondering), began to creep into my consciousness as well. The idea that I might someday work at Walmart, the store I had only deigned to shop at when I first moved there, actually filled me with an almost wicked self-loathing. It seemed a sort of cosmic comeuppance for the delusion of thinking I could hold on to my career and independence in a traditional blue-collar environment.

When I brought up my money anxieties to Jake, his solution was to work even harder to earn more money to keep the bills paid and presumably, me happy.

There was a possibility I was just being hard on myself. Perhaps the solution was to abandon the pretense of finding a job altogether, get pregnant and become a mom. That seemed to be the trajectory of a good number of women, and for the most part they seemed perfectly happy, if not downright giddy, about their lives—save for the occasional battle over cheese on a husband's sandwich. Why should I be any different? We *were* scraping by on Jake's fencing salary. And as long as I didn't mind him buying himself fancy tools and equipment while I made do with Excalibur Estates Boxed Chablis, we'd be fine.

Except I did mind. A lot. Not having a job or my own money was anathema to my being—what do you expect from a woman whose mom had "UNCLBARB" on her vanity license plates? At the risk of sounding like one of those self-aggrandizing jerks who blather on about how hard or how much they have worked, I really had been working more or less steadily since the age of twelve, beginning with the paper route and ending—I dreaded—with an underperforming egg business. And now I feared that part of me was going the way of my Lancôme lipstick pipe—tossed into the bottom of my sinkhole.

I decelerated as I entered Lexington city limits and made my way toward Katrina's house. A group of buff military cadets, clad in their ubiquitous exercise togs (gray T-shirts, red shorts) and sporting eraser haircuts, jogged on the sidewalk. Even in the midst of an afternoon run, with no upper classmen around to torment them, the cadets looked stressed and anxious.

Farther up the road, four or five guys from the elite private college walked from their fraternity house to campus across the street, all carrying plastic cups without lids (I often wondered what was in those cups—water? Juice? Milk? Beer?), without a care in the world. I remembered insisting to Jake that for me to move out of New York I required a university town; he boasted about Lexington having two. What he didn't mention is that the two side-by-side colleges were quite possibly the oddest in the nation. One represented masochistic self-denial, the other Waspy contentment . . . like G.I. Joe walking arm-in-arm with a guy named Chauncy Poindexter.

Katrina opened the door before I could knock. She was dressed, per usual, like a lady on her way to a Junior League charity luncheon: bright cornflower toothpick pants, black velvet slippers, a light gray sweater, and a chunky gold watch. I wore a pair of Jake's old Wranglers and my scuffed riding boots. I tried to smooth my static-y helmet hair as we entered the living room and I tucked my helmet into the corner. On her way into the kitchen, Katrina asked if I would like a glass of wine, which she knew by now helped lubricate my Christian assimilation.

Megan and Amber were in their usual positions around the coffee table. They were both dressed like they were on their way to the same charity luncheon: Megan in a schoolboy blazer over a polka dot blouse and a pair of slouchy trousers; Amber wearing a sherbet orange shirtdress and leopard loafers. The three of them looked put together and polished and I made a mental note that perhaps I'd been wrong about the preppy look and Southern belles in general. I'd come to admire these ladies—we didn't always see eye to eye but they were smart and opinionated and kind (and stylish)—and I realized that my early assumptions about this "type" was testament of my own glaring provincialism—my own need to make sense of my environment—than anything else. I was the only one in this little worship circle who wasn't gainfully employed. Megan worked at the library. Amber worked for an interior decorator and Katrina was employed by the university. And they all still found time to look amazing for Bible club.

Amber perched on the edge of an easy chair, briskly flipping through the latest issue of *Real Simple*. "Who on earth has time to dust under the bed?" She laughed as she tossed the magazine on the coffee table with an impressive thud.

I raised a finger. "Um, me?"

She gave a throaty laugh and crossed her legs. Her nails were lacquered red. One leopard loafer bobbed impatiently. From that one offhand gesture, I saw Amber was a power broker's wife in training. Sure enough, she revealed that she would be fleeing Lexington for greener pastures. Her husband, an ultra-confident VMI alumnus with a smooth baritone and a lush sweep of anchorman dream hair, was going to work for a senator in California. They planned to move in a couple of months. I figured it was only a matter of time before I would hear his voice interrupt my favorite radio station during election season, saying something like, "I'm Chas Tillman, and I approve this message."

Katrina returned with cheese and crackers, accessorized by an assortment of grapes, and took a seat next to me on the couch. Four glasses of wine were poured. As we clinked glasses, I commented that Anna Bundance could make anybody drink. I fished my battered workbook, *Strong Queens, Tough Choices*, from my bag. Many of the pages were by now covered in doodles and hearts and flowers interspersed with line after line of completed fill in the blanks, multiple choice questions and my attempts at Scriptural analysis. I turned to the chapter about Eve. We were studying the book of Genesis and Adam and Eve's ill-fated pit stop under the apple tree in the Garden of Eden.

Katrina stood up and slid the DVD into the machine. She darkened the lights and resumed her seat next to me on the couch. Anna Bundance took the stage to another round of wild applause from her adoring acolytes. I noticed she sported a slightly updated hairstyle in this DVD—more sculpture, less puffy. Or maybe I had been in Lexington so long she—and the girls—just seemed more stylish than she actually was. As she paced the stage like a frantic squirrel, spitting Scripture into her headset, she segued into a discussion of identity.

"So many women are confused about who they are," she cried, then turned to the audience with both hands near her face. "You know what I say to those women? I say, hallelujah, sister! Hallelujah, amen! Why do you have to know who you are? Because once you think you know who you are, you start acting like it. You conform to a role, to an idea about who you think you should be. And what is acting, beloveds? It's pretend."

After the DVD ended, Katrina suggested we take turns reading the corresponding Biblical passages aloud, ostensibly to facilitate a deeper understanding. I opened my Bible to Genesis 3:14.

"Amber, would you like to start?" Katrina asked.

Amber picked up her Bible. "And the Lord God said unto the serpent, Because thou has done this, thou are cursed above all cattle, and above every beast of the field; upon thy belly shalt thou go, and dust shalt thou eat all the days of thy life."

Megan read next: "And I shall put enmity between thee and the woman. And between thy seed and her seed; it shall bruise thy head, and thou shalt bruise his heel."

I traced the following words with my index finger: "Unto the woman he said, I will greatly multiply thy sorrow and thy conception; in sorrow thou shalt bring forth children; and thy desire shall be to thy husband, and he shall rule over thee."

Katrina read the next passage, something about Adam's punishment, but I wasn't really listening. I was engrossed by the last sentence of the preceding passage, which I slowly retraced with my finger. *And thy desire shall be to thy husband, and he shall rule over thee.*

Wha—?

"Are there any questions before we continue?" asked Katrina, who over the months had assumed the role of spiritual leader and moderator.

"Yes, I have a question." I looked up from my Bible. "What does it mean, 'Thy desire shall be to thy husband and he shall rule over thee'?"

Katrina thought for a moment. "I think there are many ways to interpret the passage," she said. "Not all of which are meant to be taken literally."

I was surprised by Katrina's all-inclusive response. As a dyed-in-the-wool Christian, wasn't she supposed to take this stuff somewhat seriously? "I'm not sure what you mean," I chuckled. "Since it *says* Eve is *cursed* to desire Adam. God doesn't mince words."

Katrina shrugged. "The Bible contains a variety of writings—history, mythology, legends, parables, poems, short stories," she said. "You can't interpret all writings the same way."

"Besides, it's the Old Testament," said Megan from across the coffee table.

"I don't understand," I said.

"The Old Testament is full of rules and restrictions and ways of thinking that don't apply to our New Testament lives," she explained. "I prefer to think of how *Christ* treated women—he traveled with them, he had female friends."

"Uh-huh," I said skeptically.

There was a lull. The girls studied my dissatisfied expression.

"But we can discuss the passage literally, Jessie, if that is what you would prefer," offered Amber quickly.

"It's not that I *want* to read the Bible literally," I said. "It's that this particular passage seems to demand it." I reread the words aloud, enunciating *"and he shall rule over thee."* "As written, it seems like Eve is cursed to have a deeper yearning, a deeper psychological dependence on Adam than he has for her. The implication is that Adam doesn't love Eve to the same extent."

"I think I understand what you're saying, Jessie," said Amber, cocking her head slightly. "Sometimes Chas *does* rule over me. I am 'subject to him' in a way I have absolutely no control over. He has the power to wilt me with a few sharp words or make me bloom with some nourishing and cherishing."

I nodded slowly.

"You do realize that is the fundamentalist interpretation," said Megan. "Eve represents *humankind*, not just womankind. We are *all* cursed because of the sin she *and* Adam committed. We need to move beyond the idea of Eve as seductive temptress or repressed wife. It's so reductive."

Reductive—my all-time favorite academic-sounding word now being used against me and my theological analysis. I cringed at the thought that I—me, progressive, liberal, open-minded, city person—had wrung the oldest, frumpiest, reactionary interpretation from the passage.

"No, no, what I'm—" I blurted.

"While I agree with you, Megan," Amber cut in, "that *desire* and *rule* can be reductive, they can also be redemptive by bringing marriage into closer semblance with garden intimacy. Don't you agree, Jessie?" She looked at me to backup her thesis.

"'Garden intimacy?'" I said. "Is that a douche?"

"Jessie!" said Amber.

"Sorry," I said. "'Feminine wash.'"

Amber's wounded expression conveyed I had offended her but I was urgently trying to distance myself from this "garden intimacy" and "nourishing and cherishing," which gave me a not-so-fresh feeling just thinking about it.

Katrina cleared her throat. "We may want to consider that different interpretations serve as a reflection of where we are in our own lives."

I glanced around the room, looking for the bottle of wine, as if I had exposed myself in some way. I was mortified for having made the beginner's mistake of a literal interpretation.

"As for me," Katrina sighed, rising from the couch to remove the DVD from the player. "The passage has always meant there is a hunger in a woman's heart that cannot be nourished by man, only by Christ."

"I'll drink to that. Amen," said Megan. "Pass the Yellow Tail."

That night, I sprawled half on the couch and half on the floor, depositing cold slabs of Coca-Cola ham into my mouth, droplets of glaze dribbling onto my shirt. I was thumbing through Flaubert's *Madame Bovary*, about a restless French housewife who becomes disillusioned with her stable marriage and quiet country life, grows dull and listless, becomes reckless, then dies. Sad. The book had caught my eye at the library. I was hoping to find some helpful tidbit about how I might avoid a similar unfortunate end, but all I felt was a startling kinship to the madame. At one point in the story, Emma Bovary bemoans being left alone while her solid, stable husband works day and night.

"[Her husband] increasingly felt like a memento, a keepsake, a feeling to sustain her as she tried to navigate through the boredom and idleness of her days."

I looked at the clock—nine o'clock. Jake and Cowboy still weren't home. No phone call to tell me he'd be late. All of my messages to him went to voice mail. The table had been set for two, a vase of fresh lilacs between the two place settings, but the ham was cold. My faithful companion Sunny rested her little head, eyes wet with adoration, on my thigh, waiting for an affectionate nuzzle or a piece of meat.

Jake and Cowboy eventually burst through the door. "Hey, baby, baby!" Jake called. He plopped his lunchbox onto the table between the two place settings and dug around the refrigerator for something to drink. His face was sooty. His pants were rubbed in dust. I noticed there was a fresh rip in the sleeve of his snap-front shirt. "Wha'ja get up to today, pretty girl?"

I hated that question. It sounded like a test, a reproach.

"Nothing," I grumbled. "Went to Bible school."

"Wha'ja learn?" He walked over to me on the couch. The treads of his boots left clumps of dirt on my newly polished bamboo floors. He leaned over to kiss me.

"What are you doing?!" I cried. "Your boots!"

He stood up, taken aback. "Chill out, woman." He walked back to the kitchen and began sorting through the mail.

"Where were you?" I asked. "The ham came out of the oven two hours ago."

"I'm sorry, babe," he said. "I tried to call a bunch of times, but I couldn't get any cell phone reception. I was on top of a mountain. You eat?"

I looked down at my soiled shirt. "What does it look like?" Another whine. God, I hated this behavior. I hated the woman I was turning into—that *he* was turning me into. "And next time you *think* you're not going to have cell phone reception, the *least* you could do is let me know *before* you leave for work. Is that too much to ask?"

"Uh, okay."

Cowboy scampered over and planted his face on my other thigh. Both dogs stared up at me hopefully, hungrily. I fed both the remaining cuts of meat, picked up my book and walked into the kitchen. Jake removed his boots and padded over to me in his socks. "Jessie, I'm trying." He placed both hands resolutely on my shoulders. "I really am. But sometimes you give me mixed messages. First you complain about never having enough money, then you complain when I go out and try to earn more money. You're hard to read sometimes."

"I know," I said reluctantly. "But I feel like I'm turning into someone I hate."

"I know it's not always easy for you here," he said. "But all in all, I think we got it pretty good. I know I don't make a pile of money but we do alright . . . a lot better than some. And sometimes I think you need to try to focus on what's right about our lives instead of fixating on what's wrong. Because there's always going to be something that's wrong."

Objectively, I couldn't argue with this, but it sounded preachy and patronizing since his life hadn't been the one to change. It hadn't changed one iota, in fact. I inserted an index finger in my mouth and made a gagging sound.

"It's true," he said, with what sounded like the slightest bit of melancholy, producing in me a feeling not unlike victory over finally puncturing his relentless good cheer.

"Thank you, Joel Osteen." I released from his grasp. I didn't want to discuss it anymore since it appeared I was on the wrong side of righteousness again.

Jake sighed, quickly remounting the happy horse. "Well, do you want to try some of this tomato wine?"

"Oh. Yeah."

We went into the mudroom where I helped him retrieve a bottle of his latest batch of tomato wine from the cistern-turned-wine cellar beneath the house. The cistern by that point resembled a small wine and beer shop—shelves stacked with horizontal bottles of merlot, peach wine, rhubarb wine, bottles of IPA, pilsner and ginger beer. For whatever reason, Jake had developed a special fascination with tomato wine and had been tinkering with the recipe for over a year. Each batch he made was surprisingly tasty. Tomato wine, I was shocked to discover, wasn't half bad.

He brought the unadorned bottle back into the kitchen. I fetched two wine glasses and took a seat at the table while he poured. He sat down next to me. We held up our glasses by the stems to check for clarity against the light; there were hardly any floaty bits in the rose-colored liquid.

"To the good life," he said, clinking my glass.

We sipped. The flavor was light and crisp and tangy without any obvious overtones of tomato. It reminded me of a two-buck Chardonnay: nothing I'd serve at a fancy dinner party. But for the two of us at home, during a recession, it was another example of Jake's ability to create something from nothing—to improvise and deliver. He was the master of making lemonade from lemons. Or in this case, tomato wine from tomatoes.

I brought up the reading of Genesis 3:16. I wanted to know his thoughts on whether I might be a closet fundamentalist.

"The girls think Eve's curse isn't applicable to 'our New Testament lives,'" I said while Jake poured more wine. "They don't think it's a big deal that Eve is cursed twice—once in childbirth and once for desiring her husband. While Adam is cursed to, what, 'working too hard,' which sounds to me like 'eating too much' or 'catching too much sun.' And since when is desiring your husband a curse? And why doesn't Adam desire Eve?"

"I'm pretty sure he does, hon."

I smirked. "It's like God hates women, or something."

I waited a beat to see if Jake would respond to this admittedly outrageous statement, but all he said was, "Do you mind if I watch a DVD?"

I made a face. Jake got up to go take a shower while I sat there. I craved a heated, heavy discussion about theology; Jake wanted to watch a DVD. Therein lay our differences, distilled to the essence: I was abstract, Jake was concrete; I was theoretical, he was actual; I was ruminative, he remained above it all. The dissimilarity filled me with longing that widened my loneliness.

He returned cleaned up and showered, wearing sweatpants and a T-shirt, the smell of dirt and grime replaced by Old Spice body wash. He walked into the living room. Jake, who had never in his life been much of a television watcher, had recently become enthralled by reality programs chronicling the trials and adventures of the working man—manly men who fished the Bering Sea, manly men who drove big trucks, manly men who cut timber.

"Hon, you gotta come watch this!" he hooted from the living room as an Alaskan king crab fishermen was nearly swept overboard.

"A show about crabs," I said dryly. "Yeah, no. Sounds more like the deadliest scratch to me."

I drummed my fingertips on the dining room table. One knee

was propped under my chin, a foot resting on the cushion of the chair. The nail beds on my feet were inexcusably ratty. A professional pedicure was an unimaginable luxury, right up there with buying a Bentley or getting a lip wax. I was far too lazy to give myself a pedicure, too restless to go to bed, too tired to sew. I got up to put away the dinner dishes. I flopped back on the chair and studied the back of Jake's head, visible over the couch. He was in a reclined position; one hand was tucked casually behind his head, the other holding his tomato wine.

Madame Bovary was on the table. I picked it up and read:

She resented [her husband's] settled calm, his serenity, his ability to make the best of whatever was at hand, never wanting or striving for more. She began to resent the very happiness she herself brought him.

I set the book down. Something was wrong. Jake loved me, but I wasn't happy. I was very unhappy. I was so unhappy it was all I could do not to throw the book across the table. But I was incapable of discussing it. I was choking on guilt—guilt over not being able to fully embrace this life I had chosen. Guilt over marrying the world's most loving and devoted man whose happiness always seemed to elude me.

Jake exploded in laughter as a meth-faced fisherman slipped and crashed on the frozen deck. "Babe, c'mere, c'mere, you gotta come see this!" He turned to me with a gigantic grin.

My guilt guided me over to the couch. I sat down and watched the show that Jake found so entertaining, feeling the hairs on the back of my neck prickle at the realization that maybe there was another reason for my unhappiness. Maybe all of this was a big mistake. Not just moving to the country, but marrying a cowboy, a man I had—if I was completely honest with myself—nothing in common with, who didn't get me at all and who never expressed the slightest inclination to do anything outside his comfort zone.

Suddenly the thought of hightailing it back to New York with my tail between my legs became a stunning possibility, carrying with it the stain of divorce. Divorce. I was appalled and terrified by how quickly that word come to me, so I sat there, saying nothing, and slowly sipped my wine.

Nineteen

Queen of the County

As summer turned to fall, I tried to suppress my growing agony by throwing myself into an onslaught of baking. This evening, in preparation for what would turn out to be the last potluck for a long time, I was putting the final touches on a tray of lemon bars. Not only did lemon bars put a dent in my yolk supply, but I had developed a weird fascination with the ratio of creamy lemony custard to crunchy shortbread. The perfect bar, I had concluded, was composed of three parts gooey custard to one part shortbread—a pillow of lemon atop a thin wafer bed. Any deviation from this ratio upset the balance of flavor but I still ate them all anyway.

I ate a lot. I was hungry. My weight was up. I tried to suck in my gut as I zipped into my homemade cherry red, ruched

Halston jersey dress that used to fit not quite so tight. My hair was quite long at that point so I managed to wrap one thick braid around my head like a Bavarian milkmaid. I slipped my feet into a pair of white high-heel ankle booties and turned sideways before the full-length mirror in my bedroom to evaluate this quirky ensemble. I grabbed a fistful of custard that was my abdomen. I looked fat and hopelessly overdressed for holding a paper plate around a campfire in the cold but otherwise totally on-trend, which meant absolutely nothing here but still somehow gratified my ego. Jake wore dirty army boots, a canvas Carhartt coat and a cowboy hat.

The hostess, a thirty-something Smith graduate named Lauren who was married to one of the more successful contractors in town, opened the door and gave our clashing looks the once-over. She wore jeans, black Dansko clogs and a tight T-shirt that read "Well-behaved women seldom make history." Jake must have read the shirt too because a look of apprehension crossed his face, like he had accidentally crashed a menstruation symposium. Strong male voices could be heard in the background, signaling neutral gender territory though probably skewing toward progressive earth people. Lauren buried Jake in one of her tight bear hugs. As I waited for her breasts to detach from my husband's chest, her six-year-old daughter MacKenzie tugged at her pant leg, asking the location of the Pirate's Booty. From the living room could be heard the piercing twang of a bluegrass quartet. Bluegrass. Always bluegrass. It was impossible to go anywhere in Virginia without hearing the bluegrass. Young children raced and screamed around the house. Moms clustered around the island in the kitchen, sipping wine and chatting. I spotted Alice, Lucy and Carrie and waved. A glance toward the floor revealed a tapestry of Dansko clogs—black, red, straps, no straps, studded, floral leather appliqués, white. A few women sported the least flattering Dansko look of all—clogs with bare legs and pretty dresses. It was a look that tried to claim the best of both worlds—light and feminine on top, an H-1 Hummer with blackened windows on the bottom. I averted my gaze and transferred my lemon bars to a plate, arranging them so the perfect ratio of custard-y plumpness could be admired by all. I casually listened in over talk of kombucha tea and energy fields, gluten allergies, Montessori versus charter schools, local versus organic. As the women chatted, I was reminded again that the nomenclature of progressiveness was not confined to liberal urban enclaves. It was part of a broader social movement that had burrowed down even in the back hills and farms of rural Virginia—Confederate flag country—populated by a surprising number of educated, liberal, ridiculously well-intentioned folks who bit the bullet as I did to live off the grid in the hope of becoming more wholesome, more authentic, more pure than they were in Madison or Boulder or Manhattan or wherever it was they came from.

Lauren showed off her collection of canned goods, boasting about her success with heirloom tomatoes that year. I resisted telling her about the many quarts I myself had canned and instead nodded in faux-wonder while glancing around for Jake. I saw him through the kitchen window. He had already slipped out the back carrying a six pack of his home brewed I.P.A. He had congregated around the campfire with the rest of the manly husbands where they were almost certainly discussing some manifestation of manual labor. Also standing around the camp-fire, rocking on his heels of his boots, was Scratch—who at the moment was living up to his name near the crotch area.

Lucy sidled up to me, nursing a drink. "My little one finally started sleeping through the night," she sighed, apropos of noth-ing. "I think it's because of the cod-liver oil I've been giving him before bedtime. So many Omega 3s."

"Uh-huh," I said, fine-tuning the M.C. Escher–like arrange-ment of lemon bars on the tray.

"That's a . . . neat dress," she said. "I suppose you made it yourself."

"Yeah."

She looked at the plate of lemon bars. "And I suppose you made these too? From your own yolks?"

I nodded.

"You need to get knocked up already," she smirked. "You're like the queen of the county."

"I need to get knocked up like I need a hole in my head," I said. It was an uncalled for and unnecessary comment—I didn't even mean it—and I'm surprised Lucy didn't throw her freshly squeezed limeade in my face, but I was tired of being baited, of feeling like it was my duty to live up to and beyond the old timey lifestyle I had chosen.

Her smirk didn't go away though—she knew she had got to me.

Scratch came in from the outside holding an empty Tesco cup

and strode over to the snack table. "You guys know where the Jack is?"

"Jake's outside," I said.

"No, Jack—Jack Daniel's."

Lucy and I both shook our heads as she picked up one my lemon bars, which I found surprisingly intimidating because of her ultra-refined palate. She took a small bite, carefully evaluating the quality of each ingredient with each of her discriminating taste buds. Once the medley of flavors had passed inspection, she ventured another nibble.

"These are actually pretty good."

"Thanks."

"Is that raw sugar?"

"Yes, I stripped it from cane in the fields this morning."

Scratch picked up a bar and sunk his teeth into the lemony custard. Flecks of shortbread stuck in his beard.

"Good, right?" Lucy asked.

"Eh." He chomped with his mouth open, giving us both a glimpse of custard sloshing around his chew hole. "It'll make a turd."

I made a face like he had farted, which, figuratively speaking, he had.

"*What?*" Lucy snickered.

"I said, it'll make a turd." Scratch polished off the rest of the bar and brushed his beard with his hand, somehow missing the entire nest of crumbs that had bedded down there.

I was, quite frankly, too shocked to say anything.

"What is it with the women around here?" he said, shaking his head in disbelief. "Everyone so anal about their food. It's like they don't have nothin' better to think about."

Lucy made a face. "Don't you need to go shave your back or something, Scratch?"

I happened to glance over my shoulder and spotted, out the kitchen window, none other than Miranda the sexy horsewoman standing in front of the bonfire, wearing a peasant top, cowboy boots and cutoff denim short-shorts, the frayed ends dangling down her thighs like some kind of hillbilly garter belt. Her long black hair shone almost blue against the flames and her slender neck and wrists were wrapped in an assortment of beads and braiding of varying lengths, making her look like Kate Beckinsale on her way to a funky outdoor music festival. She coyly faced the fire, palms outstretched to warm them. Jake stood by her side. They were engaged in an intimate conversation that the other guys standing around the fire weren't privy to, though it was evident that most were leering at her from behind their Tesco cups.

My eyeballs dried in their sockets. My heart dropped into my butt. I emitted a tiny squeal of terror. My instinct was to run outside and casually (but wrathfully) bust up the cozy conversation. But even I was perceptive enough to know such a move would brand me forever as Crazy Old Jealous Bitch Wife, desperate and preening enough to wear fräulein hair and retro career-casual to a potluck! But that wasn't the most horrifying realization. The most horrifying realization was this: She and Jake looked happy together. I sensed it the first time I saw them; I sensed it now. They *belonged* together. They were made for each other. They were of the same world. They spoke the same language. They both loved horses. They were both so pure, so wholesome, so healthy, hardworking and alive! They were both younger than me. *And who the hell wears short-shorts in the fall?* My throat tightened. My tear ducts switched from "single drip" to "rapid flow" position.

"Hey, aren't you a cougar?" asked Scratch.

My head swiveled from the window to his hirsute face. "What?"

"A cougar. You know, an older lady who goes after younger guys."

"I don't know what you're talking about."

My pained expression must have been obvious because he pointed an oil-stained fingernail in my face and said, "You are! I knew it."

My forehead tingled. I actually grasped the counter for balance. All of my iterations, my guises, my attempts to conform and fold so that my life fit more seamlessly into Jake's, reduced to one stupid, ridiculous *Us Weekly* word. That's all I was to these people: A cougar. A G.D. cougar! My brain strained for a response. "I—?"

"You're a lot older than Jake, right? How many years? Let me guess—seven? Ten?"

"Can't . . . under . . ." Agh! Short-circuiting! Stand back! This bitch is going to blow!

"Oh, geez, I hurt your feelings." Scratch slapped a hand on his mouth, feigning remorse. "I'm sorry. Really. So sorry. Didn't mean it."

"Scratch, you're an asshole," Lucy said.

"Excuse me," I said. I rushed past him and Lucy and pushed out the front door. Once the door had clicked behind me, I sat heavily on the wood steps and hung my head in my hands. Large swaths of hair had come unbound from my fräulein braid. I unwrapped the braid, dug my fingers through my hair to allow my tear curtain to fall around my face. I inhaled deeply, trying to prevent drops from squeezing from my eyes while drowning out the manly chatter and laughter drifting from the backyard. The air smelled damp and clean and cool. *How the hell did he know how old I am? Oh, that's right—because I live in a town so small no one has anything better to talk about!* I inhaled again until I couldn't inhale anymore, then held the breath at the top of my lungs, like Kaur Maur Khalsa Amsala had taught me so long ago. I could almost hear her breathy childlike voice telling me that *"Love is like the wheel of a bicycle, and round and round it goes until . . . one day . . . you hit a rock . . . and go flying . . ."* Or something like that. I couldn't remember. That life seemed so long ago. I tried to visualize wisps of rejuvenating, revitalizing oxygen circulating through my rib cage, coursing through my veins, expanding my cells, calming me, relaxing me, bringing my heart rate down to a more reasonable level.

The door opened behind me. I turned around. It was Alice and Lucy.

"Hey, Jessie, are you alright?" Lucy asked nervously. They both sat down next to me on the steps. "You can't take Scratch seriously. I mean, the guy's name is *Scratch*."

"I know, I know," I said.

"And you know I'm just giving you a hard time, right?" Lucy looked concerned. "I don't really think you're the queen of the county."

Alice placed her hand on my back, and a jolt of Reiki energy gathered like a tornado in my lumbar spine, as if all my cells rushed to meet her soothing touch.

"Well, that's a relief," I said. "I just don't know what I'm doing here." I held up my hands to demonstrate this concept.

Alice chuckled, reaching into the pocket of her fleece vest for a tissue. "Dude, I've been in this town ten years and I still don't know what the hell I'm doing here. I hate bluegrass."

"Don't even get me started," I said, taking the tissue and blowing my nose.

"Preach," said Lucy. Her palm grazed mine in a high five.

The door opened again and Carrie poked her head outside, followed closely by hostess Lauren. Carrie spoke in a faux stern whisper. "What's going on out here? You're not leaving, are you?" They joined us on the front steps, where Lucy caught them up on events. Lauren produced from a small woven purse a swirly blue psychedelic glass pipe and held it before me. "Want some?"

"Nah," I said.

"Suit yourself," she said.

The air became heavy with the tangy perfume of homegrown ganja. I watched as Lauren acted out the slogan on her T-shirt.

"I'll tell you what's going to happen here," said Alice. "You're going to have kids and raise a family like the rest of us. And you know what, Jessie? It's not so bad." She glanced at the three women, a wise maternal connection between them. "It can be pretty awesome, actually," Lauren croaked. "Now watch this bitchin' smoke ring."

We all laughed as Carrie blew perfect doughnuts out of her mouth. I wondered if the women I'd met in Rockbridge County over the years would have been my friends up in New York too and I realized that yes, they would. Anyone who could blow perfect smoke rings would have to be my friend. The women down here were just as funny and smart and real and neurotic as my friends up north. I guess I had been a little hasty in my neat classifications of the types who populated Lexington. They were just like me—trying to get along, trying to keep their heads above water. They were also trying to be helpful, trying to make me see that "settling down" was part of the natural ebb and flow of life. And yet, why did it feel so much like resignation, like defeat? I pondered the question as I stared at the silvery outline of the roof across the road, its edges lit up by moonlight.

A cold, shivery rain came down during the car ride home, the back roads twisting into an ever-thickening fog. Jake lowered the high beams for better visibility, though there wasn't much of that.

"We sure need this moisture," he said, oblivious to the ache in my heart. "It's been awfully dry lately. It's supposed to rain all next week. Hey, you mind if I work tomorrow?"

"Do whatever you need to do," I responded.

"Hey, I got to talk to Miranda tonight," he said brightly.

The sexy horsewoman. So help me, God, I refuse to speak of her. I refuse to think of her.

"I think we're gonna try to go team penning here in the next couple of weeks," he said, as he pulled into our driveway and brought the truck to a stop. Thick drops of rain plinked and plonked off the roof of the vehicle.

I exhaled in a deeply sad, hurt and final way. "You're going team penning with her?" I said to the tiny rivulets of rain pouring down the windshield.

He eyed me warily through the darkness. I sensed his befuddlement and apprehension, as if performing a quick scan of his data banks for the source of offense and, failing to find it, was at a loss for an effective appeasement strategy.

"You're going team penning with her?" I turned to face him.

"Yes? What?"

I started to cry, a wheezing, snot-clogged cry. He didn't say anything. He just looked at me strangely. I shook my head despondently, my sorrow quickly shifting to rage. "'Oh, sexy horsewoman, you're so strong!'" I blurted, imitating a conversation I overheard during our very first trip to Lexington years ago. "'You're the hardest worker I know! Remember we said we'd get married! I'll take care of you!'"

"What are you talking about?"

"'Oh, sexy horsewoman,'" I continued. "'Come take a ride in my wheelbarrow! We have so much in common! I like horses and you look like one!'"

I groped for the door handle and stumbled out of the truck.

The rain stung my face and hands. The hurricane inside me had turned into a tsunami. I knew I couldn't enter the house, that hovel that was becoming my tomb, or my heart, my brain, my entire body would shatter into a million little fragments just like the flecks of paint that steadily blew from our shoddily painted rooftop. I stumbled through the rain across the lawn in my white ankle booties, the heels sticking in the dirt like tent stakes. I strode over to the barn and pushed open the creaking wooden door. Rain leaked through random openings in the ceiling. A red heat lamp illuminated the undersides of several hens squashed together on a metal bar suspended overhead, their only sound a gentle cooing and the occasional plop of a turd hitting the ground. I slumped onto a dusty pallet in the corner, most certainly ruining the backside of my Halston dress, but I knew I'd never wear it again. I was sunk in torpid despair. I cried for myself, I cried for Jake, I cried for our marriage. I remembered the psychic's prediction from four years ago: "But it won't last," she'd said. Fantasy had put up a good fight but reality had finally won. Being a country woman felt nothing like I'd hoped.

Jake quietly entered the chicken coop. "Feeding the chickens, hon?"

I tried to steady my voice. "Yup, feeding the chickens."

He inspected their feeder, which was clipped to a chain suspended from their roosting bar. "Yeah, looks like they could use a topper." I watched as he calmly scooped feed into the bucket, astonished by his obliviousness. He didn't feel anything. All he could say was, "Yeah, looks like they could use a topper." I was so sick of his aloofness, his steady composure. His calm serenity now worked in me like poison. He re-clipped the feeder to the chain, and turned toward me. "You coming back to the house or you going to hang out here for a while?"

"I hate it here," I said in the shadows, engulfed in gloom. "I hate this life. I hate the way you make me live. I hate everything about it."

He stood motionless before me, his strong, lanky form in silhouette against the red heating lamp. For one split-second I thought he was going to punch a hole in the wall, but instead he walked out of the barn into the night.

Let him go, just let him go. I had followed Jake much too much. I had conformed and folded my world completely upside down and inside out for him . . . for this life, for this marriage. I had ditched my entire existence—my independence, career, money, professional network, friends, access to ethnic food, *New York City*—for what? *For what?* For a closetful of aprons and a larder full of pickles? To become the town's most talked about cougar? I had done it all in an attempt to not just be closer to Jake and prove to him and myself I could make my way here, but, disturbingly, to actually be more like him, to appropriate his calm serenity and focused purpose. To become him! Jesus. I had even joined a ladies Bible club for him. A ladies Bible club! I didn't even believe in God.

The ladies Bible club. The ladies Bible club!

Eve's curse!

Goosebumps rose on my arms. A wave of nausea made standing up impossible. I leaned my head against the crumbly boards of the barn and gasped. By bending over backward to fit more seamlessly into my husband's world, I was living out my own ass-backward interpretation of Genesis 3:16—I *did* have a deeper yearning, a deeper psychological dependence on my husband than he had for me. Ha! Stupid woman! Jake had never conformed or changed or sacrificed for me. What's worse, I never expected him to. On some level, we both assumed that *I'd* be the one to do all that changing, conforming and following.

Oh my God, Jake really was a cowboy—a selfish, macho, intractable cowboy, making the core of my compliance actually this: Desperation to prove this marriage wasn't actually the biggest mistake of my life. I was no more meant to be with a cowboy than a yellow-bellied sapsucker was meant to marry a horse—a party boat mixing with an aircraft carrier. Such is the power of fantasy.

There was only one course of action: Break the curse. Screw Eve's curse! I had been playing the role of the domestic country goddess for too long and I couldn't keep up the charade any longer. Well, screw horses! Screw fences! Screw sewing! Screw chickens! Screw canning! Oh my God, screw canning. Seriously. Please. Screw canning! Screw the ladies Bible club! Screw marriage!

Yes, screw marriage. I had to get out of there. I had to get out of there immediately.

Oh, the irony of the ladies Bible club. To think it was none other than Anna Bundance's traditional teachings and conservative preaching that had illuminated this life-changing lesson to me. Anna Bundance had brought me clarity. Anna Bundance had brought me salvation. It just wasn't the kind of salvation she had in mind.

I never went to another Bible club after that night.

Part Four

Twenty

❧

Moonshine on Fire

When you've been away from Manhattan for a while, especially when "away" is a place where the shrimp feast at Country Cookin is considered for many the ultimate in fine dining, coming back to the city can be exhilarating and intimidating. It's overrun by people so busy and important they cannot possibly look up from their iPhones when you almost plow into them with your car upon ascending from the Holland Tunnel. As you make your way across Chinatown via Canal Street, you roll down your window to inhale the lovely spring air and are hit in the face with *parfum de New York*, that old familiar tang of human sweat and garbage you realize you had become desensitized to when you lived here. And as you pass kiosk after kiosk of cheap watches, fans, jeggings and footie socks of every synthetic fiber and description, you find yourself longing for similar cutting-edge fashions even though you only have twelve dollars in your pocket (perhaps you can persuade some of your rich city friends to lend you some money during your stay). You glance northward up the Bowery, and notice that buildings on both sides of the street stretch to a point on the horizon, and you think to yourself, *Wow, New York is so big! So many people!* Finally, you're on the Manhattan Bridge heading into Brooklyn and no sooner are you spit out onto Flatbush Avenue than you spot two men holding hands. *Oh my God, are they . . . gay?* you ask incredulously, then realize what a complete hick you've become.

That was pretty much my headspace as I made my way toward Maria's house in Park Slope: elated, disgusted, covetous, alarmingly homophobic and finally, ashamed. It was the first time in the past seven hours I'd been so aware of my surroundings, having spent the day in a fog replaying the events of the previous evening.

After Jake stormed out of the chicken coop, I sat on the pallet and cried for what felt like a long time, though it might have only been another ten minutes or so. Eventually—around the time I got hit on the arm with a turd from a hen who'd had me in her crosshairs overhead—I pulled myself up and dragged myself back toward the house where I stripped in the kitchen and threw the soiled Halston dress in the trash. Approximately thirty hours of labor and focused concentration had gone into that dress, but now it was nothing more than a crap-stained symbol of my own backward slide.

* * *

The moment my eyes sprang open the following morning, I knew I was leaving. Jake was already out of bed dressing for work. The once familiar snap-snap of his shirt buttons and the swoosh of his leather belt sliding through the loops of his jeans now sounded foreign. He went into the kitchen to put on coffee. He returned wearing his cowboy hat and his boots with his nylon lunchbox slung over his shoulder, ready to leave for the day. He sat down on the bed and leaned over to kiss me, robotically, out of a sense of marital duty. "I love you, hon."

"Just go."

"What's the matter?"

"What do you think?" *Because I'm living a lie. Because you've made me live a lie.* "I won't be here when you get back," I muttered.

"Where are you going?" It was so sad. He tried so hard to remain strong, a stalwart of composure, but it came across as indifference.

"Away."

"When are you coming back?"

"Don't know."

He sighed. "Okay, well, I'll give you a call later." He leaned over and kissed me on the head. "I'll bring both dogs today. I love you, hon."

I waited for the sound of his truck to roar past the house, accompanied by his characteristic *honk-honk*, before I pulled myself out of bed, threw on a flannel shirt, insulated vest, frayed jeans and fugly clogs, packed a duffel bag of equally sensible fashion choices and tossed it into the back of my car.

Me: u mind a houseguest?

Maria: why? u planning on coming up?

Me: on my way.

Maria: now? today?

Me: yes, that okay? should be there around 4

Maria: of course it's okay! bring yoga clothes. bring eggs! bring moonshine!

Maria: is everything okay?

Me: let's just say u were right about skinned gophers.

Maria: ???!?!

I walked down to the Hen Hut, gathering freshly laid eggs, which I washed and loaded into cartons. I squirreled several pints of moonshine, six quarts of various pickled products, four pints of jam and the rest of the Tropical Island Thunder (I was so sick of looking at it). I packed two of our fattest frozen broiler birds in a cooler with ice and tucked it the trunk of my car. The anticipation of going to New York made it surprisingly easy to leave my husband.

Somewhere between Pennsylvania and New Jersey, my Black-Berry chirped.

"Hey," he said when I answered. "Just called to check on you."

I didn't say anything.

"You at home?"

"No, I'm not at home," I said tersely. "I told you I wasn't going to be home."

"Oh? Where are you?" He was breathing hard, no doubt walking uphill along a fence line in some field.

"New Jersey."

"New Jersey? What the heck are you doing in New Jersey?"

"I told you I was leaving."

"I thought you meant you were going to back-to-back Body Blaster classes."

I laughed bitterly. "Jake, you are clueless."

"Well, when are you coming back?"

"Good grief, do you not hear anything I say?" I said. "I told you, I don't know when I'm coming back. I don't know if I'm coming back."

The line went quiet. "Okay," he said cautiously, slowly comprehending what was happening to his world. "Maybe you need a few days to think about things. Maybe getting out of town will be good for you."

"Golly gee whiz, ya think?" I cried maniacally. "I have turned my life upside down for you! I have morphed into another person for you! Now you tell me you're going 'team penning' with a woman who is basically everything I'm not nor ever will be! I can't believe I'm saying this, but I'm sorry I'm not more of a redneck."

"Hon," he sighed. "She's a friend. A *friend*."

"A friend you want to take care of. A friend you almost married."

"That was a conversation I had *years ago*. You and I weren't even married yet!"

"That's not a conversation a wife forgets. And at the potluck. You two looked so pretty at the potluck. Two joyful pure hearts in their prime. I almost puked!"

"Hon, we spoke for ten minutes."

"Twenty! And we may as well lay it all on the table now: Why didn't you end up with her? She's obviously the perfect woman for you. I bet she hangs gates and tosses hay bales. I bet she rides bareback!"

"Why didn't I—? Because I don't love her? Because I'm not attracted to her? Because I could never settle down with someone like her?"

"But you can settle for me?" I shouted.

"I swear, sometimes your mind," he said. "It gets so twisted up. You start imagining things, inventing things. It's like you've mapped out this entire scenario—"

"I have given up everything for you! *Everything*!"

"I know you've made a lot of changes for me, for us," he said. "I know you've given up a lot to live here. But instead of talking to me about it, you get in your car and drive to New York. The only thing you do bother to tell me is that you hate our lives together. Do you have any idea how that makes me feel? I was so hurt I could hardly talk to you this morning."

I didn't say anything, alternately irritated and chastened by his skillful deployment of the beleaguered husband card.

"I also think you have a lot to show for living here but you refuse to see that," he said.

"Jake, I deliver eggs for dollars," I said, realizing most of my clients stiffed me the paltry sums they owed anyway. "What exactly do I have to show for it?"

"Just that—selling eggs. Building fence. Installing water lines. Planting a garden. Transplanting trees. Canning vegetables. Sewing clothes. Building fires. Slaughtering chickens! How many of your friends know how to do anything with their hands? I know you look down your nose at it sometimes, but you've picked up a lot of new skills since moving here. You've become very self-sufficient, Jessie."

I remained silent.

"And correct me if I'm wrong," he said. "But it's not like you were so happy up in New York either. You complained about it too."

"What? No I didn't. I loved New York!"

"No," he said. "I'm pretty sure you hated it up there too."

"Yeah, well, it was my life to hate."

"Was it? Cause you've sure made it sound like it was dumped on you."

* * *

I eventually found a parking spot near Fifth Avenue in Brooklyn's South Slope and after three nerve-racking failed attempts, managed to parallel park into a space about two inches longer than my car. I was eager to reimmerse myself in the fabric of urban life. The plan: Proceed directly to the nearest artisanal store where I would treat myself to a nutritionally enhanced beverage and hand-crafted bread product, which I would unfortunately have to charge to my credit card. As I approached the slightly less polished Fifth Avenue, I glanced down at my sad uniform—the dumpy clogs, the rumpled flannel shirt, the puffy vest—and immediately felt conspicuous about my fashion choices. Why hadn't I had the forethought to bring along the romper? The celebrity sunglasses? The delicate jazz shoes? I looked like a middle-age mom who goes camping in a toilet paper commercial.

But as I rounded the corner onto Fifth I realized just how long I'd been out of the city. The cultural zeitgeist had apparently evolved during my absence. There, on the sidewalk, amid the power strollers and sculpted boho moms, around the spiffy young men toting Vespa helmets and shiny laptop bags, past the occasional geezer whose constipated expression made it clear he pined for the Park Slope of old, was a new breed of city person I'd never encountered before: the urban woodsman. There was one, exiting a specialized sandwich shop, tall and thin and clad in a combination of denim and natural fibers of varying scratchy textures, all artfully distressed, and anchored by a pair of low-top reddish-brown boots. He had a thicket of facial hair that extended from his nostrils to his sternum, topped by a pair of unflattering horn-rimmed granny spectacles. He reminded me of a more self-consciously styled Scratch, if Scratch were a mixologist at an exclusive speakeasy. This new permutation of hipster, the budding Adirondack mycologist, was a clear sign the pendulum had swung in the opposite direction of the helpless, manicured metrosexual of the early aughts. It was a look that referenced pre-industrial self-sufficiency and scruffy independence (and probably questionable unemployment). I half expected him to pull a longbow from his knapsack (and it was a knapsack, not a backpack; I checked).

And flannel! Everywhere, G.D. flannel! Flannel on men! Flannel on women! Every other twenty- or thirty-something gal strolling the Avenue looked like they were competing for ultimate old-timeyness. The suspenders. The floppy straw hats. The braided hair held back by handkerchiefs. So many dumpy denim overalls and . . . oh my God! What fresh hell is this? Black Dansko clogs? Hideous black Dansko clogs! Aghast, I glanced again at my camper-in-need-of-toilet-paper uniform and realized I was actually on the cutting edge of fashion.

"It's because they all want to be like you, Jessie," Maria deadpanned when I asked her a few nights later about all the "canyon people" that had infiltrated the South Slope. I had spent the last three days unburdening myself to my friend—owning up to my confusion, my isolation, my lack of purpose, my growing conviction that Jake and I might not make it. My diatribe was accompanied by an unbelievable amount of cursing, my lips wet from spitting the F, S and C words with impunity. Maria looked at me with a sad-wry smile and said, "You know you're completely insane, right?"

Maria looked good. Relaxed. Happy. Her library of instructional swimming, hiking and yoga books must have paid off because she was exceptionally svelte and toned. She herself was wearing a flannel shirt made of the lightest wool and featuring a slightly avant-garde cut. And she was in love. We were getting ready for a small gathering of friends in her apartment where she lived with her boyfriend, Oscar, a handsome, fit, successful wine consultant with long eyelashes and a shaved head who moonlighted as a Bikram yoga teacher. He was quite possibly the only person on the planet more questioning, sardonic and probing than she, though he also had a playfully curious disposition that compelled him to do things like stage dance-offs at dinner parties and play Marco Polo in swimming pools at company retreats. It was only a matter of time before these two would tie the knot.

Maria and Oscar's new apartment was most impressive. It was a spacious, minimalist floor-through on the street level of a fashionably lumpy brownstone on one of Park Slope's more sun-dappled streets. They had instituted a shoes-off policy so I was obliged to leave my scat-encrusted clogs by the front door and embarrass myself in socks I noticed had a hole in the big toe. Oscar was out back in the foliage-covered patio, nursing a cocktail and wearing old man slippers, quietly tending to the pork tenderloin and vegetables on the grill. Their patio was a nest of twinkling lights, flowers and shrubs, with a sturdy teak table and chairs in the center.

As Maria padded around the kitchen in her bare feet, arranging Burrata and truffle goat cheese on a plate, stirring a pitcher of Pimm's Royale, I walked around the living room admiring her folksy, eclectic decorating style—vintage posters of dancing ladies from the 1930s, impressionistic oil paintings of tractor trailers, a foot-high ceramic statue of a pair of Chinese communists dressed in green uniforms and holding books, striding toward a prosperous future. I picked up a Russian nesting doll—a stout babushka dressed in a sarafan—and twisted the upper half of the wood to reveal a smaller figure inside, and so on, until reaching the smallest, innermost doll lathed from a solid piece of wood. As I slowly put it back together, esoteric Eastern European gypsy music streamed over the Internet radio. The kitchen began to fill up with guests—media people mostly, as well as a quota of artsy and indie foodie sorts. The floating conversation and gentle laughter that filled the space was blithe and undemonstrative—a sign of the truly successful. I had nothing much to add to the conversation so I took a seat and quietly evaluated female guests' attire, a favored pastime. I noticed the Brooklyn *Waltons* trend had trickled up to the professional classes—a few of Maria's colleagues were also decked out in luxe flannel shirts. By way of greeting, women complimented Maria on her sinewy appearance: "Oh my God, Maria, you look hot. Bikram? Your flannel is incredible. Love the shoes." There was Hush wearing a sparkly gold minidress with puff sleeves and leggings. On her finger was a simple and elegant engagement ring, given to her the night before by Freddie, the handsome real estate agent from the Upper East Side standing next to her, his arm looped protectively around her waist. She joked that it was a constant battle trying to deprogram Freddie of his ingrained preppiness, which was why she had him decked out in cargo pants slashed at the ankle, a vintage tee and rainbow colored sneakers. Hush looked more confident, more gorgeous and in love than I'd ever seen her, her frenetic excitement replaced by a calmer womanliness, a transformation no doubt aided by being one half of a long-term relationship. I sidled up to Maria as she cracked open a few jars of artisanal pickles, dumping the contents into bowls. I noticed the pickles were store-bought, which mildly vexed me because I had been sending her and Hush jars of my own canned creations for the past couple of years and noticed three still unopened in Maria's cupboard. "That reminds me," I said. "I bring offerings. From the country."

I presented both Hush and Maria, before a small audience of guests, with my DIY bounty—the pickles, the jams, the Tropical Island Thunder, the eggs, the two seven-pound frozen chickens, and the pièce de résistance, the moonshine infused with pears and cinnamon. I wasn't all that surprised when this dovetailed into banter about the glorious self-righteousness of eating the locally grown.

"Wow, you're like a modern day pioneer woman," said one social media marketer who had a "This Is Not a Plastic Bag" purse slung across her chest. "Your life sounds so real. It reminds me of that story in last week's paper. Did you guys see that? About the urban hillbillies?"

Maria walked over to a small pile of newspapers in the living room and returned with last week's trend section, which she handed to me. I looked at the cover story, which featured a large photograph of a rakish thirty-something couple, of the same urban woodsmen tribe I'd seen that afternoon on the streets of Park Slope, standing amid a rooftop garden and chicken coop somewhere in Greenpoint with Manhattan's skyline just piercing the clouds behind them. The couple was waifish and grim-faced and very fashionable; his earlobes were stretched to capacity, festooned with giant ear plug piercings evocative of African hunter-gatherers, and he had a long, sturdy axe slung over his shoulder that looked capable of toppling him backward. She stood in a pigeon-toe posture, wearing skinny jeans and a severe Joan Jett haircut, the ends of which were jagged like lightning bolts. In her arms she grasped a chicken. The article was sprinkled with quotes containing phrases like "woolen sweaters" and "retreat from consumerism," "appreciation for people who work with their hands" and "if it's yellow, let it mellow," as if the most satisfying thing in the world was splitting wood by hand and squatting over a piss-stained toilet.

"Woolen sweater," I sneered. "It's *wool.* Just call it a wool sweater. And that axe. Is that a joke? Any real country person knows it's not possible to survive one winter in a house heated by wood without a gas-powered automatic wood splitter. And 'let it mellow,'" I laughed haughtily. "I've used leaves."

It was a strange thing—hearing myself trying to "out hill-billy" the urban hillbillies by positioning myself as somehow more "down home," more *real*, more authentically blue collar, than this glamorized interpretation served up in the style section of an urban newspaper. I'm not sure if it was contempt or competitiveness that egged me on—contempt for this couple's enviable media coverage and killer haircuts, competitiveness over the size of his axe and the ass-backward way she held her chicken. But even as I spoke, my shoulders tensed in protest over this gross display of lies, this circus sideshow of affectation—gloating over a lifestyle I had just fled, bragging about a husband I had just deserted, claiming verisimilitude for a way of life that had, in fact, proved *too* real for me (I think this is why Hush and Maria eyed me quizzically). But I couldn't stop. Even in the midst of the histrionics, it occurred to me I was only truly capable of owning my country identity when I wasn't actually in the country.

Guests took an interest in the two pints of pear cinnamon moonshine, the ultimate emblem of country authenticity. Some of the girls unscrewed the lid, and sniffed, skeptical at first, which is to be expected when presented with liquid resembling vibrant urine. Oscar came over and poured a drop into a glass and sipped while the others watched. The first thing he said after swallowing was, "It tastes like there's no alcohol in it." Actually, the first thing he said was, "It tastes like dish soap." Then, "Is there any alcohol in it?"

I scoffed at the question. "'Does it have any alcohol in it?' Of course it has alcohol in it! It's moonshine! It has so much alcohol in it it might even impair your ability to reproduce."

"Really?" He looked skeptical. "Let's see if it will light."

Light, as in, with a match; alcohol with a high enough proof will ignite into a blue flame.

We walked outside onto the patio, followed by a handful of guests. As Oscar fumbled with the matchbook, I tried to appear nonchalant, like I was having a gay old time, but inside I trembled with anxiety—*What if the moonshine doesn't light? What if Mel and Melinda didn't know what they were doing? How do I know it's not pear concentrate cut with wine cooler?*

We poured a bit of the moonshine onto the concrete patio. I held my breath as Oscar threw a lit match into the puddle of liquid. The match hissed and sent up a curl of smoke. It didn't light. I looked at the puddle, then at Hush and Maria whose expressions said, "Sucks to be you."

"Hmm," said Oscar. "Maybe there was something wrong with the match?"

I wanted to sink into the nearest teak chair but I knew that would only emphasize my indignity so I stood there, chuckling uncomfortably. "Oh, it's real," I said as guests, unimpressed by the performance, turned to go back inside. "Not all moonshine lights, you know. I got totally *wasted* on that stuff." Another lie. "Last weekend. Woke up facedown in the sink hole."

I was speaking to an empty patio. Everyone had gone back in except for Hush. She took a seat next to me. "I'm sure your moonshine is real."

"Yeah." I suddenly remembered Maria's artisanal pickles. "And why is Maria buying expensive pickles when I've been sending you guys jars and jars of my homemade dills?"

"Honestly?" Hush winced. "Freddie and I found a hair in one of your jars a while back. It was pretty gross. You should probably wear a hairnet when you make that stuff."

"Great. Sensational."

My BlackBerry chirped. I reached into my back pocket and saw Jake's smiling mug on my caller I.D. "Hey, babe," I answered with forced cheerfulness. Hush signaled she was going back inside.

"Hon, you shouldn't have left," he said harshly. "You don't leave when something gets hard. We need to talk. When are you coming home?"

"Tomorrow," I said. "I'm coming home tomorrow." I made a groaning noise that sounded somewhere between self-pity and disgust.

"Hon, it's okay," he said quickly. "You don't have to cr—"

"Hush found hair in my pickles," I said.

"Come again?"

"And the moonshine didn't light."

"What are you talking about?"

"We tried to throw a match on it and it didn't light."

"So?"

"So? It's not moonshine, Jake. It's not moonshine."

"So what?"

"If it's not moonshine . . . who are we? Who am I?"

Silence.

"Who am I, Jake?"

"Have you been doing more of that kundacrap?" he asked.

"Just come home, Jessie. Me and the dogs and the chickens miss you."

After we hung up, I looked at the half pint of pear cinnamon shine sitting on top of the table. It had evidently proved unworthy to bring back into the house. I felt squeamish and raw over having presented myself as some sort of rural ambassador: The brave/foolish outlier who took the leap of faith to live the dream of the zeitgeist—a life off the grid, by the sweat of my own brow, with a cowboy, DIY, off-the-land, buzzword, buzzword, buzzword, but whose moonshine didn't even light and whose pickles were brined with hair. What a farce. I had become so denuded of any sense of self that I now looked to moonshine—moonshine!—as validation of my country character, an identity I wasn't even that comfortable with, because I really had no clue who I was.

I sat outside for a long time and watched my friends mingle about Maria and Oscar's warmly lit apartment. Occasionally a guest came outside for a smoke or a breath of fresh air and was surprised to see my form sitting in the shadow of the large overhanging tree. They asked if I cared for a cocktail. I politely declined. I had no appetite for alcohol. The thought of booze made me nauseous. I had this queasy feeling in my stomach that wouldn't go away. Through the windows, I saw Freddie's arms clasped around Hush's waist while she laughed intimately with Maria. Hush and Maria's friendship had deepened over the years in my absence, which made me jealous even though I took a small amount of pride of knowing I was the glue that initially brought them together. It was nice to see my friends so content and in love, having successfully crossed the threshold into true adulthood. As I watched them, I wondered if it would have been the same for me had I stayed in New York. Of course it would have been. I would have eventually stumbled upon some gainfully employed, non-pervert man-like person who laughed at my jokes and shared similar taste in books and movies, and settled down with him, earning New York money in a white-collar job—even if it meant editing *Cat Fancy*—and spending our weekends in the company of such fine people as these. It would have been a fine life. My problem was that I had mistaken the natural displacement of my own heart, my tendency to look outside myself for happiness and contentment, as an indictment of my surroundings. I had failed to consider that the dissatisfaction and disappointment, the lack of purpose and shaky self-perception that dogged me in New York would follow me to the country too. It had followed me from Montana to New York initially, from New York back to Montana, from New York to Lexington and from Lexington back to New York. And now I had a headache—especially when I realized my perpetual dissatisfaction had followed me into my marriage. It would follow me right into my grave.

In some ways, I was a victim of my own insane creative energy—always running like there was somewhere I could get to, always role-playing with one foot out the door, never taking pride in anything I attempted, always adapting and conforming in one world so that I might stand apart and *really be somebody* in another. Perhaps this is the universal condition of humanity, I don't know. But I had spent a lifetime craning my neck for some new and improved, more "authentic" version of myself, and I now felt like that Russian nesting doll in Maria's living room—a shell that keeps shedding layers only to reveal a smaller, lesser version of its previous self. By trying to fill myself up I had actually hollowed myself out.

There was only one thing I was sure of anymore: I had to start being more honest with my husband, a man who would always hold my heart in the palm of his hand—to hell with Eve's Curse—by being more honest with myself. The only one shackling me to the stove was me. The only one who decided I had no future in rural Virginia was me. The only one who tried to fit more seamlessly into my husband's world was me. The only one who decided my marriage was a sham was me. I was the common denominator in all of my unhappiness (go figure!). By playing such roles, I had forced Jake into a role too: The Cowboy who cared more about his trucks and horses than me. I owed it to him to see him for who he really was: A man who had only ever followed his own heart, who had never told one untruth about himself (except for the occasional lapsed accent) and who worked his butt off to support us while I kept looking to my belly button for answers.

I had to get on with it. I had to stop undermining myself. I had to make peace with the life I'd chosen. I would never be Jake. I would never possess his calm focus, his grounded disposition, his faith in the Almighty. I would never find serenity walking in a pasture or feel stimulated discussing hay. I didn't love the things he loved. I would never overflow with his glass half full optimism. I would always be more of a glass half empty kind of gal—and he loved me for it. The only thing he had ever done was love me for it.

I slipped out of the party and aimlessly walked the streets of Park Slope until I found myself in a drug store open late. I found what I was looking for and walked to the cashier counter where I laid my money down and placed my bet. Late that night, after all the guests had gone home, I peed on a stick in Maria's bathroom and was oddly relieved by the two pink lines staring back at me—I was pregnant. Pregnant. My reaction surprised me. There would be no more running.

Twenty-one

※

June Born in July

I turned left at the blue mailbox just after the old church, as directed, and lurched for two miles along a road—really more of a wide strip of grass flattened by tires—until the road sloped upward to expose a brand new four board fence. I parked the car and climbed over the fence, taking note of its construction: solid, straight, strong, deeply rooted, capable of withstanding the test of time—just like the man who built them. The fence encircled an expansive pasture of hay stubble that nestled up to a wall of mountains, their blanket of trees showing flecks of red and copper as autumn bloomed. It was late afternoon and the sun was in my eyes, making the pasture burn gold. In the middle of it was Jake's blue work truck and another half-finished fence line that would soon bisect the field. Two black spots were barely visible in the grass—Cowboy and Sunny enjoying an afternoon nap. Kneeling before the fence-in-progress was Jake, so content in his working solitude. He wore his cowboy hat and heavy work gloves, and was building a brace for a section of woven wire fence.

"Hey," he kind of smiled when he saw me, as though I hadn't run away from home. His ability to detach from bad feelings could be maddening at times but as I watched him work, I conceded there was solace in it too, since it meant one of us was firmly anchored. One of us would never leave. "You have any trouble finding this place?"

"Nah, came straight here."

"How was traffic?"

"Fine," I said. "Sorry about leaving."

He stood up and faced me. A hardness flashed across his expression. "You know I love you more than anything. But you probably should have married a rich man."

I looked away. "It's not about the money," I said, trying to blink back tears. "I'm just tired of being the only one in this marriage who does all the changing."

"Jessie, have I ever asked you to be anything other than who you are?"

"No," I said. "But it's kind of implied by the life we lead. Jake, I hate manual labor. And I hate horses."

"Hate is a mighty strong word."

"Yeah, it is. And your optimism? It gets on my nerves."

"And I think you like to feel sorry for yourself."

"Perhaps." I took a deep breath. "And I 'strongly dislike' going to church. I don't think I'll ever . . . play for the Christian team."

"I know." He winced when he said this, which made me rueful. But I pushed on. "I'm not going to any more Bible clubs."

"I never asked you to join one," he said. "Jessie, I don't want you to be someone you're not. I'm not interested in a superficial relationship with my wife. But sometimes I guess I do wish you'd get right with God. Things would be a lot easier on you."

"I don't need to be right with God." I kind of laughed. "I have you."

"Well, I love you no matter what you do," he sighed, looking toward Cowboy and Sunny. "You don't have to be a country girl for me."

"But then what are we doing together? Do we have *anything* in common?"

"Jessie, I'm from Baltimore, remember? We have a farm in common. We have animals who depend on us in common. We have a chicken business, a garden, dinners, homemade wine and jerky in common. I'd say we have more in common than most. But if you still see this as a pit of despair, you gotta write your way out of it. But now, since you're here, can you hold this post and help me secure this brace?"

I went to his side. He slipped his arms around my waist and we kissed.

As I helped steady the post, I realized how much Jake loved me—he was willing to set aside his core values, his most sacred belief by accepting that his wife would spend eternity engulfed in the flames of the devil's inferno. I was deeply touched. I also grasped that there was an inherent contradiction in having a big revelation about one's "real" identity and self-perception when there was still fence to be built, yard work to be done, chickens to be fed and eggs to be sold. The daily business of life made the revelation itself a moot point.

"A little higher, hon," he said, three screws sticking out of the corner of his mouth.

I figured this was as good a time as any to tell him. "I'll try, but I have to be careful how much I lift now."

"Why? You wimping out on me?"

"No," I said. "I have to protect the fencer-in-training."

He cocked an eyebrow. "Are you—?"

"Pregnant?" I laughed. "Yes!"

He dropped his tools and stood up. "You hear that, Cowboy? You're going to have a little brother! Or sister!" The dogs wagged their tails so fiercely their whole bodies shook. Jake stomped over to my end of the post, picked me up and twirled me around until I yelled at him to stop.

"Well, that's great news! Let's celebrate! I'll make you dinner tonight. Miss Roberta dropped off some filets from one of the steers they just butchered. I can make homemade tortillas and we can crack open your canned salsa and I think my new pilsner is ready to try—well, pilsner for me and milk for you!"

"That's the other thing I wanted to get off my chest," I said. "I'm sick of do-it-yourself eating. The baby wants McDonald's."

Jake's eyes widened. "You know I can't say no to McNuggets."

"Yeah, they always get the chemicals just right."

That night we dined on a twenty-pack of Chicken McNuggets dunked in barbecue sauce. I was blown away by how good it tasted.

I want to say my circumstances vastly improved once I stopped pretending to be Country Woman on Fire, but that would be an exaggeration. We were still financially strapped, I was still jobless and still a work widow, I still grudgingly (but gratefully) pocketed Jake's walking-around money, he still had to work harder than ever. As October turned to November, the house was still freezing, my customers still stiffed me on my egg money and Adolph still tried to kill me. But there were changes of a subtler though crucial nature. I stopped trying to rise above my surroundings and accepted what I was: a rural housewife, but only insofar as I was a "wife" in a "rural" community who spent a lot of time in the "house." I resisted further explication. I even occasionally made Jake's lunch. I was learning that being a good wife, a caring spouse, was sometimes about nothing more than just that: putting cheese on your husband's sandwich. Turns out it wasn't necessarily a sign of subjugation, a symbol of oppression by the patriarchy. It just tasted good. I even still occasionally went to work with him (in my limited capacity—first trimester pregnancy fatigue is a killer!), not because I wanted to impress him or compete with him but because he needed my help and the bills kept coming.

We stopped going to church. Nothing much more was said about it. We simply woke up on Sunday and didn't go. Jake took it a step further by ceasing the nightly prayers. Instead of reaching for my hand as I placed the ten thousandth plate of eggs in front of him, he just smiled, shrugged and dug into his supper. I was surprised by how much this upset me. The dinner prayer had become such a fixture of our marriage that sitting down to the table without one felt like a sacrilege, a betrayal of our commitment to one another—a clue there was a glimmer of spirituality in me. I couldn't bear a meal without a prayer so I took up the cause myself, beseeching the Almighty along the lines of: "Dear God, please allow us to live another day and keep blessing us with so many eggs. Please watch over my husband as he works, especially on old man Palmer's place—that guy can be such a cheap bastard and he still owes us sixty-four dollars from the last job. Thanks, God. Amen." Speaking eloquently to the Man Upstairs wasn't as easy as Jake made it sound—he resumed prayer duties the following evening and has never stopped.

I stopped going to the YMCA because it depressed me. In deference to being with child, I began taking long, slow, wheezing hikes in the woods that opened up to a brilliant sloping field behind my house. I often pondered Jake's remark, "You gotta write your way out of it." I knew what he meant: I was the only one who could save myself. It wasn't Jake's job to make me happy. Moving to a new city or a "better" small town would only present a new set of obstacles and distractions for me to try to conquer, then rail against. I had no choice but to give in to the quiet, to accept the stillness, to live inside the fence. Funny—for as long as I had professed to not like vast empty fields I sure spent a lot of time in them. I suppose they were where I truly belonged, the link to my Montana heritage. Walking across that field, with nothing but the sound of the dogs whooshing through the tall grass ahead of me, the birds overhead and the occasional deer that leapt across my path, was where I finally saved myself.

As the flower inside me grew, I sat down at my computer and began writing again—not paid assignments, since I still didn't have any of those (full disclosure: I wasn't exactly hustling for them). I wrote for pleasure—something I hadn't done since college, something I had forgotten how to do. Writing was the only thing I had ever done, it was the only thing I knew how to do with any real proficiency (though some may beg to differ). I wrote all that fall and through an unbelievably snowy winter and kept writing through the blooming of the redbud and forsythia into spring. I wrote about all the things I had learned in the country—the canning, the chicken farming, the people I had met, the moonshine, the man I had married. And it dawned on me around my sixth month of pregnancy that being a rural housewife wasn't so bad. While I stayed home stringing sentences together for pleasure, Jake was happy enough to make sure the house didn't slip into foreclosure. Traditional marriages have their perks, people.

My pregnancy went off without a hitch—no morning sickness, no excessive weight gain—and I wondered what the heck I had been so afraid of all along. We learned we would be having a girl, and I had vivid dreams about her. I could already see her face. I felt her personality. The only blip during the entire nine months was the day I had to go for some non-pregnancy-related test administered by a local doctor, a man who veered toward the more natural end of the medicinal spectrum. While I lay on his exam table, the good earth doctor surveyed my charts and asked me where I planned to deliver. In a hospital, I said.

"You don't need a hospital," he chided. "There's no reason you can't deliver at home."

I made a face. I was never more thankful I had waited so long to get pregnant as at that moment. Had such a remark been made to me when I first moved to Lexington, I probably would have taken him up on the challenge, assuming that's the way it *must* be done in the country (and in Brooklyn), and tried to pop out a kid in the woods with nothing but a handmade crown of pansies and baby's breath to alleviate my woman pains.

"Yeah, no," was all I said, vowing never to return to a natural doctor's office.

"Alright," he said coolly. "You go ahead with your hospital birth."

I did have my hospital birth—though it almost ended up a natural childbirth because I was in labor for eleven hours without the epidural. My cervix refused to dilate—what can I say, I was locked up tighter than a whorehouse in Utah down there—and the doctors wouldn't give it to me until I did.

Our daughter was born in July but we named her June anyway—June Rose, a transposition of her great grandmother's name, the original Montana pioneer woman—a woman I had grown up admiring as strong, wise and fiercely independent. Great Grandma Rose's namesake came into this world at an even six pounds, looking the same as she had in my dreams—adorably cute with curvy lips, big blue eyes and freakishly long fingers (my brother told me to watch my valuables). Her giant head and skinny body made her look like a tadpole, and I knew she would grow up to be as beautiful and strong as her great grandma.

I was introduced to that strength the first month of her life—June squawked a lot. She squawked before feedings. She squawked after feedings. She squawked during diaper changings. She squawked when I tried cradling her. The only time she wasn't squawking was when my nipple was shoved in her mouth or Jake swaddled her so tight in a blanket she couldn't move. Even though I breastfed every two hours around the clock, ten minutes after each feeding she was back to making her Gollum face—bug-eyed, bone-white, skin taut over bones and a big blue vein bulging from her forehead—and screaming viciously. June wasn't turning out to be the gurgling flesh packet of my dreams.

As Jake dug up the last of the season's purple potatoes in the garden and I sat off to the side nursing June with a blanket tossed over my shoulder, I wondered where in the world I would get the strength to make it. June had only been alive three weeks but it felt like one hundred Yoda years. Just then Mel and Melinda drove into the yard and parked their truck alongside the garden. Sunny and Cowboy romped around their vehicle hoping to attract attention. Jake ambled over to Mel's open window. The men talked while Melinda scurried over to get a look at the baby. She got down on her hands and knees and edged her face closer to my bosom.

"Now don't you be embarrassed, Mama. You ain't got nothing I ain't got. I got titties just like you. A tittie ain't nuthin'. Now listen, Jessie, I got to tell you something." She raised a finger. "Don't you beat that baby in front of the dogs."

I pried June off my chest to piercing squalls and quickly re-fastened my nursing bra.

"Because if you do, they might attack her. When you done got to beat her, Jessie, you make sure to lock the dogs in the other room."

I filed this wisdom away. Over the next six months, I received plenty of other colorful parenting tips from my well-intentioned neighbor. Three that stood out:

1. Don't let June sleep in bed with you or she'll turn into a sex-crazed maniac.
2. When teaching her about firearms (Melinda was adamant about wanting to teach June to hunt), let her touch the weapon while saying, "Don't touch!"
3. To calm her when she's crying, moisten her lips with beer.

There were times I came close to trying that third strategy—especially on those afternoons when Jake would come home from work and I'd be sitting on the couch topless, wild-eyed and sallow while June screamed in my ear. I'd look at Jake like a murderess banshee and he'd say, "Oh, it's not that bad, hon," and I'd want to throw a lamp at his head.

I was at my wit's end over the crying. In hindsight, it actually wasn't so bad because there was a definitive end point. It happened at around three o'clock in the morning a month after she was born. I was trying to calm my rattled nerves by reading the totally depraved and gratuitous rape scene in *The Girl With the Dragon Tattoo* when I looked down at the scrawny body permanently clamped to my chest, ravenously sucking my breast inside out, and something finally clicked: My daughter was starving. My breasts weren't the bountiful kegs of butter I had hoped. I had to do something immediately. Friends suggested I "pump" to "keep my milk supply up" but I didn't need to strap a medieval frappe machine to my chest to know my lactation output was the equivalent of two leaking cans of old Shasta. The first time I supplemented with formula, June gulped down four frothy ounces in a matter of minutes and collapsed in a sweet Enfamil coma. Two weeks later, she had three chins.

I stopped nursing.

I was finally settling into the business of life. In some ways, I was finally becoming an adult. Alice, Lucy and Carrie were right—motherhood *was* pretty great (once Enfamil had banished the *Bride of Chucky* anyway). Watching June's progress—her first smile, her first hand clap, her first banana smashed into a fine mousse and rubbed in her hair—was very gratifying, or at least perversely entertaining. Or maybe it was because I was finally too busy to think about myself.

I finally understood that identity comes once you stop searching for it, once you stop looking to conceptual thought for definitions of who you are or think you should be (this was the residual lesson from Anna Bundance, who had turned out to be quite the sage life coach.) It *is* possible to bend and sway in the breeze too much, endlessly tossed by questions of who you are and what does it all mean; sometimes the most courageous thing a person can do is stand straight and strong. There was freedom in this—freedom from no longer bothering to ask myself such ruminative questions. This impression was especially acute on days when I found myself removing the empty bladder from my Excaliber Estates Boxed Chablis, cutting a corner with a pair of scissors to tease the last remaining drops into my glass.

"It's just boxed wine," I'd whisper. "Don't overthink it. It's just . . . boxed wine."

The subtext: We would never be rich. We would never live "authentically," insofar as it was even possible to define such a word. But we lived an honest life, Jake and I, not because we slaughtered chickens, sold eggs, sipped moonshine and built fence, but because we were finally honest with each other; I was finally honest with myself.

Funny then—just when you think you have it all figured it out, life comes along to remind you once again you're merely along for the ride.

In October, June and I flew out to Montana to spend some quality time with my mom, who was hungry to bond with "her" baby. While we were there, we got a call from Jake telling us that Sunny had died. He called me from the job site, ten minutes after it had happened. In halting speech, he said she didn't get out of the way in time when he put the skid steer in reverse, followed by a a blood-curdling yelp. He immediately pulled forward, jumped out of the cockpit and saw her run under his truck nearby, where she collapsed. Jake scrambled under the truck and grabbed her to take her to the vet but she started convulsing and died moments later. Cowboy, sensitive Cowboy, was so frightened he tore off into the woods, where he hid, huddled in a thicket, before Jake was able to eventually coax him out hours later.

Without verbalizing it, we both acknowledged that we were responsible for our animal's death by allowing her free rein on what could be a dangerous job site. Sunny just wasn't a working dog. She had no aptitude for such things, reinforcing my understanding there was occasionally a price for venturing too far outside the comfort zone. The freedom we'd tried so hard to provide for our dogs—the freedom to run, the freedom to be dogs—was what ultimately killed her. Had she been on a leash or fenced in a yard, she'd still be with us.

But that wasn't the worst news. During that same trip, I received another phone call from Jake, who informed me he'd just been called up.

He was deploying. To Afghanistan.

Twenty-two

※

Blue Tags

Winter hunkered down and with it, my health. The stress of the impending deployment combined with new parenthood meant I succumbed to the worst cold of my life. I was stuffed up to my brain and my throat was lined with razor blades. A sprig of cauliflower sprouted from my lower lip, preventing me from kissing my own family. When I did venture in for a nuzzle, Jake cautiously eyed the pulsating cold sore and gave me an avuncular little hug instead.

As soon as we found out he was deploying—a short two months hence—every other weekend, it seemed, was already booked with another military debriefing or Army training, requiring Jake to leave home for a long weekend or more. It gave me plenty of time to ponder just how I was going to survive a year or more out there by myself with a four-month-old and a slew of chickens. The years in Rockbridge County had taught me a thing or two about tenacity and getting by on less, but doing so with a baby—with no family present—was a game changer. Little tactical scenarios played over and over in my head: How would I mow the lawn? Clean the chicken coop? Shovel snow? Stock the fire? Dispatch Adolph . . . with a baby who cried nearly every time I set her down?

When Jake was around, he was so busy and preoccupied—scrambling to finish jobs, clearing more acreage to make way for a future pasture for horses, slaughtering another batch of broiler chickens, splitting and stacking enough firewood for the following winter, installing an outdoor wood furnace so I would finally, after all the winters in Rockbridge County, be warm—that I mistook it for indifference, that perhaps he wasn't upset about leaving us to go to Afghanistan. He insisted he was simply trying to set June and I up for success.

I finally went to the doctor to seek treatment for the cold. While waiting for the doctor, I nonchalantly mentioned to the nurse that I had a cold sore.

"I see that," she said as she strapped a blood pressure bag onto my arm.

"It's because I'm stressed," I said. "I recently had a baby. And my husband is leaving me. Not *leaving me*-leaving me, but he's leaving me to go to Afghanistan."

"Uh-huh."

"For a year. He leaves in a couple of months. And he doesn't seem too broken up about it."

"Uh-huh."

"Seems kinda psyched about his mission, actually."

"Well, your blood pressure is fine." She smiled as she removed the inflatable bag. "The doctor will be in to see you shortly."

I sat on the hospital bed, my legs dangling over the end, and it felt like the edge of a precipice. The old loneliness burbled up inside of me. My heart was breaking—for myself, for June losing her daddy in the first months of her life. For Jake too—he would miss so much: her first words, her first step, her first hug. June wouldn't even know who he was by the time he got back.

I had moments where I almost wished I was the one deploying instead of the one left behind. At least in Afghanistan there was the adrenaline-addled rush of being in a foreign land trying to do good, working with Afghans, whereas on the home front, I knew I could look forward to a year of dirty diapers and lonely nights playing online checkers. But it was an illusion. I knew that. I was right where I belonged. Still, I craved an outlet for these emotions, but I had nowhere to express them (definitely not at the doctor's office). Jake was so preoccupied. He was incapable of expressing the change as a loss, preferring to see it as "an opportunity for a better tomorrow." I couldn't help but roll my eyes over these Boy Scout proclamations, but I had to accept Jake was a soldier. And at the end of the day, a man. He would never feel things as intensely as I did. He would always express his love more through deeds and actions than through thought or words. All I had to do was look around our property to see that love in tangible form. It was in everything he had built and fixed and grown.

He had to go again, leaving June and me for a week by ourselves while he underwent another round of training at an Army base in another state. June and I were home alone one night. I cleaned the day's clutch of eggs, June was tucked into her crib, Cowboy was outside checking the perimeter. A knock came at the front door.

A young couple stood on my front porch, telling me they thought they'd just hit my dog. They thought they'd hit Cowboy. I steeled myself, wanting to believe the use of the word "thought" meant they narrowly missed Cowboy before he dashed off into the trees, frightened as anything. But it was false hope. They had hit him. I found him just across the road, about six inches outside the white line, near the mailbox. The three of us crouched down beside him. He was huddled and shaking. I'll never forget the look in his eyes as I knelt before him. He was so scared. Not from being hit, but from breaking the rules. He knew he had messed up. He knew he had disappointed us in the most terrible and tragic way. He died in my arms. I could barely bear to tell Jake. The pain was as searing as losing a son. Cowboy had been part of our story since the very beginning. The weekend I met Jake all those years ago in Miles City was the weekend I met Cowboy—looking up at me with his happy little smile outside a Kum & Go in Forsyth, Montana, without a care in the world except unconditional love for his master. And now he was gone. In an instant. All those years of faithful companionship, just gone. As Jake was prone to say, we are never promised tomorrow. I didn't roll my eyes when he said it. There was too much to learn from a dog as good and true as Cowboy—he was as pure as a child, pure as a horse. All of my fretting over self-fulfillment, when the lives we value most in this world—the guileless, the innocent, the helpless—are those the least aware of their place in the hierarchy.

Over the loss of not just one dog, but two—incredibly—within three months, and the impending loss of my husband, the world seemed less certain than it had before. I retreated inward. I couldn't help but frame the deployment in cold calculations, dollars versus cents—what was in it for me? I found myself working out this question aloud to Jim and Roberta's son-in-law Gerald who came over the following day to help me bury Cowboy in Jake's absence. While Gerald dug a grave, I mused whether the deployment meant we'd be able to send June to college on the new G.I. Bill. Maybe Jake would come home a major. Maybe we would be able to save six figures of tax-free money.

"No, what it really means," Gerald said, "is there are people out there who still believe in this country."

I turned away. My husband was going to Afghanistan because he was a patriot. He went where his country called him, at the expense of his business and his family. He did it because someone had to, and he figured it may as well be him and I for one couldn't think of a better ambassador for the United States overseas than Jake. I was part of the war effort too, regardless of my politics. If I didn't man up at home, Jake couldn't man up over there, and I really needed him to come home—*our* home, the home we had built one egg, one chicken, one canning jar, one fence post, one trip to the Walmart Supercenter, one child, at a time.

I needed to learn to protect myself. I already knew how to fire a weapon, as demonstrated at the shooting range in Terry, but I made Jake show me how to load, unload and reload the Glock, using a stopwatch so I could time my reflexes. It was a painful exercise. I have always hated guns. Anytime anyone would tell me they were thinking about purchasing a firearm, I'd trot out my favorite rebuttal: "But you're engaging in a culture of violence! Violence begets violence, friend! And you'll probably shoot your eye out!"

Which is true, but the thought of June and I alone in a house along a quiet rural highway—I needed more than my progressive values and a sharp butter knife to protect us (and I probably could have done without reading *Bind, Torture, Kill: The Inside Story of BTK, the Serial Killer Next Door* two weeks before Jake left).

My heart raged until the last week Jake was home. A local chapter of the Ruritans, a club of do-gooders in small communities, of which Jake was a member, threw him a going-away party that attracted what seemed like hundreds of people. Every subculture of Rockbridge County was represented. (You can tell a lot about a man's reputation by the number of people who show up to his going-away party.) A local Italian restaurant donated a huge pasta dinner. Local bakers brought in thirty artisan loaves. A restaurant up the road provided vats of ice cream. The chapter's president gave a touching speech. A collection was taken up in our honor. A "task force" of club members, friends, neighbors and VMI cadets was formed to help with the upkeep of our place during Jake's deployment. We didn't ask for any of it, but friends, even strangers, wanted to help me plant the garden, care for the chickens, move the Hen Hut, haul firewood, shovel snow, ensure a serial killer wasn't lurking in the bushes outside the house. It was such a huge outpouring of love and support that when Jake, June and I arrived home that night, we looked at each other slack-jawed and I almost felt ashamed for having fantasized for so long about ditching this place for greener pastures. I was an entrenched part of the community, whether I liked it or not. People knew what was going on with me. It was home.

The call came Wednesday afternoon. Jake's flight was scheduled to leave at first light Thursday morning. As he rushed around the house that evening finishing up last-minute paperwork and phone calls, shoving fatigues into duffels and laundry sacks, he asked me to sew some tags made of nylon webbing for his green army bags. The bright blue tags would enable him to identify his luggage among all the others, and he wanted enough reinforcing thread in each tag so he could conceivably carry the bag by the tag if necessary.

"Who in their right mind would try to carry a seventy-pound duffel by a tag?" I asked, removing the hard case from my sewing machine.

"You'd be surprised," he said. "Bags come around the carousel, guys grab wherever they can."

It felt good to use my sewing machine—to make something with my own hands. It was a small thing, but significant. Independence and self-sufficiency are fuzzy words. I realized I'd been blinded by my own reactive biases about those terms when in fact I had become self-sufficient in a new way. I had the courage to rely on my husband. And I wasn't helpless. When the world all went to hell, I knew could take care of myself. Or at least make deer neck tacos.

I finished the tags and held them up to admire my handiwork. Jake complimented my efforts as he fastened one tag to a boulder-size duffel and heaved it off the ground by the blue webbing. The tag held. He said every time he saw his blue tags, wherever he was in this world, he would think of me.

"And if they're strong enough, they should last a lifetime," he said. "Just think, we might still have these tags when there are grandkids running around."

I'll be looking for those tags a year or so from now, coming around the carousel at the airport near our home.

June and I kissed Jake good-bye at 4:45 a.m. on a wintry Thursday. I drove home from the airport listening to country music in a fog, literally and figuratively. The roads were icy. Snow pressed down. June slept the whole way. During the drive, I thought about my long ago quest for purpose and adventure—the force that had pulled me to Miles City in the first place. Well, I had found my purpose. My life was an adventure. Every single day of it. And nobody ever said adventure was easy.

When we arrived back home at six, I didn't know what else to do with myself so I tucked June into bed with me and we slept for a few hours. When I awoke, I walked around the house in my bare feet, faintly conscious that the floors would be free of dog hair and clumps of dirt from muddy boots for some time. The bar of soap in the soap dish would no longer be smeared black.

There would be no more cans of Beefaroni and canisters of Pringles and boxes of Pop-Tarts messing with my feng shui on top of the refrigerator anymore.

I cleaned out all the cupboards and the refrigerator, and gathered all of Jake's food-like substances in a sack and brought them down to the chickens. I threw it all into the snow just inside their pen, where they dashed toward it and inhaled it. I felt a pang of guilt for doing this; like I was trying to rid my husband's presence from the house as quickly as possible. But I *was* trying to rid his presence from the house as quickly as possible. I had to. It was a survival tactic. I checked the outdoor wood furnace. I came back inside. I put on Ryan Bingham's "Southside of Heaven." In the absence of anything else to do, or any way to express the loss, I ate an Almond Joy bar I had missed during my initial sweep and slathered it with a repulsive amount of peanut butter. As I chewed, I considered that this could be a good year for an explosive weight gain.

As the weeks and months passed, my life as a single parent got underway. It snowed harder and harder but I did the chores and carried on. There was nothing else to do but carry on. I stacked wood. I fed the fire. I shoveled the walk, but I also had a lot of people around who cared enough about our family to help me. I fed the chickens. After feeding the chickens early, early one wintry morning, I walked across the road to check the mail and found a letter in a white legal-size envelope. On the front was an APO return address written in a small, precise rightward slanting print that had become more familiar to me than my own handwriting. I ripped it open and read:

I pray for years of peace and prosperity when this is finished. I pray that you and I can grow old together, raise a family, enjoy life and each other. I hope to have lots of adventures with you and June when I return. I hope to train Yamaha to be a great horse. I hope to one day have another great dog. I hope to grow the business into something professional and successful. I hope to make some good wine and some better shine.

I live to make you smile, Jessie, and hopefully I am able to do that. I want to make the most out of life, and to do that I need to be with you. That's why I can't wait to be together again, back with the one I love, one Jessie K.

I love you forever and two days.

I folded the letter back into its envelope and tucked it into my pocket. I looked at my little house across the road, and was reminded that this life we had built together was worth it—the war in Iraq, the sacrifice and uncertainty, financial struggle, feelings of purposelessness, the loss of our two wonderful dogs, the threat of death in Afghanistan—it was all worth it. I would lose myself again and again and again for a love this big.

I walked back to the house and kicked off Jake's size eleven muck boots in the mudroom.

June wailed from her crib.

"I'm coming, kid; your mom's coming—whoever the hell she is."

I had come so far—from aimless wanderer with money in her pocket to a resourceful, self-sufficient woman with none. I was strong. Not strong like Jake, I would never be as strong as Jake, but I was tough in my own way, which is all I would ever be. This was freedom—what derives not from the absence of sacrifice, but from the hard-won ability to meet it.

As I leaned over the crib and looked into those hopeful blue eyes, the answer to my own question finally came to me—I'm alive and I'm free. And who wouldn't want to be me?

ACKNOWLEDGMENTS

I never thought I'd write a love story, least of all my own, so I have many people to thank for bringing this book to life. First off, my editor, Denise Silvestro, and the entire team at Berkley Books for believing in me. My agent, Maura Kye-Casella, for telling me she laughed out loud when she read my proposal. My good friend and earliest reader Paula Szuchman, for her superior life-coaching skills and for introducing me to the concept "creative destruction." Kitt Harris, for years of loyal friendship; there's no one I'd rather face down a Russian mobster with (*"slikha!"*). And my dear friend, fellow lady magazine veteran Anna Holmes, for convincing me I had a story worth telling in the first place.

To all the friends and acquaintances who were gracious enough to let me write about them—you know who you are—thank you so much. To my blog readers—there are so many places to waste time online; thanks for wasting a portion of yours on my site.

To my family—Dad and Theresa, Mom, Davey, Cassie, Grandma Kate, Grandma Rose, Jack and Gale, and the entire extended Wilson clan—for all the love and support over the years. My father, Dave Knadler, the keenest writer and reader I know, is owed special consideration for editing the early manuscript even though this isn't exactly his kind of book (he's more of a Cormac McCarthy kind of guy). And to my wonderful stepmother, Theresa Johnson, for helping me shape key dialogue and steering me to the work of Betty Mac-Donald.

Finally, to my husband, Jake Wilson, the love of my life. You push me to be better every day. Thank you for always burning the ships for me. And to my precious little Junebug—please don't read this until you're thirty.